Trauma-Responsive Practices for Early Childhood Leaders

Specifically designed for administrators and leaders working in early childhood education, this practical guide offers comprehensive resources for creating trauma-responsive organizations and systems. Throughout this book, you'll find:

- Exercises and tools for identifying the strengths and areas in need of change within your program, school or agency.
- Reflection questions and sample conversations.
- Rich vignettes from programs already striving to create healthier, trauma-responsive environments.

The guidance in this book is explained with simple, easy-to-implement strategies you can apply immediately to your own practice and is accompanied by brainstorming questions to help educational leaders both new to and experienced with trauma-informed practices succeed.

Julie Nicholson is Professor of Practice in the School of Education at Mills College and Co-Director at the Center for Equity in Early Childhood Education.

Jen Leland is Director of Partnerships for Trauma Transformed (TT), a seven county trauma-informed regional system of care.

Julie Kurtz is CEO at the Center for Optimal Brain Integration®. She coaches and trains on trauma-responsive and resilience building practices and social-emotional skills across the lifespan. She also operates a small private practice in California.

LaWanda Wesley is Director of Quality Enhancement & Professional Development at the Early Childhood Education Department, Oakland Unified School District and Co-Director at the Center for Equity in Early Childhood Education.

Sarah Nadiv is CEO at Global Health and Education Strategies.

Other Eye on Education Books Available from Routledge
(www.routledge.com/k-12)

Creating Inclusive Writing Environments in the K-12 Classroom: Reluctance, Resistance and Strategies that Make a Difference
Angela Stockman

Culturally Responsive Self-Care Practices for Early Childhood Educators
Julie Nicholson, Priya Shimpi Driscoll, Julie Kurtz, Doménica Márquez and LaWanda Wesley

Implementing Project Based Learning in Early Childhood: Overcoming Misconceptions and Reaching Success
Sara Lev, Amanda Clark and Erin Starkey

Advocacy for Early Childhood Educators: Speaking Up for Your Students, Your Colleagues and Yourself
Colleen Schmit

Grit, Resilience and Motivation in Early Childhood: Practical Takeaways for Teachers
Lisa B. Fiore

Sexuality for All Abilities: Teaching and Discussing Sexual Health in Special Education
Katie Thune and Molly Gage

Trauma-Responsive Practices for Early Childhood Leaders

Creating and Sustaining Healing Engaged Organizations

Julie Nicholson, Jen Leland, Julie Kurtz, LaWanda Wesley and Sarah Nadiv

NEW YORK AND LONDON

First published 2022
by Routledge
605 Third Avenue, New York, NY 10158

and by Routledge
2 Park Square, Milton Park, Abingdon, Oxon, OX14 4RN

Routledge is an imprint of the Taylor & Francis Group, an informa business

© 2022 Taylor & Francis

The right of Julie Nicholson, Julie Kurtz, Jen Leland, LaWanda Wesley and Sarah Nadiv to be identified as authors of this work has been asserted by them in accordance with sections 77 and 78 of the Copyright, Designs and Patents Act 1988.

All rights reserved. No part of this book may be reprinted or reproduced or utilized in any form or by any electronic, mechanical or other means, now known or hereafter invented, including photocopying and recording or in any information storage or retrieval system, without permission in writing from the publishers.

Trademark notice: Product or corporate names may be trademarks or registered trademarks and are used only for identification and explanation without intent to infringe.

Library of Congress Cataloging-in-Publication Data
A catalog record for this title has been requested

ISBN: 9780367355326 (hbk)
ISBN: 9780367362942 (pbk)
ISBN: 9780429345142 (ebk)

Typeset in Palatino
by KnowledgeWorks Global Ltd.

Contents

A Note about the Cover xi

Introduction 1
An Urgent Need for Trauma-Sensitive Early Childhood
  Programs, Schools and Systems................................ 1
What Are the Benefits of a Trauma-Informed Organization?........ 3
What Does the Research Say about Trauma-Informed Practice? 3
Trauma-Informed versus Trauma-Responsive 7
Balancing a Focus on Trauma with Coping, Resilience and Healing......... 8
Unique Features of This Book 11

1 Understanding State Dependent Functioning: The Importance of Maintaining Regulation in Trauma-Responsive Environments 15
State Dependent Functioning 15
When the Cortex Is "Open" for Business 17
The Pre-Frontal Cortex or Neo-Cortex (Executive or
  Thinking Brain) 17
When the Smoke Detector Is Set Off and the Brain Detects
  Danger 19
The Brainstem (Primitive or "Lizard" Brain) 19
The Limbic Brain (Emotional or Mammalian Brain) 20
Navigating Triggering Events 26
The Triggering Event Cycle 28
Cecilia Fernandez: "I Was Aware that I Was Triggered."
  Facilitating a Training for an Early Learning Advocacy
  Program 36
Reflection/Discussion Questions 37
Megan Paul: "It Is Important to Be Mindful of Triggers and
  to Have a Toolkit of Strategies Available." Training a Group
  of Quality Rating and Improvement (QRIS) Assessors 38

Reflection/Discussion Questions 39
The Complexities of Building Body Awareness 40
A Lifeline: Learning the Pathways to Regulation 42
The Foundation: Relational Regulation 43
*Programs, Schools and Organizations Are Impacted by State
    Based Functioning Too* 46
Reflection/Discussion Questions 49

2 Moving from Stress and Trauma-Inducing to Trauma-Informed and Trauma-Responsive Healing Centered Early Childhood Programs, Schools and Systems 53

*Trauma-Responsive Organizational Continuum for the
    Early Childhood Field* 54
Stress and Trauma-Inducing Organizational Environments 57
Example 1: Growing Strong Roots Early Learning Public Agency 60
Example 2: Shooting Star Learning Centers 62
Example 3: Circle of Care Center for Child Development 64
Example 4: One Way Family Child Care Program 65
Daily Schedule 65
*Example 5: Jen Leland, Director of Partnerships, Trauma
    Transformed* 66
Trauma-Informed Organizational Environments 68
*Example 1. Aracely Nava, Family Engagement Coordinator
    for Child Development Resources* 70
*Example 2. Including TIP in Early Childhood Coursework
    in Higher Education.* 74
Reflection/Discussion Questions 75
Example 3. Old Elm Preschool 75
Reflection/Discussion Questions 78
*Trauma-Responsive Healing Centered Organizational
    Environments* 80
Little Sun People 82
Reflection/Discussion Questions 86
What to Expect in Working for Organizational Change 87
Key Steps in the Process of Becoming Trauma-Informed 87
Common Barriers to Implementing Trauma-Informed Approaches 94
One of the Biggest Barriers: "They Could Never Find Substitutes" 95

Reflection/Discussion Questions 95
Trauma-Responsive Resilience-Building Principles for Early Childhood Programs, Schools and Systems 96

3 Core Principle—Build Mutually Respectful and Trusting Relationships 102

Consistent, Trusting Relationships that Buffer Stress and Support Coping, Resilience Building and Healing 103
Respect: "Differences Do Not Make People Wrong" 103
Reflection/Discussion Questions 104
Reciprocity: "Diversity Is Always Life Enhancing" 105
Reflection/Discussion Questions 105
Responsiveness: "There Is Always a Third Choice" 106
Reflection/Discussion Questions 106
"Paperwork Can Wait, You Can't" 110
Reflection/Discussion Question 111
Core Principle—Understand Stress and Trauma 111
Communicate the Message that Understanding Stress and Trauma and Using a Trauma-Responsive Approach Is a Priority for Your Early Learning Organization 121

4 Core Principle—Acknowledge Systems of Privilege and Oppression and Take Actions to Disrupt Inequity 124

Increase Awareness about Oppression 125
What Is Oppression? 126
Examples of Different Forms of Oppression and Minoritized and Dominant Groups 126
Structural Racism Is a Particular Form of Oppression 128
Elements of Oppression 128
Elements of Oppression 128
Understanding How We Are Positioned Within Systems of Oppression and Privilege 134
Oppression as Interlocking Systems 135
The Birdcage Metaphor 136
Reflection/Discussion Questions 137

*Take Individual and Collective Actions to Disrupt Inequity
and Strengthen Healing and Wellness* 138
Reflection/Discussion Questions 140
*Characteristics of Dominant/White Supremacy Culture and
Antidotes for Creating More Trauma-Responsive Healing
Centered Work Environments* 146

5 Core Principle—Create Environments that Reinforce Messages of Safety and Predictability 158

Intellectual Safety—"I Feel Engaged" 159
Emotional/Psychological Safety—"I Feel Supported" 159
Social Safety—"I Feel Seen" 160
Physical Safety—"I Feel Safe" 160
*How can Early Childhood Organizations Reinforce Messages of
Safety and Predictability for Children, Families and Staff?* 161
Core Principle—Focus on Strengths and Assets 168
Providing Effective Strengths-Based Feedback 173
Reflection/Discussion Questions 177
Core Principle—Provide Opportunities for Agency and Control 177
Reflection/Discussion Questions 184
*"One Side Is Red and Says 'STOP' and the Other Side Is
Green and Says 'GO'": Agency and Control for Young
Children in a Hospital Setting* 186
Reflection/Discussion Questions 189

6 Core Principle—Intentionally Promote Coping, Resilience and Healing 193

*What Factors Support Children and Adults to Cope,
Heal and Build Resilience?* 194
*How Are Early Childhood Organizations Building
Resilience among Staff and the Children and Families
They Serve?* 198
Reflection/Discussion Questions 200
*"Creating a Mindful Organization Is Like the Layers
of an Onion"* 202
Reflection/Discussion Questions 205

Core Principle—Implement Culturally, Linguistically
and Contextually Responsive Practices 206
How Does Culture and Language Influence People's
Experiences of Stress, Trauma, Mental Health and Healing? 207
Adopt, Adapt, Align: The Importance of Being Contextually
Responsive 211
Reflection/Discussion Questions 212
Core Principle—Create Power-Sharing Partnerships and
Community-Centered Solutions 213
Reflection/Discussion Questions 215
Reflection/Discussion Questions 219
Building Power-Sharing Partnerships within an Agency 219
Reflection/Discussion Questions 220

7 Core Principle—Use Evidence to Build Insights and Learn Collaboratively 224

Using Data to Build Insights and Learn Collaboratively 229
What Happens when We Collaborate with Community
Members and Center Their Voices in the Collection
and Use of Data/Evidence? 230
Core Principle—Work toward Sustainability and Scale
Innovation with Flexibility for Local Adaptation 232
Core Principle—Engage People Working Within Every
Part of the Program, School and/or System 234
Reflection/Discussion Questions 236
Core Principle—Acknowledge Today's Realities While
Maintaining Hope and Imagining Justice for Tomorrow 236

8 Case Study: "Do You Mind if I Bring Plants into the Center?" The Power of Grounders for Regulating Stress 244

Reflection/Discussion Questions 246
Case Study: "What's the Context of the Child?" Creating a
Trauma-Responsive PreK 246
Reflection Questions 249
Case Study: "I Would Go Home and Remind Myself
that My Job Was Not to Judge" 249
Reflection/Discussion Questions 251

*Case Study: Trauma-Responsive Environments Everywhere
(TREE Project, Humboldt County)* 252
Reflection/Discussion Question 255
Tree Project Materials Master List 255
*Case Study: "I Think We can Make This a Better Experience
for Children."* 256
*Jonathan's Approach as a Child Life Specialist Reflects
Several of Our Trauma-Responsive Principles* 258

Conclusion 262

Resources 265

A Note about the Cover

Rainforest with Animals
Source: Hannah Shack

The Rainforest Metaphor

Throughout this book, we use the metaphor of a rainforest to represent the complex and dynamic process of shifting early childhood programs, schools and systems into trauma-responsive, resilience building and healing centered environments. Why use a rainforest metaphor?

Rainforests are all over the world (on every continent except Antarctica) **but each rainforest is a unique ecosystem with specific plants and animals that have evolved to thrive in different environmental conditions.** Although rainforests are all different, they share certain elements that define them as rainforests—e.g., certain percentage of rain every year and a canopy of trees.

This is similar to the early childhood field where every early learning program, school and system is dedicated to serving young children and families yet there is spectacular diversity in the local contexts and ecosystems that have evolved in response to a diverse array of people, communities, policies and cultural practices.

Rainforests are complex interdependent systems. Although each layer of the rainforest is distinct, they all exist in an interdependent system. The processes and species in one layer influence those in another. All rainforests thrive on symbiotic or mutually beneficial relationships—e.g., because there is a lack of wind in the forest interior, canopy trees often enclose their seeds in fruit. This fruit provides food for animals who through consumption, help bring the seeds to lower levels of the rainforest for germination. Because the soil itself lacks enough nutrients to support the canopy trees, "decomposers" (insects & fungi) on the forest floor support the canopy by quickly returning nutrients from decomposing plants and animals.

Just like the rainforest where all parts are interconnected for survival, so is the field of early childhood education. The most important trauma-responsive and resilience building elements are the human connection. First, we promote attuned human relationships and provide feelings of inclusion, significance and belonging. Second, we provide safe, predictable environments. Finally, we promote spaces that include voices at all levels of the system. When we include these core elements the organization promotes resilience, buffers stress and thrives toward health and well-being.

The biggest threats and sources of trauma to the rainforest are things or events that disrupt interdependent systems as seen with deforestation where the rainforest is cleared for ranching and agriculture.

We can see the same with early childhood programs, schools and systems. The biggest threat to the health of a child, adult, family, community, organization or system is when relational trust is disrupted as this has ripple effects that impact development, learning, wellness and short as well as long term functioning for people and organizations.

The **Canopy Layer** is a dense system of leaves and branches that form a **protective cover over the forest interior**. Shielding the interior from wind, rain and sunlight makes the environment below less volatile, more consistent, "still," protected.

This is the same as attuned responsive adults that can buffer stress for trauma-impacted children and adults. Trauma-responsive early learning environments can buffer stress and support coping, resilience and healing for children, families and the early childhood workforce.

Emergent Layer. Descriptions of the rainforest describe a **competition for access to a very limited amount of sunlight**, the very few trees that make it to the emergent layer have the "privilege" of abundant sunlight which helps them to be more stable/stronger than trees and vegetation in the forest interior.

Our early learning organizations and systems are positioned within larger systems of privilege and oppression creating inequitable access to resources and opportunities for children, families and early childhood educators.

When an emergent tree falls, it creates a **light gap**, through which sunlight becomes accessible to plants at the forest floor. This gives opportunity for hundreds of hardwood seedlings that have adapted to wait at the forest floor in a state of dormancy for this event to begin **new growth, new possibility**.

We always focus on the possibility for change, growth, improvement, resilience and healing for people and programs and institutions. One small change can create a "light gap." One nurturing and responsive relationship can support others to feel safe, to buffer stress and to promote a capacity for new growth.

Introduction

> Our program had so many natural disasters this year that were impacting the staff and the families that we serve. So what our management did, which I thought was extremely trauma informed is we paused to make sure that everybody is okay. We wanted to make sure that the staff were taken care of. So, they first and foremost checked in with all of us to see what we needed. And then after the staff were taken care of, we came together and we supported the families. It was a whole trauma-responsive and comprehensive approach. We partnered with our local mental health agency here in the county and we offered crisis intervention groups for families and staff who were impacted by the fires.
> —Aracely Nava, Family Engagement Coordinator

An Urgent Need for Trauma-Sensitive Early Childhood Programs, Schools and Systems

Children, families and the early childhood professionals serving them are living in a world where the risks and realities of experiencing trauma are growing exponentially. Racism, poverty, homelessness, food insecurity, deportation, natural disasters, school shootings, community violence, child maltreatment and domestic abuse, the health pandemic—these factors and others are creating an urgent need for trauma-responsive early childhood environments. We must increase our individual and collective understanding of how to create programs, schools, organizations and systems that are sensitive to trauma and actively work to reduce stress and prevent harm and re-traumatization. The chorus is growing louder that the time is right for implementing trauma-responsive approaches at the system and organizational level across the early childhood field.

Investments in early childhood teacher training on trauma and trauma-informed practices (TIPs) have been gaining in popularity. However, teachers and providers cannot be effective in creating trauma-responsive approaches if they work in programs, organizations and systems that are stress and trauma inducing. To be truly effective in supporting children and their families impacted by trauma, the many systems and agencies that touch the lives of young children and families—home visiting and early learning programs; infrastructure organizations; local, regional, state and federal agencies; early intervention/special education and parent education/family engagement programs; child welfare and more—need to become trauma-sensitive, trauma-responsive and healing centered. This book—which builds on our first two books, *Trauma Informed Practices for Early Childhood Educators: Relationship-Based Approaches that Support Healing and Build Protective Factors in Young Children* (2019) and *Culturally Responsive Self-Care for Early Childhood Educators* (2020)—guides readers who are interested in embarking on this journey.

Trauma-responsive environments and service systems integrate and sustain awareness of trauma and its impact and trauma-sensitive approaches into organizational culture, practices and policies in order to create a climate of empathy and respect (Melz, Morrison, Ingoldsby, Cairone, & Mackrain, 2019). This requires administrative buy-in and support, strength-based and restorative responses to behavior, policy and procedure changes, teacher and staff professional development at all levels of the organization and strong cross-system collaboration (e.g., education and mental health professionals; Oehlberg, 2008; Thomas, Crosby, & Vanderhaar, 2019).

Early childhood organizations and systems have a critical role to play in providing children and families impacted by trauma with stability, safe spaces, connections to caring adults and links to supportive services and interventions. Through understanding and responding sensitively to stress and trauma, administrators and staff can help reduce the negative impacts they can have on children. Trauma-sensitive environments are also critical for the early childhood workforce as many have their own trauma histories and are at risk for secondary traumatic stress or vicarious trauma as a result of working with a growing number of children and adults impacted by trauma.

What Are the Benefits of a Trauma-Informed Organization?

Although the research base is still new and emerging, several benefits are associated with trauma-informed organizations including (Sharp & Ligenza, 2012):

- Increases safety and predictability
- Strengthens the quality of relationships
- Provides care for the "carers" (reduces burnout and impacts of vicarious trauma)
- Improves the quality of services
- Reduces negative encounters, workplace environments and events
- Increases success and satisfaction at work
- Promotes organizational health and wellness
- Improves program outcomes
- Creates a community of hope, inclusion, significance and belonging
- Promotes reflection and self-awareness

What Does the Research Say about Trauma-Informed Practice?

Empirical research is not yet well established for TIP. It's too new. While trauma work in clinical settings has robust evidence, research on TIPs in educational settings is just beginning to be conducted. The first studies published on TIP in education were in 2012, so the literature and research evidence base is relatively new and to date, very limited. Drawing conclusions across these studies is difficult as there is no standard or formally agreed upon definitions, terms or frameworks for the implementation of TIP in educational environments across the United States. Instead, there are dozens of different approaches and interventions used in programs, schools and districts across the country described as TIP (Thomas et al., 2019). In fact, there is currently no agreement about what is meant by the terms "trauma-informed approach," "trauma sensitive," or "trauma-informed system" (Hanson & Lang, 2016; Maynard, Farina, & Dell, 2017).

Clearly there is a need for further refinement of terms and future interdisciplinary research to document which approaches are beneficial for different individuals, groups, communities and/or contexts. Despite the significant limitations of the research on TIP, there is a growing agreement that TIP should not be perceived as "just another thing that will come and go" (Thomas et al., 2019, p. 445). To the contrary, there is a significant, urgent and growing need for trauma-informed approaches in education beginning in early childhood and continuing through higher education.

> **TIPs in schools should not be perceived as just "another thing that will come and go"**—rather due to the ever-increasing levels of adversity facing children and youth in our society, the need for providing environments where students feel cared for, safe and empowered will continue to be tremendous ....
>
> Out of necessity, schools have pursued TIPs and interventions through partnerships with local mental health agencies and universities (e.g., Anderson, Blitz, & Saastamoinen, 2015). However, *the core components of TIPs should also be considered at every level of the educational system.* If schools are finding ways to ensure they are responsive to trauma, then districts, state and federal education offices and colleges of education should also consider how they are supporting widespread TIPs both internally and externally. This includes attention to all **protocols and procedures, forms, accountability systems, partnerships, and trainings** (Thomas et al., 2019, p. 445).

What else can we glean from the most comprehensive review of literature on TIP in education? Following are some of the key findings and implications for the implementation of TIP in early childhood:

- **We need to shift from deficit notions of trauma to strength and asset-based views** that emphasize people are more than "the bad things that happen to them" (Ginwright, 2018, para. 5) and shine a light on individual and collective strengths, forms of resilience and pathways to healing (Thomas et al., 2019, p. 446).

- **Using culturally responsive approaches to teaching and leading within trauma-informed classrooms and schools** is thought to be a promising avenue toward dismantling deficit approaches and improving equity for children and youth (Thomas et al., 2019, p. 447).
- **Educators need proactive support from leaders to manage stress and to be supported through organizational care policies and practices** (SAMHSA, 2014). There is more need to consider the reality and impact of working with trauma-impacted children and adults on the workforce. As Thomas et al. (2019) state:

  > Secondary/vicarious trauma needs to be considered at every level of the system (federal, state, district, schools)...While self-care is promoted as a component of trauma-informed practice, administrators at school and district levels should take responsibility for embedding approaches and practices that encourage self-care and regulation for all adults in schools, including teachers and staff. (p. 447)

- **Many TIP studies do not measure what leads to changes in educators' practice.** We don't currently know if learning about trauma (e.g., in trainings) leads educators to translate this knowledge into the use of TIP in their classrooms and workplace. We also do not know which types of supports (e.g., coaching, communities of practice, reflective supervision, mental health consultation, etc.) are most likely to support teachers to shift their beliefs and behaviors to become more trauma-informed. Finally, we need more research to document *how* teachers use TIP in their classrooms. (Melz et al., 2019).

Naming the Elephant in the Room

Early childhood programs may avoid addressing trauma for many reasons including:

- Lack of time or too busy
- Uncomfortable with the subject of trauma
- Lack of awareness of the widespread impact or the definition of trauma
- Lack of training
- Fear of opening a Pandora's box (unexpected consequences of opening up this topic)
- Do not have the resources or tools
- Unsure of impact on classroom instruction

We have a profound under investment in early childhood education. When we're doing trauma informed trainings and trainings on secondary trauma, we don't see early childhood educators. Even though we know early educators are often the lowest paid, have the least access to training and workforce development and who have the most amount of time and opportunity to be in relationship with children at opportune, optimal brain development times. Early educators have the greatest opportunity to really shape the neuroplasticity and the healing from developmental trauma for young children and yet, they have the least connection to resources and investments to support that relational healing. To me, this is one of our biggest crimes against humanity. We understand early adversity and Adverse Childhood Experiences (ACES), we understand developmental trauma and peak opportunities for repair and for healing and for growth. **And yet our investments haven't reflected that knowledge or those values.**

–Jen Leland, Director of Partnerships,
Trauma Transformed

Reflection/Discussion Questions

- What are some of the barriers or fears you face as you explore bringing trauma-informed practices to your program?
- What are some of the benefits you would imagine would come to fruition from beginning to include trauma-informed practices to your program?

Trauma-Informed versus Trauma-Responsive

To be informed is to receive information. To be transformed is to be changed or altered as a result of this new knowledge.

–Brandt (2020)

Why do we use the term trauma-responsive and not trauma-informed? Because we're not just aware, we're responding. You can be trauma-informed and do nothing about it. We are more than trauma-informed, we are trauma-responsive. That means that we are able to actively respond to a child or adult who is in crisis. And I think that that is so much more meaningful when you can say, "we know what to do when a child or adult is having a really big emotion and we do it." That is the shift from informed to responsive.

–Heather Richardson, Director of Early Childhood Education

Although the more familiar and commonly used term in research, professional literature and professional development is "trauma-informed," we have opted to primarily use the term "trauma-responsive" throughout this book. We believe that building awareness of trauma and its impact and trauma-sensitive organizational strategies to become *trauma-informed* is an essential first step, but not sufficient. Instead, we advocate for going beyond a process of building awareness and understanding toward applying this knowledge in practice. **To be *trauma-responsive* is to take actions for positive change**, to use knowledge of trauma and resilience to make changes to language and beliefs, to audit and revise policies and to make shifts to practice. To be trauma-responsive is therefore, to be trauma-informed; however, the reverse is not necessarily true. As Dr. Brandt states, our goal is to be changed or altered as a result of our new knowledge, not simply to receive information.

Balancing a Focus on Trauma with Coping, Resilience and Healing

We believe it's essential to balance any discussion of trauma with an equal if not more robust naming of resilience, coping, healing and strengths. No individual, family, community, cultural group or organization wants to be defined by the bad things that happen to them (Ginwright, 2018). This reflects a paradigm shift as "early literature on the impact of trauma positioned individual responses to trauma as moral weakness …[it is] essential to disrupt deficit notions of trauma affected children [and adults] toward asset based perspectives and actions." (Thomas et al., 2019, p. 446). Focusing on our vulnerabilities and traumatic experiences can prevent individuals and groups from perceiving a felt sense of safety, agency and control and instead, can perpetuate cycles of trauma and oppression. In contrast, when stories of stress and trauma are honestly acknowledged but balanced with discussions of coping and resilience, we create the conditions to buffer stress, prevent negative impacts from trauma and support healing.

We draw on Dr. Shawn Ginwright's discussion of healing centered engagement as a central construct throughout the book.

Dr. Ginwright is an Associate Professor of Education and African American Studies at San Francisco State University and the author of *Hope and Healing in Urban Education: How Activists are Reclaiming Matters of the Heart* and *The Future of Healing: Shifting From Trauma Informed Care to Healing Centered Engagement* (Ginwright, 2018). Dr. Ginwright explains that although the idea of trauma-informed approaches in education is important, he believes it is incomplete. He states this is the case for several reasons:

- Trauma-informed education correctly highlights the specific needs for individuals who have exposure to trauma but incorrectly assumes that all trauma is an individual experience rather than a collective one
- Our current focus on trauma-informed approaches in education does not address the root causes of trauma in neighborhoods, families and schools. And because trauma is a collective experience in many cases, we need to disrupt the environmental contexts (the toxic systems, policies and practices) that caused the harm in the first place
- Instead of emphasizing the experience and impact of trauma, we need to spend more time fostering healing and strengthening the roots of well-being

Dr. Ginwright advocates for a more holistic approach and a wider a range of healing centered options—inspired by the fields of positive psychology and community psychology—for responding to trauma and fostering well-being. This approach shifts the focus from a treatment-based model which views trauma and harm as an isolated experience to an engagement model which is strengths-based, emphasizes a collective view of healing and re-centers culture as a central aspect of well-being. Additionally, a healing centered approach acknowledges that well-being comes from participating in transforming the underlying causes of harm within our societal structures and institutions.

Articulating Your "Why" for Trauma-Responsive Organizations

Understanding and clearly communicating your program, school or system's rationale—your "WHY"—for embarking on the journey to become trauma-responsive and healing centered is essential. This work is difficult and requires a long-term commitment. It can only be sustained when people understand and are committed to the values, mission and vision driving the work. It's easy to fall into a trap of focusing on the *what* (content) and the *how* (operations and implementation). While these are important, this work can only be successful and sustainable if people take time to identify the "whys" that will fuel their passion, effort, investment and commitment to this work.

As authors, what is driving our fight for transformative justice and imagining a future where all children, families and early childhood professionals have access to trauma-responsive healing centered environments and systems? Making our "Why" Visible:

Support the flourishing of *all* children, parents/families and the early childhood workforce serving them

We want every adult working in early childhood and every child to have:

- Consistent, trusting, attuned and caring relationships
- A felt sense of belonging, dignity, worth and affirmation of their identities and cultural ways of being and knowing
- A value and respect for human diversity
- Opportunities for agency and control
- A felt sense of safety and protection from the systems, structures, policies and people that cause harm. And when harm does occur …
- Support to cope, build resilience and heal

Reflection/Discussion Questions

Each program, school and community will have their own "why" that is rooted in your local contexts and conditions.

- How will you bring people together to collaborate in articulating your "why?" Who needs to be involved in this conversation for it to be truly inclusive?
- How can you clearly communicate your "why" to various individuals and groups who will be affected and involved in the work?
- If you had a magic wand and could fast forward five years, what would your program look like if it was to be trauma-informed, trauma-responsive and healing centered?

Unique Features of This Book

Everything in this book is written explicitly for the early childhood workforce especially prospective, emerging as well as veteran leaders in early childhood. This includes program directors, site supervisors, principals, infrastructure staff and individuals working in state or federal early childhood policy or quality improvement and/or systems building initiatives, community college and university faculty, researchers and others working directly with, or on behalf of, infants, toddlers, preschoolers and early elementary-aged children. Although there are other books and resources available on trauma-informed programs and systems, this is the first written specifically for professionals working in early childhood (pre-natal to early elementary).

Throughout the book we include rich vignettes and case examples that provide many windows into early childhood programs, organizations and systems striving to become trauma-informed, trauma-responsive and healing centered. We highlight stories of environments where people are in various stages of their hard work and journeys for change. We share honest narratives—reported from directors and staff members working in diverse contexts across the country committed to this work—that acknowledge their strengths, small wins and progress as well as the many barriers they face and the different ways they are responding to these challenges. We want readers across all points of the continuum—those brand new to trauma-informed work and others whose organizations and systems may be farther along—to "see" firsthand exemplars that are **mirrors** validating their experience as well as **windows** that provide inspirations for what they can strive to become over time (Bishop, 1990). In addition to the authentic case examples and vignettes, we include reflection questions, sample conversations, practical strategies and a range of resources and tools readers can use to support them in their journeys for transformative change.

The narratives of early learning environments included throughout the book were created from interviews we completed with dozens of educators and early childhood leaders across the United States as well as the authors' collective authentic experiences working in the field for decades as educators, social workers and non-profit leaders. When vignettes and case examples are composites instead of representing a specific program— in order to protect confidentiality—they are entirely authentic.

We provide practical tools and ideas that are accessible, adaptable for local communities and contexts and action steps readers can take right away. Given the realities of our under-resourced field, we offer many ideas throughout the book that do not require significant resources and investments. We aim to demystify trauma-responsive organizational practices. As early childhood leaders read through this book, we believe they will discover they are already using many TIPs and we hope that everyone—whether they are just beginning this journey or are quite far along—will learn new ideas and strategies they can use right away with staff, community partners and systems-change initiatives to shift toward healing-oriented and wellness-based organizations and systems in early childhood.

As maintaining regulation is essential for learning, wellness and healing, throughout the book, we include examples of different strategies to support regulation. We encourage readers to integrate these regulation activities into meetings, professional learning opportunities, higher education coursework, parent and family engagement events and other early learning contexts to support individuals and groups to ground and regulate themselves and de-escalate and calm people's stress response systems.

It is important to note that the focus of this book is trauma-responsive approaches that strive to shift organizations and systems to be more trauma-sensitive in their work with children and families and for the early childhood workforce. **We do not discuss trauma-specific treatment interventions** that can be implemented at the individual-level to address trauma and its symptoms.

References

Anderson, E. M., Blitz, L. V., & Saastamoinen, M. (2015). Exploring a school-university model for professional development with classroom staff: Teaching trauma-informed approaches. *School Community Journal, 25*, 113–134.

Bishop, R. S. (1990). Mirrors, windows, and sliding glass doors. Originally published in *Perspectives, 1*(3), ix–xi. Accessed on January 22, 2019 at https://scenicregional.org/wp-content/uploads/2017/08/Mirrors-Windows-and-Sliding-Glass-Doors.pdf

Brandt, K. (2020). *Reflective supervision.* Bruce Perry office hours. Retrieved from https://vimeo.com/406307258

Ginwright, S. (2016). *Hope and healing in urban education: How urban activists and teachers are reclaiming matters of the heart.* New York, NY: Routledge.

Ginwright, S. (2018). *The future of healing: Shifting from trauma informed care to healing centered engagement.* Medium. Retrieved from https://medium.com/@ginwright/the-future-of-healing-shifting-from-trauma-informed-care-to-healingcentered-engagement-634f557ce69c

Hanson, R. F., & Lang, J. M. (2016). A critical look at trauma-informed care among agencies and systems serving maltreated youth and their families. *Child Maltreatment, 21*, 95–100.

Maynard, B., Farina, N., & Dell, N. (2017). *Effects of trauma-informed approaches in schools.* Retrieved from https://campbellcollaboration.org/media/k2/attachments/ECG_Maynard_Trauma-informed_approaches.pdf

Melz, H., Morrison, C., Ingoldsby, E., Cairone, K., & Mackrain, M. (2019). *Review of trauma-informed initiatives at the systems level: Trauma-informed approaches—Connecting research, policy and practice to build resilience in children and families.* U.S. Department of Health and Human Services.

Nicholson, J., Driscoll, P., Kurtz, J., Wesley, L., & Benitez, D. (2019). *Culturally responsive self-care practices for early childhood educators.* New York, NY: Routledge Press.

Nicholson, J., Perez, L., & Kurtz, J. (2019). *Trauma-informed practices for early childhood educators: Relationship-based approaches that support healing and build resilience in Young children.* Routledge Press.

Oehlberg, B. (2008). Why schools need to be trauma-informed. Originally published in *Trauma and Loss: Research and Interventions, 8*(2), 1–4. Accessed on January 22, 2019 at http://www.traumainformedcareproject.org/resources/WhySchoolsNeedToBeTraumaInformed(2).pdf

Sharp, C., & Ligenza, L. (2012). *Is your organization trauma-informed.* National Council for Community Behavioral Healthcare. Retrieved from https://www.thenationalcouncil.org/wp-content/uploads/2012/11/Is-Your-Organization-Trauma-Informed.pdf?daf=375ateTbd56

Substance Abuse and Mental Health Services Administration (SAMHSA). (2014). *SAMHSA's concept of trauma and guidance for a trauma-informed approach.* Rockville, MD: Author.

Thomas, M. S., Crosby, S., & Vanderhaar, J. (2019). Trauma-informed practices in schools across two decades: An interdisciplinary review of research. *Review of Research in Education, 43*, 422–452.

1

Understanding State Dependent Functioning: The Importance of Maintaining Regulation in Trauma-Responsive Environments

State Dependent Functioning

Trauma-responsive practice (TRP) is guided by an understanding of the neurobiology of stress and trauma or what Bruce Perry (2020a) describes as **state dependent functioning**. State dependent functioning means:

- ♦ **Our internal state is always changing along an arousal continuum** (Perry, 2020a):

    calm → alert → alarm → fear → terror

AROUSAL CONTINUUM.

- **The perception of threat and fear are especially impactful in shifting our internal states.** Our lower brains are continually receiving input from multiple sensory domains (e.g., what we hear, see, smell, taste etc.) to monitor our internal state and the external environment to scan for safety or danger.
- **The more distressed and fearful we are, the more we move up the arousal continuum** (shifting away from a calm state into an alert state, then alarm and into a state of fear. The state of terror is the most stressed state we can be in).
- **We perceive, process and store information in different ways depending on our current internal state.** When we are in different states of arousal (e.g., calm, fear, sleep) different neural systems are activated in our brains which increases neural connections to some parts of our brain while decreasing access to others (Perry, 2020a).

We know from decades of research on stress that several characteristics amplify a stress response for individuals and for groups and move us farther along the arousal continuum. These characteristics include:

- **Novelty.** Events or experiences that are novel, unfamiliar or that create uncertainty for us activate our stress response system.
- **Unpredictability.** Events or experiences we go through where there is a significant level of unpredictability and a constant sense of change elevate our stress.
- **Lack of personal agency and control.** When people do not perceive a sense of agency and control, feelings of fear, anxiety and hypervigilance increase.

> In the same way that children exhibit state dependent functioning, so do adults, families, programs, organizations, schools, communities, businesses, governments and countries.
> –Bruce Perry (2020a)

The brainstem and limbic brain are continually receiving input from multiple sensory systems (e.g., what we hear, see, smell, taste etc.) and monitoring a person's internal state and the external environment to determine if they are safe or in danger.

When the Cortex Is "Open" for Business

When adults perceive that they are safe and not threatened in any way, as Bruce Perry describes, "their cortex is open for business."

The Pre-Frontal Cortex or Neo-Cortex (Executive or Thinking Brain)

Mammals and reptiles do not have a neo-cortex. Only humans have a neo-cortex allowing us to have more advanced processing capabilities. The neo-cortex is considered the **"Boss or Chief Executive Officer"** of the brain.

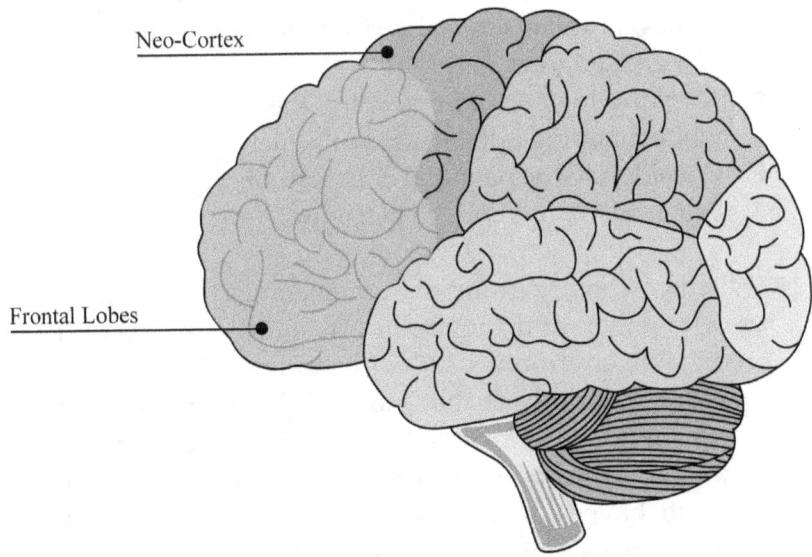

FIGURE 1.1 Neo-Cortex
Source: Courtney Vickery

When adults are calm and regulated, have their basic needs met (e.g., enough food and water, neither hot nor cold), do not have excessive demands on their attention, are in a familiar environment with people they trust and they have a felt sense of belonging and safety, they can engage the full range of their cognitive reasoning and capabilities including:

- Engaging in reflection
- Identifying how they feel and how intense their emotions are
- Thinking abstractly
- Creating and inventing
- Learning new information
- Relating to time in complex ways (Considering the past and dreaming into the future)
- Making thoughtful decisions after considering different ideas and solutions
- Examining different perspectives (other than one's own)
- Problem-posing and problem-solving
- Using strategies to self-regulate emotions and behavior
- Aligning their beliefs and behaviors with expressed values, an organizational mission and/or an understanding of a greater good
- Thinking logically and keeping the big picture in mind while mapping out the steps to achieve a goal
- Considering the potential or actual consequences of one's beliefs, decisions and/or behaviors

"When you have a group of human beings that live and work together, and they're in a resource surplus and predictable environment, the prevailing affective tone is calm, which means that more of the people in that group are going to be able to be abstract and creative, they're going to be more future oriented and they're going to have a whole variety of recommendations, rules, policies, and supervisory practices that are healthier."

–Bruce Perry (2020a)

> Arousal is a state of physiological and mental alertness. Each adult has an individual **zone of optimal arousal**. Optimal arousal is a state of physiological and mental alertness that is optimal for adults' behavior and their ability to be attuned, responsive, reflective and self-regulated.

When the Smoke Detector Is Set Off and the Brain Detects Danger

If the brain detects any information that suggests a potential threat (internally: E.g., adults are hungry, thirsty, cold or worried; externally: E.g., they are in an unfamiliar environment with people they don't know or trust), our brains will automatically and subconsciously activate a survival response that engages the brainstem and limbic brain and other systems throughout the brain and body.

The Brainstem (Primitive or "Lizard" Brain)

The brainstem is responsible for the FLIGHT, FIGHT and FREEZE response humans have when they perceive danger. This part of

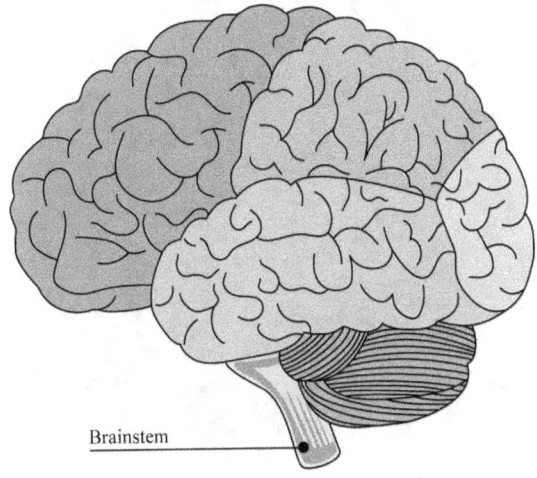

FIGURE 1.2 Brainstem
Source: Courtney Vickery

the brain is referred to as the **"alarm center"** or **"smoke detector"** and it continually scans the environment for red flags and sends messages that lead us to perceive whether we are safe or should mobilize to prepare for danger.

The Limbic Brain (Emotional or Mammalian Brain)

We share this part of our brain with mammals. It generates our feelings, emotional intensity of feelings, and creates our desire for attachment, significance and belonging. The limbic brain includes the amygdala which controls our survival responses and allows us to react within fractions of a second to the presence of anything we perceive to be threatening or dangerous. The amygdala supports our ability to feel emotions and to perceive them in others around us and the physical sensations in our bodies that result when we are fearful or threatened (e.g., racing heartbeat resulting from a sudden and very loud siren). The amygdala is the reason we are scared of things that are out of our control. It is the alarm center of our brain and responsible for the triggering of fear.

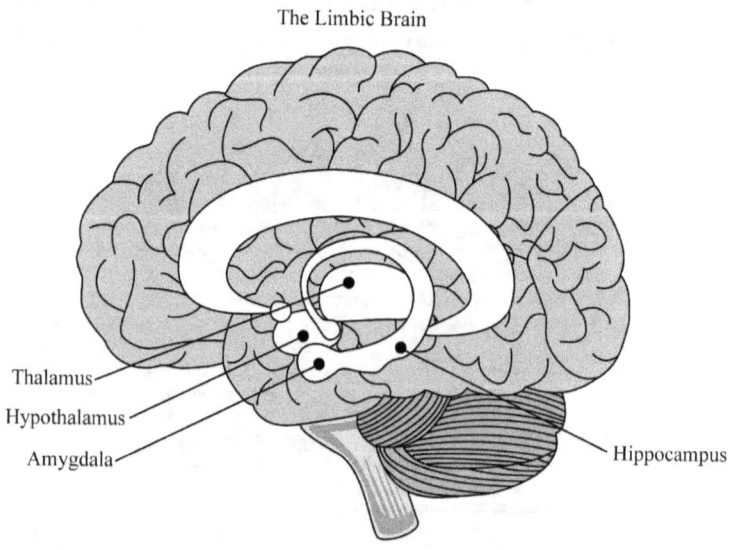

FIGURE 1.3 Limbic
Source: Courtney Vickery

What happens to adults' functioning as their state shifts and they move up the arousal continuum?

> "Implementation of trauma informed practice in early childhood classrooms, it really is about self and co-regulation.
> —Jen Leland, Director of Partnerships, Trauma Transformed

When our brains detect a threat, because of state dependent functioning, our core regulatory networks will set off a cascade of changes in how we think, what we feel and the way we behave. Certain systems are "turned on" in our brains and bodies while others are "turned off" or less accessible. **The greater the threat, the less access adults will have to their cortex.** When we are under stress, the thinking parts of the brain are less functional as faster more primitive survival systems take over. There are several consequences for adults' functioning.

When the cortex is "closed for business" and less accessible, Perry (2020a) reminds us that you will observe adults who are more:

- ♦ **Reactive, emotional, anxious and activated.** Reactivity, highly emotional and worried states are common characteristics of people when they are distressed all signs of state dependent regression.

> "the further that you escalate up the arousal continuum, the more you have what we call state dependent regression. You act less and less and less like an adult and more and more and more like a child and at some point you regress and get to the point where you're completely self-referential... you just care about your comfort. You want your needs met, and you want them met now... you are hard to reason with, you're emotional and reactive in the way you do things... the more you get threatened, the less access you have your cortex, and the more you basically functionally regress."
> —Bruce Perry (2020a)

- **Externally focused and vigilant.** Scanning for danger is a characteristic of this state of hyper-vigilance. Increase sensitivity or reactivity to sound, light and touch is common. Also misreading the intentions of others during interactions or when reading and responding to written communication.
- **Emotionally and physically exhausted.** Having a stress response system that is continually activated and scanning the environment for danger takes a toll emotionally, physically, socially, psychologically and spiritually. And this translates into less productivity and less ability to focus. The longer this hypervigilant state lasts, the more adults will see their learning and work negatively impacted as they will not be as productive and their ability to learn new skills and information becomes more challenging.
- **Less capable of being creative, inventive and reflective.** When stressed, adults may be capable of hearing or receiving new information, but they will struggle to engage in reflection, deep analysis or thinking creativity and innovating.
- **Difficulty sustaining focal attention: Focused on survival.** Perceiving stress—especially at the high end of the arousal continuum, impacts adults' ability to focus on anything but the "here and now." As a result, strategic planning and other activities that require thinking into the future are more difficult.
- **Less capable of thinking through the potential or actual consequences and impact of individual and group thoughts, decisions and behavior** (e.g., the consequences of a new policies or practices). When people and groups are stressed, decisions can become impulsive, irrational or overly focused on meeting immediate needs instead of considering what is best long-term and/or for the greater good. Reflection on the potential impact of the choices being made is less likely to take place.
- **Making lower quality decisions.** The quality of people's decision-making begins to deteriorate—they experience

decision fatigue (Perry, 2020b)—when their brains detect stress (e.g., when they are hungry, tired, thirsty, worried etc.). As people become stressed, dysregulated and/or in a state of alarm, their decisions and ability to problem-solve are compromised. They are not as thoughtful or future-oriented (they are focused on the present moment) and they are more likely to react based on their biases and prejudices and/or to be simplistic in their thinking and solutions (e.g., less likely to focus on nuance, context or specific circumstances). Decision fatigue is most impactful when people have to make lots of decisions in a row.

- **Showing a range of behavioral changes.** Some people will be hypervigilant and constantly scanning the environment for more information including observing what other people are doing and saying and gauging how they are behavior. Others will be openly defiant and aggressive. And the majority of adults will respond to stressful situations with compliance, a dissociative response that supports coping in the face of threat.

> "This is why it is more critical than ever that leaders who are making decisions that impact children, families and the early childhood workforce, need to be in a state to make thoughtful, ethical and reflective decisions. When leaders can keep their cortex open and make ethical and high quality decisions and recommendations, people's compliance does not have to be a drawback or vulnerability. However, the more leaders are activated and working without the aid of their cortex, the more likely we will see poor decisions that are not logical, not future-oriented but instead, focused on short term fixes, and likely to lead to negative consequences with people most likely to be impacted unable to fight back or advocate effectively due to their state dependent reduced functioning"
>
> –Perry (2020a)

- **Resistant to new initiatives, changes, recommendations, feedback and suggestions.** The more threatened people feel, the more likely they are to be resistant to change, feedback, recommendations or suggestions because to feel safe, their brains and bodies need to reduce the factors that increase the stress response: Novelty, unpredictability and lack of agency and control. Therefore, maintaining the status quo—even if they find aspects of it problematic—is likely to feel safer as it is familiar, predictable and their understanding/knowledge of continuing with the ways things have been done, leaves people feeling a greater sense of agency and control.

> "It's is really hard to implement any best practice in a system that is in hyperarousal because the staff are in hyperarousal. The kids are in hyperarousal. We have seen this as the biggest challenge in implementing trauma-informed practice in an early childhood setting. And yet they are the people that spend six to eight hours per day with kids. The people who have the most opportunity to heal and to bring that relational medicine to bear with an early childhood population in public education.
> –Jen Leland, Director of Partnerships, Trauma Transformed

Stress is Contagious. So is Calmness.

"Human beings are relational, and therefore, we absorb the emotions or affect of those around us. Our capacity to instinctively and immediately understand what another is feeling or experiencing is due to our mirror neurons. In this way, the mirror neuron system is the neurological foundation that supports humans' ability to empathize, socialize, and communicate our emotions to others. Mirror neurons are activated when an individual observes someone else taking an action (e.g., walking toward them, gesturing that they need help) or when they observe someone experiencing an emotion (e.g., fear, anger, happiness, surprise) as they help us perceive other people's intentions (Acharya & Shukla, 2012; Conkbayir, 2017). **One person's emotional state is "mirrored" by the neuronal system of another** as the mirror system of one person alters their emotional and physical state to match the emotional and physical state of the person they are interacting with. An example of this is when we see someone crying and feel sad knowing that they are hurting, or we sense someone is stressed and this creates our own feeling of internal distress. This process of taking-in another's emotional state happens at a subconscious level, which means individuals are neither aware of this process nor in control of it" (Nicholson, Kurtz & Perez, 2019, p. 41).

Drew Giles, Director of Educare Programs with Franklin-McKinley School District at Educare California at Silicon Valley describes how he reinforces with his staff the power of using mirror neurons to calm and regulate adults in the context of daily interactions:

> "I talk to my staff about being a mirror. I am basically saying when someone comes at you with a lot of escalated energy, we don't want to absorb that energy but instead, if we stay calm, they will then begin to absorb that calm. In this way, we can lead them to more regulation rather than dysregulation."

Drew uses a metaphor to explain to his staff that remaining calm externally in their interactions with others does not mean that they won't be managing a range of feelings and sensations inside their bodies. He explains this in the following way, "We need to pretend that we're like ducks gracefully swimming across the pond, but underneath the water, our feet are flapping and may be going 90 miles an hour."

Navigating Triggering Events

Sometimes when doing trauma-responsive work, we can trigger those we are working with, and we can become triggered ourselves. This means that we can be in the middle of working in a classroom, providing professional development or facilitating a meeting, and find ourselves feeling overwhelmed and losing focus. This is a natural reaction but can be counterproductive to our goals and lead us to behave in ways that are out of line with our values. When we have a triggering experience, we can react in ways that cause those we are working with to shut down, feel hurt, frustrated or angry.

As we do the work of building trauma-responsive environments, it can be helpful to understand what triggers are and how to navigate our response to them. Trauma and resilience work can be very difficult, and it is very likely that at some point we will become triggered which can be a very uncomfortable and intense experience, so for many of us, it can be helpful to know that it is common and even expected when doing this type of work.

A triggering event is defined as:

> "…an unexpected, intense emotional reaction that seems disproportionate to the original stimulus. Triggered reactions are like an automatic reflex that occurs in a split second without conscious thought. People can feel so overwhelmed and thrown off balance that they are consumed by their triggered reactions and lose touch with the comments and actions occurring around them. During a triggering event, [adults] may feel disoriented and deskilled and have difficulty making conscious, intentional choices about how to respond effectively in the moment…It is common to experience a strong wave of negative emotions when triggered, including anger, fear, sadness, anxiety, shame, guilt and embarrassment. When [adults] feel triggered, the current stimulus has usually reactivated an area of intrapersonal roots, including

unresolved conflict, personal issues or suppressed emotions from their past or current life experiences... Triggering events are a mirror reflecting parts of ourselves that need attention and healing"

—Obear (2013, pp. 152–153)

We can often tell we are being triggered because our reaction might be disproportional to what is going on around us. These reactions are automatic and overwhelming and may even seem to come out of nowhere. Triggering events may be connected to something deeply personal such as unresolved issues or past experiences including our own past traumatic experiences or having too much stress in our lives.

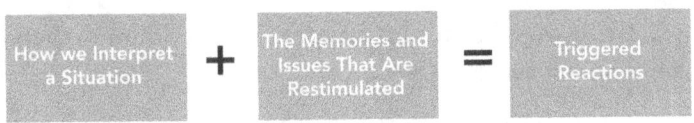

FIGURE 1.4 How We Interpret a Situation
Source: Hannah Shack

When triggered, it is really common to immediately be hit with a rush of strong negative emotions such as anger, shame, embarrassment, hurt and so forth. Most of us aren't able to control *when* we feel triggered, but we can develop tools to help us navigate these situations.

Who we are and what we bring into the work we do including our multiple dominant and marginalized social categories of identity and group membership (e.g., race, gender, class, ability, sexuality, immigration status, formal role and level of authority, etc.) and our fears, prejudices, biases, unconscious needs, values and life experiences impact how we perceive and navigate triggered reactions within our ourselves and in our dialogue and interactions with others (Obear, 2013). Adults who are striving to create trauma-responsive environments have an ethical obligation to build self-awareness and skills in productively managing triggering events so their words and actions can calm and de-escalate versus harm or re-traumatize themselves and others.

It is helpful to **learn about the steps in a triggering cycle** (Obear, 2013). Knowing the steps will help early childhood professionals increase their self-awareness in triggering moments so they can interrupt harmful and/or unproductive reactions and *intentionally choose healing and effective ways to work through the triggering event.* Learning how to react effectively when triggered is challenging and will likely be something you work on throughout your lifetime. The following steps can occur in any order in the brief moments between the time we are triggered and the time we react.

The Triggering Event Cycle

Step 1: Stimulus Occurs. You experience a comment, behavior, image, personal thought, etc.

- *A director loses her temper at a staff meeting*

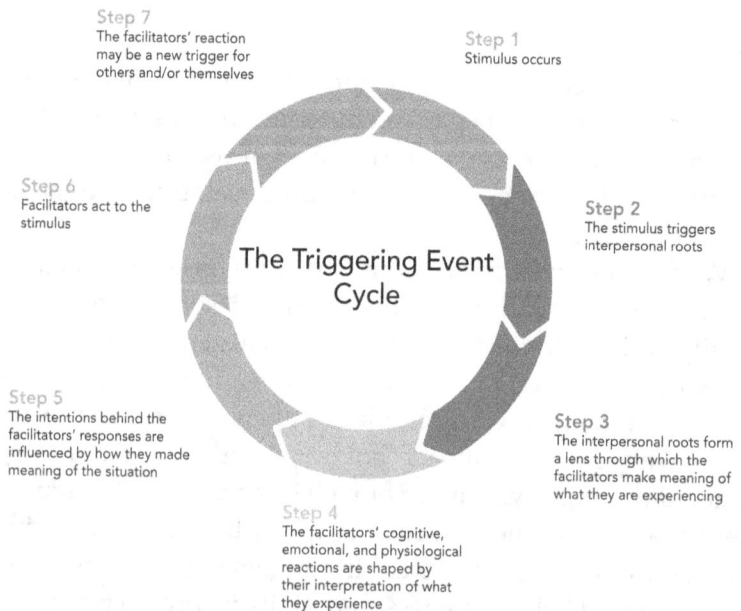

FIGURE 1.5 The Triggering Event Cycle
Source: Hannah Shack

- *A parent arrives to find her child in a "calm down" area*
- *Evaluations of your recent training include several low ratings and critical comments*

Step 2: The stimulus triggers you. This stimulus reactivates some current issue, a past memory or emotion for you.

- *The director's loud voice triggers painful memories of growing up with an abusive and alcoholic father who yelled whenever he was drinking*
- *As a teen, the parent dropped out of school because of the racism she faced. She does not want her child to experience the same discrimination. Seeing him separated from the other children brought up deep and uncomfortable feelings and fears.*
- *As a new trainer, you are worried these low ratings will raise questions about whether you are the right person for the job. If you are not hired back, you will be at risk of losing your housing.*

Step 3: Your perspective forms a lens through which you make meaning of what you are experiencing. You gather selective information and draw a conclusion or make meaning of what you believe just occurred. This can be likened to creating a story about the person or events based on your experiences.

- *The director doesn't like me. My job is on the line.*
- *These teachers are no different than the teachers I had as a child. They are hurting my child. He is not safe here.*
- *[Ignoring the fact that 90% of the evaluations returned had positive ratings]. I'm so bad at this. I knew I never should have accepted this position.*

It's challenging to notice "I am triggered" in Step 1 or 2, however, in Step 3 where we are constructing meaning about what we think happened, we have the opportunity to create a pause that can interrupt our reactivity, assumptions and biases and create space for responding in more effective, attuned and empathic ways.

> "We create narratives in our minds about what happened and what people's intentions are and these interpretations can lead us to feel anger, frustration and resentment toward others. *This is an important point to interrupt the triggering cycle so we don't react in ways that causes harm and undermines their sense of safety in our presence.* I can suspend my initial assumptions and judgments and create a different narrative that opens up great possibilities for connection. "I wonder if…." We have the option of creating other narratives that allow us to feel compassion for others. And then from a more grounded stance, we can choose to respond in a way that is regulated"
>
> –Obear (2013, p. 158)

Step 4: Your mental, emotional and physical reactions are shaped by their interpretation of what you experience. You experience strong feelings related to your immediate mental, emotional and physical reactions to your perception of the stimulus.

- *My heart starts to beat rapidly. My chest gets tight. I can barely breathe.*
- *I can't be here in this place. I can barely make eye contact with the teachers. I quickly grab my son and run out the door. My fists are clenched, I'm grinding my teeth, I'm running to the car and not noticing sights or sounds around me.*
- *I feel numb, my mind starts to race through all the scenarios that could happen if I lose my apartment. I hear my name, but I can't move or talk, I'm frozen in place.*

Step 5: The intentions behind your responses are influenced by how you made meaning of the situation. You may be unaware that you are triggered and you may begin to choose a response to the stimulus based on perception and your emotional state.

- *I'm noticing that I'm triggered and I start raising my voice or make an unkind comment.*

- *Wow, they are having a bad day and taking it out on me. I'm going to pause and take a few deep breaths before I respond.*
- *When things are this out of my control, the only thing I can do is to take a moment to pray.*

Step 6: You react to the stimulus. And, your reaction may then trigger others in the group.

- *I notice that I might be triggered and I become anxious and avoidant of others. Those around me start to treat me like there is something wrong with me and they avoid me.*

Step 7: Your reaction may be a new trigger for others and/or themselves. And when others around you are triggered, they may trigger you further.

- *I feel so upset that I leave the meeting. This triggers others in attendance. Some are worried about me and run after me, others are angry the meeting was disrupted and one person is pacing around the room with her palms sweating and her heart racing.*

Tip: *It can be helpful to have someone you trust provide you with feedback. They can gently help you recognize when you are feeling triggered and help you reflect and regulate.*

Identify warning signals. Our goal in learning about the triggering event cycle is to learn to recognize when we are triggered *before* we have an automatic reaction (Obear, 2013). Once we learn how to notice the warning signs in our *body sensations* (heartbeat, breathing etc.), *emotions* (fear, shame, sadness etc.), *behavior* (snap at someone, close my body language off by crossing my arms and avoiding eye contact) and *thoughts* ("why is this person so difficult?" "why can't they just leave me alone?" "I've got to get out of here!"), we are in a position to choose more productive strategies to navigate triggered reactions and to facilitate the conversation in ways that align with our values. Try to observe and document your personal warning signals: Ask yourself:

- How do I feel when I'm triggered?
- What does it feel like in my body?
- What kinds of thoughts run through my head?

"Common **physiological reactions** that can serve as early warning signals include a racing pulse, pounding heart, fidgety energy, blushing, an urgent sense to respond and difficulty breathing…in addition a variety of unconscious behaviors… clicking pens, eye twitches, pointing their fingers, pacing, rolling their eyes, tapping their feet, and making fists" Other warning signs to become aware of his inner dialogue, the thoughts that are influence how we are defining the situation…"for example, **judgments of others** ("He's so arrogant" "They are so rude and immature"), **judgments of self** ("They are so much smarter than me" "This is all my fault," and "I am letting people down"), **expectations of what self or others should do** ("I should know how to handle this," "I have to maintain control"), **thinking in absolutes** ("I am totally incompetent"), and **taking the stance of the victim** ("My boss is out to get me.")"

–Obear (2013, p. 159)

> **Tip:** *Open an honest dialogue with your colleagues. Share your warning signals with one another and strategies for helping one another to de-escalate in a triggering moment.*

Identify common triggers: We are often triggered by the same things over and over again. Begin to notice when you are triggered and take note of the themes. You may begin to notice a pattern.

- Can you remember a time in the recent past where you felt triggered or had a strong emotional reaction to something that maybe wasn't that big of a deal?
- Do you notice any patterns?

"Common triggers from others include belittling comments, disruptive and controlling behavior, arrogance, offensive comments, challenges to one's credibility, bullying, refusal to self-reflect or engage in dialogue, denial of privileged status, dismissing the conversation as political correctness, portraying themselves as the victim of reverse discrimination…the expression of deep pain, grief, or anger" or through one's own actions and thoughts including "making a mistake, thoughts of self-doubt, saying something biased, and not responding effectively in the moment"
—Obear (2013, p. 160)

Understand common reactions: Begin to understand how you typically react when you are triggered. Notice how intense your emotions are on a scale of 0–10 (0 = no emotional reaction and 10 = significant or highest level of emotional intensity). If you are feeling really strong or intense emotion, it can be hard to respond appropriately.

> "When my emotions are more intense, around a level 6–7, I am far more likely to react without conscious thought…If I feel triggered to a level of 9–10, I rarely have capacity to respond effectively. Or, if I am numb and my feelings are shut down, I may be a 1-2 but so disconnected that I am unable to respond.
> —Obear (2013, p. 161)

There are many ways you can intentionally choose to respond when you are triggered that will slow down or interrupt the activation of your stress response system. Following are some of the many ways you could respond effectively *when* you notice you are in the middle of a triggering event:

- Use self-disclosure to share a personal thought, feeling or experience to make a relational connection with the participant(s) ("I'm feeling really overwhelmed right now. I appreciate you sharing your thoughts with me, but I need a moment to process what I heard.")

- Ask a question to gain time to get more centered, accurately understand the participant's perspective, and intentionally choose a response ("Tell me a little bit more about what you mean by that."). Having to respond to your question may help the person reflect on what they said and not only their intended message but also the impact their words or actions had.
- Ask the person to talk you through their thought process so you can better understand how they arrived as their statement, assumption, belief etc. ("Wow, I'm really interested in knowing more about your perspective. Can you tell me a little more about the context/where you are coming from?").
- Ask a question to clarify a person's intent ("I wonder what you mean by that comment, are you just wanting to process something out loud or are you open to feedback and discussion?").
- Acknowledge the triggering moment and invite others to share how they are feeling ("I really appreciate this conversation, but I am actually feeling triggered right now. I wonder how others are feeling?").
- Describe (without interpretation) what you agree/disagree with
- Stop the conversation and center attention on the group's living agreements and norms for conversation and work together
- Invite people to write down their thoughts and feelings and reflections
- Use humor to de-escalate the situation
- Provide a regulation break (movement, go outside and get fresh air, lead group in taking five deep breaths) or agree to revisit the topic at another time
- Redirect the topic of conversation to the focus and intention of the original discussion. (Adapted from Obear, 2013)

Calm and ground. If you find that your stress response is activated (you are triggered and in a state of fight, flight or freeze), there are several strategies you can use to calm and ground yourself so you can have agency to choose an intentional (and trauma-sensitive) rather than a reactive (and trauma-inducing) response.

- **Conduct a "systems check."** Do a quick scan of your body and notice the intensity of your sensations and emotions. Also, notice the assumptions and interpretations that are influencing how you are creating meaning about the experience. Are there any memories or personal experiences that are impacting your reaction?
- **Use calming/grounding techniques.** If your breath has sped up, if your heart is racing, if your thoughts are racing, begin to calm yourself down by taking deep belly breaths, or noticing your environment (even naming to yourself the color of the walls, the feeling of your clothing, the placement of your hands). Get a drink of water, look at pictures of friends and family or nature, hum to yourself or listen to one minute of a calming song.
- Then, **remind yourself of your core values** and **shift your inner dialogue**. Remind yourself why you are in the field of early childhood. Noticing your negative thoughts and reframing them can be a really powerful tool.

  - Repeat a mantra ("Everything happens for a reason" or "Trust the process")
  - Use a visualization technique to imagine responding effectively; or
  - Quickly check in with a colleague or write out your feelings or intentions as a way to get more centered.

> **Explore Yourself.** Trauma and healing work is hard. It is valuable to use self-reflection often. Ask yourself:
>
> - What current life issues and dynamics are at play for me right now?
> - What unresolved issues are in my past that might be interfering with my professional work? Are there past traumas or wounds that are influencing me to "lead" from a place of hurt?
> - What are my fears?
> - What things do people do or say that are triggering for me?

Following are two authentic vignettes describing triggering events in the context of early educators' daily work. Read through the vignettes to see how many of the ideas and strategies described in this section you can identify.

Cecilia Fernandez: "I Was Aware that I Was Triggered." Facilitating a Training for an Early Learning Advocacy Program

I was facilitating a workgroup to discuss our early learning program's new trauma-informed strategy. This group was comprised of community members, families, social workers, health providers, teachers and paraprofessionals. Many in the workgroup had survived their own traumas and were invested in sharing their experiences and knowledge. For many reasons, the group dynamics were difficult. Many of the participants felt strongly and their ideas often seemed to be at odds with one another. I called on a participant to share their thoughts about one of the strategies we were debating ("Taking actions to disrupt inequity"). I was met with complete silence. The participant looked down at the ground and hunched over in their chair. My thoughts started racing, my heart started pounding, and I could feel my whole body starting to tingle. I was feeling embarrassed and angry. I started telling myself that I was incompetent and that I should have never tried to facilitate a group like this. I immediately blurted out "Silence is not an option in equity work. We need everyone's input if we are going to move forward." At that point, all of the energy in the room became intense and angry. This made me feel even worse, even more fearful, even more angry. I could feel the emotion overwhelming me and I noticed how shallow my breath was, how my heart was pounding through my chest and I couldn't think clearly. **I was aware that I was triggered.**

I took a deep breath and noticed how my feet felt in shoes, I noticed the tree outside of the window, the texture of the notepad in my hand and the sound of the children playing outside. I took just a moment to check in with myself, the thoughts and feelings I was having about the current situation, how I was perceiving the group dynamics and the situation around me. I asked the group if we could pause the meeting for a moment. First, I apologized for my comment and told the group that my reaction was out of line with my values. I let the group know that I was interested in creating a safe and secure space that allowed for honesty and openness. I asked the group for permission to pause and clarify our vision, values and intentions. We took five minutes and wrote down our collective vision for the working session. I made a point to acknowledge some of the common ways we react when triggered—our natural negative responses in group dynamics: We want to gain everyone's approval, make everyone happy, prove our own competence or win every argument. The group found it really empowering to talk about negative intentions openly and authentically. We were then able to pick back up where we left off. The participant that I called on explained that they were feeling triggered too and was now ready to share her thoughts.

Reflection/Discussion Questions

- ◆ Did the facilitator move through the steps of the triggering event cycle sequentially?

- How did the facilitator become fully present in the moment? What has worked for you in the past?
- What triggered the facilitator? Facial expression, comments, even silence can be triggering.
- What skills and values did the facilitator model and how were her intentional actions a powerful learning experience for the participants?
- What do you notice in this vignette that reflects trauma-responsive practice?

Megan Paul: "It Is Important to Be Mindful of Triggers and to Have a Toolkit of Strategies Available." Training a Group of Quality Rating and Improvement (QRIS) Assessors

I was training a group of QRIS assessors. I knew many of them were working in childcare settings with some of the city's most vulnerable populations. I felt it was important to include some information about triggers as part of their training. I began this particular training session by sharing about a time I felt triggered. I shared that I had just arrived to assess a childcare program that was attached to a liquor store. As I parked my car, I was immediately triggered by seeing the children coming into school at the same time other members of the community were coming in and out of the liquor store. I felt almost panicked and kept thinking "this isn't safe..." I tried to push past this feeling as I went into the first classroom. Shortly after I arrived, I noticed a teacher who was impatient with a child who was not cleaning up despite her many requests to do so. My palms began to sweat. I could feel my heart racing. I felt nauseous. I felt a surge of anger and I felt like yelling at the teacher. I sat in one of the child sized chairs in the corner of the room. I barely remember completing the assessment and walking to my car. Once I got to my car, I started sobbing.

After crying for several minutes, **I realized I had just experienced a triggering event**. I thought for a moment about what happened, why was I triggered? I realized that I was triggered first by seeing the children enter their classroom next to the liquor store. I was feeling worried for their safety and my mind was flooded with thoughts like "what are these children witnessing everyday as they come in and out of their classroom?" "I bet they have seen some things that have scared them or overheard things that might make them feel unsafe." Then, when I felt the teacher had been unkind to a child, I really got overwhelmed. I used this instance to confirm my beliefs that this was an unsafe and uncaring environment. Once I was able to walk myself through the events of the morning in the quiet of my car, I realized that my judgment was not likely empathy based or fair. I knew, at that point, that I would need to talk with a colleague to sort through my feelings and reaction and then return to assess the program on another date.

I shared this story with the assessors to normalize triggering events. I wanted to talk with them about it before they got into the field so we could identify some helpful strategies they could use when/if they found themselves responding to triggering events like this. In addition, I wanted them to know that when you are triggered you can lose touch with what is occurring around you (actions and comments). For this reason, **it is important to be mindful of triggers and to have a toolkit of strategies available** so you can stay calm and present as you complete your assessment.

Reflection/Discussion Questions

- What are some factors that contributed to Megan's triggering reaction?
- What are some of the warning signs that Megan could identify were indications that she was becoming triggered?
- How did Megan react when she was triggered? How do you typically react when you are triggered? It is great to catch it before you react, but sometimes watching our reactions is the only way to notice that we've been triggered.
- What are some strategies Megan could have used when she felt triggered? What works for you?

The Complexities of Building Body Awareness

As trauma is experienced and remembered in the body, when activated, our stress response systems release stress chemicals that begin a chain reaction of physiological responses impacting every part of our brains and bodies (e.g., pounding heart, redirection of blood flow away from the extremities, pupil dilation, quickening breathing etc.). Healing from trauma and learning to de-escalate the stress response system requires attending to our bodies. However, the very fact that the body is the site that holds and remembers trauma can make building body awareness very difficult for people impacted by trauma. In many cases, children and adults with histories of toxic stress and trauma have an automatic "freeze" or dissociative responses where they disconnect from the intense emotions and physical sensations associated with traumatic experiences as their body's automatic (sub-conscious) survival skill. Disconnecting from one's body (sometimes called "disembodiment") is therefore, a powerful coping strategy for many trauma survivors. **Many trauma survivors may find that reconnecting to their bodies** (e.g., embodiment) and strengthening sensory literacy and body awareness—**is a deeply painful, unsettling and triggering process.** As Berila (2016) explains, this requires that anyone guiding early educators to reclaim their embodiment—to strengthen body awareness and sensory literacy—must take extra care to understand the risks and special considerations involved:

- "It can be an overwhelming process to learn to sink into our bodies when we have long been disconnected from them" (p. 49)
- "Reclaiming our embodiment is a slow and often unsettling process. To become embodied for many of us means to counter a lifelong process of disembodiment. It requires learning new skills and practicing them constantly, in the face of the barrage of cultural messages that encourage the opposite. Reconnecting with our embodiment will not happen" quickly. (p. 57)

- Some people will not be ready to "sink into their embodiment or may not feel safe doing so" in a group setting. They may need the "additional support of counseling services, depending on where they are in their healing process." It's important when we talk about body awareness that we prepare people for this reality. We can "let them know the range of reactions that might arise and why [and] give them a lens for making sense of those reactions." We can also suggest mindfulness practices as ways to handle triggering reactions in the moment, or alternative activities for those who are not yet ready to engage in somatics/body awareness work, and we can direct people to information about additional resources and services if they need to seek additional support. The most important thing we will do is to **provide them with choice**, "even being able to tune in enough to their own needs to discern which embodiment practice they wish to choose is a big step" (p. 58) in becoming trauma-responsive and supporting a healing process.

Disembodiment is also described as a consequence of the oppression we all experience as a result of the dominant belief systems in our society that places value on cognitive knowing (e.g., thinking, writing) and dismisses emotional and embodied forms of knowing (e.g., body awareness, expression through movement etc.). Berila (2016) states that we are socialized to perceive bodies as "something we have,' objects that exist in the service of cognitive goals" (p. 40). We see this in Western perspectives on trauma—strongly influenced by psychology and psychiatry—that treat the mind and body as separate entities where the mind (and thinking) are emphasized and the body is too often ignored (Letendre, 2002).

For these reasons, trauma-responsive anti-oppression work aims to "reclaim" the wisdom of the body, to guide individuals and groups to **"reinhabit our bodies as sites of knowledge"** (Berila, 2016, pp. 39–40). This involves strengthening awareness of our bodies' ways of knowing—*interoception*—including "sensing our breathing, digestion, hunger, arousal, pain, emotion, fatigue" etc. and awareness of the movement and coordination between different parts of our bodies and/or between our bodies and the environment around us (p. 44). This is distinct from a conceptual or thinking awareness of oneself (a way of knowing that is rational, abstract and rooted in language) which is a cognitive process. Instead, **building body awareness is about building awareness of the present moment and the sensations and feelings in one's body** (p. 44).

As many people impacted by trauma find difficulty in processing their thoughts, feelings and memories verbally, providing opportunities for body-oriented, non-verbal activities can be helpful. Embodied activities (e.g., art, theater, dance, movement, music, breathing, mindfulness etc.) can strengthen coping and healing by reconnecting people to their bodies and providing ways to manage strong feelings and calm activation of the stress response system (Guarino, Soares, Konnath, Clervil, & Bassuk, 2009).

A Lifeline: Learning the Pathways to Regulation

To function in the workplace, adults need to be regulated to access their cortex (thinking, reasoning and relationship part of the brain). It is critical that early educators learn how to use various strategies to reduce their stress and calm their stress response systems when activated. *The key to attuned, responsive equitable and high quality practice is regulation.*

> **What is the most effective and powerful pathway to regulation? As Perry (2020c) states:**
>
> Relational Regulation
>   PLUS....
>   One or more of the following forms of regulation:
>
> - Top Down Regulation
> - Bottom Up Regulation
> - Intentional Disconnection Regulation

The Foundation: Relational Regulation

Relational regulation is the most powerful way to buffer stress. People feel safest when they are with others who provide them with a sense of belonging and with whom they experience mutual feelings of care and respect. This is due to our relational neurobiology, that is, the ways in which our brains are wired for connection. When we are in the presence of others we care for, love and respect, we can tolerate more stress and adversity and we are also more likely to have opportunities to build resilience and heal from the impact of previous adversity and trauma (Perry, 2020c). And the reverse is also at play, when people are in environments that lack a value and focus on caring relationships, they are more vulnerable to the negative impacts of stressors and less likely to build resilience and heal from trauma.

As Perry (2020c) states, the most powerful and effective approaches to regulating our emotions and behavior happen when adults are in the presence of others they trust and feel safe with (relational regulation) and use one or more of the following strategies:

Top Down Approaches: "Using your cortex (thoughts) to regulate and calm."

One way to regulate and reduce stress is a "top down" approach. This is using your cortex to help calm your stress response system by thinking or telling yourself that you are safe, that you are ok, you can handle a stressor, you may felt sense of being in danger but you are *really* safe. Top down strategies use the intellectual parts of our brains, our thinking/reasoning, to help us calm our stress related emotions and behaviors. Top down strategies are effective in some situations, however, they require use of the cortex. Once someone is already dysregulated and their lower brainstem is activating a survival response, it is extremely difficult to use top down regulation strategies as the cortex can drop to as low as 10% of its efficiency (Perry, 2020c). This is why, although quite popular, top down strategies are the least efficient pathway to regulation. Examples of Top Down regulation strategies include:

- Thinking of grounders (people, places, objects, activities associated with safety, belonging and calm)
- Mapping out different solutions to a problems
- Repeating mantras or sayings ("I got this!")
- Noticing and addressing the thinking patterns that become distorted. Instead of "I am all bad", "No one likes me" or "this is the end of the world" reframing these thought to be, "I regret the mistake and am eager to learn from it" or "Her comment was upsetting but she had some interesting points" or "This was a frustrating situation but I can get through it."

Bottom Up Approaches: "Using patterned repetitive somato-sensory activities to regulate and calm."

Bottom up approaches are the fastest and most effective and direct way of regulating stress for children and adults (Perry, 2020c). Bottom up approaches directly reach the core neural networks in the lower brain responsible for regulation. Repetitive somato (movement) sensory (sight/sound/touch etc.) activities engage these core regulatory networks and help people calm their stress and regulate their brains and bodies. Examples of Bottom Up regulation strategies include:

- Rocking back and forth (in a rocking chair or just in place)
- Walking or running
- Swimming, riding a bike
- Jumping (e.g., on a trampoline)
- Petting a dog or other pets/animals
- Listening to music, dancing singing or chanting
- Humming
- Deep breathing exercises
- Stretching, yoga, Tai Chi or Qi Gong
- Drumming and rhythmic use of musical instruments
- Mindfulness activities

Krystal Lewis, a Head Start Director, soothes herself and buffers her stress by **ironing her clothes**, a coping strategy she started in her childhood and continues to use to this day. Learning about the science of trauma and resilience helped Krystal discover why ironing has been so healing for her and how engaging in this rhythmic repetitive somatosensory activity has been a powerful protective factor for her throughout the years. She explains:

> "I iron everything, everything. It doesn't matter what it is. My son always asks me, are you going somewhere? No. Well, why are ironing? That's something that as a child that stuck with me, that's how trauma impacts us. And you know, somebody sees that as crazy. I see it as something that is necessary for me to manage. Having pressed clothes. That's very important to me. I iron everything. I never realized the impact of my childhood trauma until recently when I could verbalize why I do what I do. Now I recognize that I literally iron everything, and that's just who I became after my childhood experiences of trauma."

Intentional Disengagement Regulation Approaches: "Proactive intentional disengagement to regulate and calm" (Perry, 2020c). Disengagement approaches to regulation are the most common way that we as humans regulate and calm ourselves when we are impacted by stress. Disengagement is essentially when a person's brain momentarily withdraws from focusing on the external (outside) world and shuts off. During this time of intentional withdrawal, people can shut off in healthy ways momentarity in order to take a break and restore their energy (The Child Trauma Academy, 2011, p. 4). Examples of Intentional Disengagement Regulation strategies include:

- Daydreaming or mind-wandering
- Disengaging/tuning out for brief moments during a meeting (e.g., to think about how what you are hearing relates to you/your life)
- Guided imagery

- Prayer or meditation
- Taking a nap
- Taking some quiet space
- Cooking
- Gardening
- Taking a shower or bath

Programs, Schools and Organizations Are Impacted by State Based Functioning Too

"All decision making is state dependent, and you want somebody to be regulated and you want them to have full access to their cortex when they make their decisions... Your job is to make the working environment where they make decisions safer and more regulated and give them opportunities for self-regulating activity and make sure that the policies and practices of the organization and your leadership style are regulated."

–Bruce Perry (2020b)

In trauma-responsive environments, strategies are actively and intentionally used to support adults and children to maintain emotional and behavioral regulation. Stress related behaviors and dysregulation are met with relational support and activities that tap into core regulatory networks to calm and de-escalate people's bodies and brains. Perry (2020c) recommends several **"organizational care" strategies** that support people and organizations to be "regulated:"

- **Build in short regulation breaks throughout the workday.** The more stress people are experiencing, the more frequently they will need short regulation breaks throughout their workday to avoid burnout, high turnover, dysregulation and poor quality and inefficiency. Short regulation breaks—from 30 seconds to 5 minutes—should be built into meetings and trainings. It's important to create a brief time and space an invite everyone to stretch, take a collective deep breath, get a glass of water, listen to a minute of music together, or to participate in a guided imagery. Right after people have regulation breaks is the time their cortex is most likely to be open, so this is the time to invite them to reflect, problem-solve or engage in the most cognitively demanding work. Additionally, be intentional about building in time to be playful, have fun and lighten the environment (e.g., have check-ins at the beginning of a meeting that are fun and help break the ice and build relational connections).

- **Decrease the number of decisions people have to make on a given day or during one meeting.** When people have to make too many decisions at once, decision fatigue can set in (Perry, 2020b). What does this mean? They have less ability to utilize the full range of cognitive abilities in their cortex which translates into less thoughtful and more reactive decision-making. By simply reducing the number of decisions people have to make (and engaging them in regulatory activities just before they need to make those decisions), the cognitive load on adults is reduced and they are more capable of making responsible and responsive decisions.

- **Match the stakes of decision-making with the length of regulation-breaks.** There is a direct relationship between the importance/complexity and stakes associated with decisions and the amount of time needed to regulate so adults are able to access their cortex. The bigger, more consequential or complex a decision is that an individual or group needs to make, the longer amount of time people will need just prior to the decision for a break to engage in regulation strategies. Perry (2020b) describes this as "dosing" decision-making. And conversely, important decisions should not be made when people are least likely to be in a regulated state (e.g., just before lunch or at the end of the day when they are hungry or tired or when they are highly stressed).

- **When people are stressed, reduce their workload.** Because of state dependent functioning, people are not as productive or efficient in doing their work (and they are unable to learn as efficiently) when they are stressed, especially if their stress response systems are activated over a long period of time which is emotionally and physically exhausting. It is important to anticipate this reduction in efficiency and effectiveness and adjust the expectations for what individuals and groups can accomplish. Giving yourself and others grace and recalibrating expectations prevents or minimizes the chance that people will have feelings of self-doubt, guilt and/or shame.

- **As stress increases, provide more opportunities for people to partner to accomplish their daily work.** Because stress reduces people's capacity, the more stress adults are managing, the greater the need to create opportunities for people to work in partnership in order to maintain efficiency and effectiveness. Working together, adults can provide one another with relational regulation—acting as buffers for stress—and share responsibilities so they are able to maintain the quality of their work.
- **Delegate responsibility but minimize group decision-making.** In trauma-responsive environments, it is important for people to be involved in the decision-making process, to have a voice and to help think through the information, options and the potential consequences and outcomes of a decision. However, it can be counterproductive to ask a group to be engaged in a collaborative process of decision-making as this can, Perry (2020b) reminds us, lead to "analysis-paralysis." Leaders can provide coaching, reflective supervision and other forms of support to build capacity of staff to make good decisions in line with the program values and mission. The key is to create a working environment that strikes a healthy balance between decision fatigue and analysis paralysis meaning the inability to make any final decision, so adults have opportunities for agency and control without being overly burdened by decision-making. It's also important to resist micromanagement as this disempowers and dysregulates people and leads them to make less effective decisions.

♦ **Take time for "mind-wandering" before making major decisions.** It is important not to rush into making major decisions. Adults can engage in all the work our cortex affords us—e.g., hearing different perspectives and ideas, analyzing the benefits and limitations of various solutions etc.—however, it's important to plan time for people to allow their brains to engage in a "mind wandering" process (time for the mind to sort through and make-sense of information) by taking regulation breaks. What does this look like? After thinking and talking through an important decision—go home, exercise, watch a movie, listen to music, get a night's sleep, eat a healthy breakfast, talk with a friend and then return to making the decision. This type of break to regulate and support mind wandering often makes a critical decision easier to make as information is integrated or synthesized in a manner that brings clarity and insight.

Reflection/Discussion Questions

- Which top-down approach have you used to regulate?
- Which bottom-up approach have you used to regulate?
- Do you find these strategies are a part of your daily routine and practice? If not, what is one small step you can take to add a strategy to your toolbox of strategies that you can to use to keep yourself regulated?

Bottom Up Pathway to Regulation

Somatosensory Activities

Repetitive (patterned) **and Rhythmic** (resonant with neural patterns) **Activities**

Bruce Perry (2020c) recommends patterned, repetitive, body-based, rhythmic activities for calming an activated nervous system. For young children, these somatosensory activities help to mature the brainstem and facilitate development that was impaired or delayed as a consequence of trauma. For adults, the activities help provide regulation in times of stress or during a trauma trigger/trauma reminder. Consider using these activities as moments of "pause" throughout the day. They allow for moments to keep the activated stress response system in the "window of tolerance," prevent us from moving into the dysregulated or hyper/hypoaroused states of fight, flight or freeze and promote a sense of safety. Following are examples that are regulating for adults and children:

- **Finger and/or Toe Wiggles**—Wiggle your finger or your toes. This brief break relieves tension.
- **Using Art or Play Dough**—Nonverbal forms of sand tray, play dough, art, painting or drawing can help connect the logical brain to that part of our brain that is housing big emotions. When we draw, it allows nonverbal outlets for communicating what is happening inside of us. When we express our internal world of emotions, it can serve to calm them.
- **Rocking from Side to Side**—Imagine you are at a concert standing as you listen to the music. As you imagine listening to the music, you rock from side to side. This can be very subtle rocking yourself in this rhythmic pattern left to right.
- **Walking**—Walking provides rhythmic movement and short releases of tension in the body. It can clear the mind and the movement can allow us to think more clearly.
- **Shoulder Shrugs**—Raise your shoulder up to your ears and then release. The tension and then subsequent release of tension helps us relax our muscles associated with stress.
- **Swinging Arms and Legs**—Imagine you are tracking down a taxi and you shake your arms up and down as if you are trying to get them to see you

need them to stop (or we could say imagine you are at an airport and your loved one just got off the plane—swing your arms up and down so they can see you). You can swing both arms over your head or across your body. For your legs, this can be down seated or standing. You can shake one leg at a time or both at once. Imagine shaking all the stress out of your arms and/or legs and releasing the tension that might be inside through your limbs.

- **Spending Time Outside (Barefoot is ideal)**—Being barefoot and feeling the earth or water underneath our feet can help us feel grounded and can increase our feelings of calm.
- **Humming or Singing**—The rhythmic vocalization of humming or singing stimulates the parasympathetic nervous system which slows down the activated stress response.
- **Blow Bubbles through a Straw into Water**—Literally put a coffee straw or a regular straw into water or a liquid and blow bubbles. This out breathing can stimulate the PNS and slow the stress response.
- **Butterfly Hug**—Wrap your arms around yourself as if giving yourself a big hug. Now with your hands tap left to right or both hands at once as if you have butterfly wings gently tapping 5–6 times.
- **Use Your 5 Senses**—When you have high levels of stress it is common to leave our bodies or the present moment and be hijacked by fear. One way to bring us back into our body and the present moment to feel safe is to engage one or more of your senses: (1) *Use your sense of sight*: Look at a photo of nature/greenery or a beloved family or friend; (2) *Use your sense of touch*: Hold a piece of ice or a cold object from freezer; (3) *Use your sense of smell*: Try lavender lotion or soap or essential oils; (4) *Use your sense of sound*: Put earphones on and listen to calming music or a favorite song.

References

Acharya, S., & Shukla, S. (2012). Mirror neurons: Enigma of the metaphysical modular brain. *Journal of Natural Science, Biology and Medicine*, 3(2), 118–124. Doi: 10.4103/0976-9668.101878.

Berila, B. (2016). *Integrating mindfulness into anti-oppression pedagogy: Social justice in higher education*. New York, NY: Routledge.

Conkbayer, M. (2017). *Early childhood and neuroscience: Theory, research and implications for practice*. New York, NY: Bloomsbury Academic.

Letendre, A. (2002). Aboriginal traditional medicine: Where does it fit? *Crossing Boundaries: An Interdisciplinary Journal*, 1(2), 78–87.

Nicholson, J., Perez, L., & Kurtz, J. (2019). *Trauma-Informed Practices for Early Childhood Educators: Relationship-Based Approaches that Support Healing and Build Resilience in Young Children*. Routledge Press.

Obear, K. (2013). Navigating triggering events. Critical competencies for social justice educators. In L. Landreman (Ed.), *The art of effective facilitation: Reflections from social justice educators* (pp. 151–172). Stylus Publishing, LLC.

Perry, B. (2020a). Understanding state dependent functioning. NN COVID Series 2. Retrieved from https://youtu.be/PZg1dIskBLA

Perry, B. (2020b). Decision fatigue. NN COVID Series 8. Retrieved from https://youtu.be/Yc-Nv8eqfgM

Perry, B. (2020c). Understanding regulation. NN COVID Series 5. Retrieved from https://youtu.be/L3qlYGwmHYY

Guarino, K., Soares, P., Konnath, K., Clervil, R., & Bassuk, E.. (2009). Trauma-informed organizational toolkit. Rockville, MD: Center for Mental Health Services, Substance Abuse and Mental Health Services Administration, and the Daniels Fund, the National Child Traumatic Stress Network, and the W.K. Kellogg Foundation. Available at www.homeless.samhsa.gov and www.familyhomelessness.org

2

Moving from Stress and Trauma-Inducing to Trauma-Informed and Trauma-Responsive Healing Centered Early Childhood Programs, Schools and Systems

As described in the introduction, teachers cannot support and heal children in silos on their own as their success in meeting the needs of children and families impacted by trauma is deeply influenced by the level of trauma-sensitivity of the programs, organizations and systems they are working within. Trauma Transformed, a SAMHSA (Substance Abuse and Mental Health Services Administration) funded trauma-informed system of care initiative in northern California, created a framework that that programs, organizations and systems can use to evaluate where they are on a learning continuum in becoming trauma-responsive and healing centered. We adapted their continuum for this book to support early educators to identify the current strengths and what we call 'learning edges' (areas desired for growth, change or improvement) within their organizations. On one end of the continuum are environments that are stress and trauma-inducing, then moving to the center are environments that are trauma-informed and moving all the way to the right—what we can envision as a Northstar for programs, schools and systems—are trauma-responsive healing centered environments.

Trauma-Responsive Organizational Continuum for the Early Childhood Field

Adapted from Trauma Transformed (www.traumatransformed.org). Graphics: Hannah Shack

FIGURE 2.1 Stress Inducing
Source: Hannah Shack

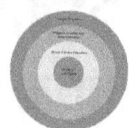

FIGURE 2.2 Trauma-Informed
Source: Hannah Shack

FIGURE 2.3 Healing Centered
Source: Hannah Shack

Stress and Trauma-Inducing Environments	Trauma-Informed Environments	Trauma-Responsive Healing Engaged Environments
- Unsafe - Relationships lack trust and/or are frequently disrupted - Fragmented, silos - Authoritarian, top down decision-making - Reactive - Overwhelmed and under-resourced - Rigid and inflexible - Fear driven and punitive - Reproduces inequities - Re-enactment/re-telling of trauma-related stories - Self-care not supported	- Developing awareness of trauma and resilience - Common language and shared values - Focus on reflective and relationship-based practice - New knowledge begins to inform policies, procedures and practices - Value on collaboration - Acknowledge historical and cultural trauma and other forms of oppression - Culturally responsive self-care is beginning to be supported and integrated	- Values human connection and ethic of care for self and others - Safe and predictable environments - Work is collaborative, focused on a greater good, power is shared - Learning, growth and optimism - Honesty, authenticity and vulnerability - Pausing, reflecting, meaning-making - Joy, creativity and innovation - Transforming underlying causes of harm within structures and institutions - Strengths, assets, well-being - Culturally responsive self-care valued and integrated

STRESS AND TRAUMA INDUCING → TO → STRESS AND TRAUMA REDUCING →

FIGURE 2.4 Arrow
Source: Hannah Shack

It is essential to recognize that programs, schools and systems do not fall neatly into one of these categories. This continuum was developed as a tool to support individual and group reflection, dialogue and identification of strengths and areas for learning and growth as well as tracking progress against desired goals. Programs, schools and systems are complex and dynamic and will identify themselves up and down the continuum for different indicators. For example, a child care program may identify that a strength of their program is their value for and commitment to relationship-building and a learning edge is beginning to implement organizational care routines and more intentionally supporting self-care in the workplace.

This tool is not intended to be punitive. We do not intend for this tool to be used to blame, shame or criticize program staff or administrators. Instead, this continuum is intended to support educators to create reflective learning organizations where there is an honest acknowledgement and appreciation of people's work and efforts and an understanding that healthy organizations engage in a continual process of collaborative learning.

We encourage individuals and teams to use this continuum to promote cycles of reflection, dialogue, goal setting, progress checking, learning and continuous improvement. In alignment with a commitment to continuous learning and quality improvement, we encourage leaders and groups to be integrating the use of this tool into Results Oriented Cycles of Inquiry:

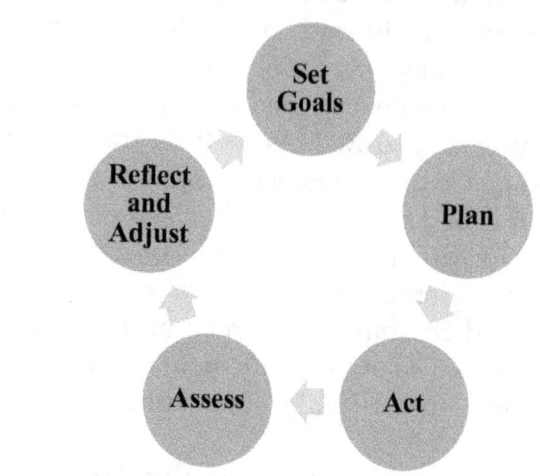

FIGURE 2.5 Roci Cycle

Source: Hannah Shack

The Results-Oriented Cycle of Inquiry (ROCI) was designed as a process to support the capability for continuous organizational learning and improvement. ROCI is a set of five steps that develop educators' habits of mind to engage in continuous improvement. The five steps include:

Set Goals: Working together as a team, identify values and define clear goals and desired outcomes.

Plan: Collaboratively create plans for interventions and organizational change.

Act: Take actions to change policies, procedures, practices and/or programs.

Assess: Collect feedback from all impacted by the changes as well as evidence of intended and unintended impacts and their consequences.

Reflect and Adjust: Compare feedback, impact and consequences against stated values and goals and make adjustments to be more responsive and effective.

Source: http://www.partnersinschools.org/wp-content/uploads/2012/06/ROCIOverview.pdf

Stress and Trauma-Inducing Organizational Environments

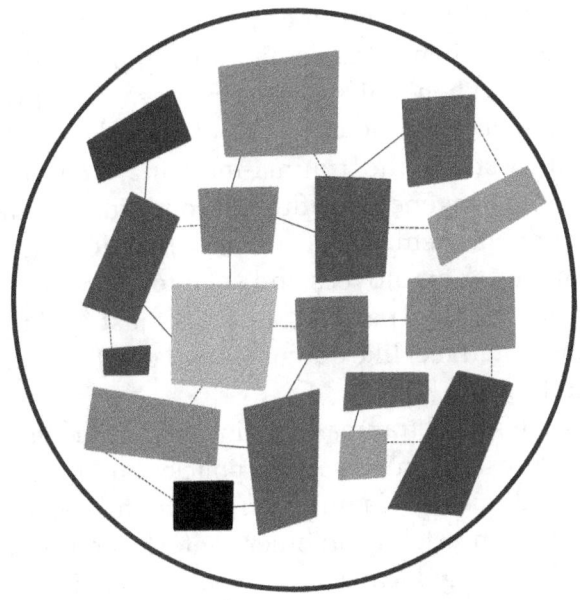

FIGURE 2.6 Stress Inducing
Source: Hannah Shack

People working within stress and trauma-inducing early learning settings, or impacted by their services, do not feel an inherent sense of safety. There is not an expressed value for developing and strengthening relationships. Many relationships lack attunement, responsiveness and trust (or are frequently disrupted before trust can be adequately built). Information, communication and work feels fragmented, people and systems/processes are continually overwhelmed and under-resourced.

Leadership is most often authoritarian (e.g., "power over") and decision-making is typically top down, directive and more reactive than reflective. The climate in these environments is fear driven, competitive and punitive and there is little, if any, value for sharing power and collaboration. Significant inequities and power differentials exist that are often based in social categories of identity (race, class, gender etc.) and the policies, practices and relationships in the setting reproduce these inequities without any recourse for those who are marginalized by them. It is common for those with power to feel threatened when staff suggest changes or improvements as they perceive them as critiques of their leadership. As a result, staff in stress and trauma-inducing environments do not feel a sense of agency to influence conditions in their workplace that impact them. This can, and often does, lead to lack of engagement for employees and such feelings as numbness, hopelessness, rage, despair and a sense of just "going through the motions." Staff feel like outcomes and deadlines are valued more than they are.

In some stress and trauma-inducing environments, change is a constant with shifts in personnel, policies and practices made frequently and quickly leaving staff having to manage a lot of disruption and uncertainty. In other contexts, policies and rules are tremendously rigid leaving no room for flexibility and adaptation (e.g., a "one size fits all" and "this is the way we do things" norm prevails) and there is significant resistance to any change or innovation. Many staff do not feel valued or understood due to cultural differences and therefore, often feel at odds with the leadership and/or the norms of their working environment. Further, self-care practices are not valued nor supported within these environments and barriers exist that make it difficult for employees to practice self-care at work.

These environments increase stress for those spending time within them and can be trauma-inducing, re-traumatizing and/or triggering. Employees in all stress and trauma-inducing environments spend valuable time re-enacting or retelling stories of the stressful/traumatic experiences they endure working for the organization.

Leading from Hurt

Brené Brown's (2018) description of leaders who "lead from hurt" is a pattern seen in many stress and trauma-inducing environments:

> "The most common driver of hurt that I've observed is from our first families. The first family stuff can look like seeking the approval and acceptance from colleagues that we never received from our parents. Also, if our parents' professional failures and disappointments shaped our upbringing, we can spend our careers trying to undo that pain. That often takes the shape of an insatiable appetite for recognition and success, of unproductive competition, and, on occasion, of having zero tolerance for risk. Identifying the source of the pain that's driving how we lead and how we show up for other people is important, because returning to that place and doing that work is the only real fix. Projecting the pain onto others places it where it doesn't belong and leads to serious trust violations"
>
> (pp. 112–113)

Reflection/Discussion Question

- Sometimes we react and end up leading from hurt. Can you reflect on a time you reacting in that way? What happened? How did the other person react? What could you have done differently? What can you do now to repair the hurt?

While referring to the continuum and description above, read through the following examples of early childhood environments and identify elements of these environments that are stress and trauma-inducing:

Example 1: Growing Strong Roots Early Learning Public Agency

Growing Strong Roots is an independent public agency with a goal to support the safe and healthy development of young children in a local county. Charged with creating an integrated and coordinated system of services and supports to strengthen families and improve child outcomes. Ashley Connors was the former Director of Community Partnerships for Growing Strong Roots. Ashley describes her experience working for the agency:

> "I felt like I was under a microscope where I could not make one move, speak one word, make any decision without permission. The CFO would do rounds to make sure everyone was working and monitoring if all the jobs were getting done and report back to the Executive Director (ED). Random meetings would be called where the ED would proceed to shame and blame the leadership team about something. We sat in these meeting in silence waiting in fear to learn who would be called out publicly in front of the team. She marched around the table with a stern face and a loud tone thinking her style would motivate us to perform, to submit or to 'get in line.' **It was not safe**. All the staff learned quickly that power was gained from finding some bit of information they could report to the ED so they could gain her favor. If you had anything you could report, real or perceived that would make her feel like she had 'spies' then you could have power and would be included in her inner circle. Growing Strong Roots is a place that only staff who submit to these conditions can survive. It was a place where you cannot directly share any thoughts, ideas or opinions. The tales that circulate within the agency are stories of staff who were let go previously because they voiced differing ideas or suggestions. I often felt triggered into a feeling of being numb and too scared to make any move. Over time, I stopped trusting anyone as I worried they might smile

at me but then throw me under the bus to protect themselves. No voice, no choice, no trust, no relationships, no idea, no opinions and walking on eggshells every day. Even if I had a word, I was too scared to share anything. Following is a memory I have that reflects the way my ED treated me:

I attended a community collaborative meeting on behalf of the Executive Director. At the meeting, the partners unanimously voiced concerns about a particular curriculum that was being used county-wide. The concern was that it was behavioral and reward-based rather than relationship and strength based. When I brought the update back to the ED during a meeting in her office, she began to raise her voice, 'Why would you even allow them to say those things? This is an evidence-based curriculum and our agency is deeply invested in integrating it into our program.' I proceeded to share my concerns about this curriculum based on some of the current research in the early childhood field. I explained that I spoke up and shared these concerns at the meeting. She said, 'So are you the one that instigated all this at the meeting? Did you tell them we use it and like it?' The line of questioning came in rapid fire. She then said in an exasperated angry tone, 'I can't trust you again to represent me or our agency at these meetings in the future! I can't even handle that you would speak on behalf of me or this agency without consulting with me first.' I could feel my body shutting down and starting to freeze during this meeting. I did not even know the right words to say any longer. I felt like I could not have a healthy conversation with her. Whenever I say something she does not like or agree with, instead of listening and learning, she begins to attack me with words, using an angry tone of voice or making threats."

Reflection Questions: Stress is increased in environments where adults perceive that they have little agency and control. When supervisors micro-manage employees, reducing their opportunities to perceive that they can provide input or influence in decision-making and other aspects of their daily work, they are actively increasing the level of stress and dysregulation of their employees

- What are some ways you could productively disrupt a system like this?
- Throughout the year, how often do you seek input from those throughout the organization? Do you take their input into consideration in the decision-making?
- Before you roll out a new policy or procedure, do you seek the input of others throughout the organization?
- How can you create an environment where everyone's voice can be heard?
- Can you list out three to five benefits of increasing the ability for staff at all levels of the agency to have voice and input?

Example 2: Shooting Star Learning Centers

Shooting Star Learning Center is an organization with 50 child development centers which include Head Start, school age programs, infant and toddler programs and mental health and early intervention services. Samantha Thompson, Deputy Director, describes her first day working at Shooting Star Learning Centers:

> "I started my first day of work. No one emailed me in advance what to do. No one welcomed me. I had no idea where to go or what to do. I found my way to the mailroom. I ran into a staff member, Jennifer, I explained who I was and asked if Laura, my supervisor, was in the building and where I could find her. Jennifer looked shocked. She told me that no one on staff was aware that I was hired for the Deputy Director position. She mentioned that she applied for the job, but no one told her anything until this morning when she saw my name on a mailbox. After an hour of wandering the property I finally found someone

who could guide me to Laura. When I was brought to her office, she looked surprised that this was my first day. She said, 'Oh no, I totally forgot that today was your first day. I am so sorry!' She led me to an office that would be mine. The office was filled with construction items and boxes and a few trails from some snails wandering through. I lasted 9 months. This was a sign as to what was to come. I never had scheduled supervision. I could rarely find Laura anywhere on the campus. I tried to leave her emails or voice mails with requests to arrange times to talk or ask questions. If I was lucky, she would respond a week later. On days we were scheduled to meet, I would walk down to Laura's office and often waited 15–20 minutes before learning that she was not going to show up. I felt invisible, unsupported, lost and had no guidance as to how to do my job. Every day, I felt like I had a blindfold on and had to lead myself and had no one to check out if I was doing the right thing. The experience of having a supervisor like Laura who was consistently unavailable and unsupportive, created a lot of anxiety for me."

Reflection Questions: Stress is increased in environments that lack a commitment to building relationships among staff and where adults do not perceive they have access to the support they need to feel capable of fulfilling the requirements and responsibilities of their jobs.

- What aspects of a stress and trauma-inducing environment do you see represented in Samathan Thompson's description of the Shooting Star Learning Center?
- How do you welcome and onboard new employees to help them build relationships, learn expectations, and feel safe?
- What ways do you help others know they are cared for?
- As a supervisor, you may be feeling overwhelmed by all the tasks and meetings you have to complete. What are some small ways you can make sure your supervisees are supported? Are there larger structural things you can shift to better create space to support your supervisees?

Example 3: Circle of Care Center for Child Development

Circle of Care Centers for child development are state and federally subsidized child care programs in a Midwestern city. Matthew Gomez is the Regional Director and responsible for overseeing seven Circle of Care early childhood sites. Matthew provides a window into a program that is very stress inducing for staff because of the constant flood of new programs and initiatives adopted by the agency's Executive Director that are pushed down to staff in rapid succession leaving Matthew and others feeling little sense of predictability or grounding:

> "Our Executive Director loves change. Any new shiny object, new grant, new change is her passion. She did not like things to be the same! I am part of a large organization that continually rolls out new programs. The changes happen so fast that we struggle to keep up. We never know what is coming next. We keep getting more and more work and we are constantly overwhelmed. There is no time to create a healthy foundation, a solid team, manuals, policies and procedures or to bring the staff together to understand the expectations for implementing the new programs. The changes come down from the top unexpectedly, rapidly and monthly. Even my direct supervisor does not know what is coming next. This constant change and the conditions of uncertainty leave me and my staff feeling unsafe. All of the employees in our organization feel a high level of stress due to the unpredictability and never having a voice in the decisions to make these changes."

Reflection Questions: Stress is increased in environments with a high degree of uncertainty and unpredictability. This can be the result of too much change without ample time for planning and implementation of new programs, policies, procedures and/or practices.

- ♦ Before a new change is rolled out, how do you seek input from others?

- How do you communicate the change? How do you communicate the "why" behind the change? Then, how do you clearly communicate the specific steps to roll out the new change?
- How can you create ways for people to share their opinion and voice?
- Are there opportunities for shared decision making?

Example 4: One Way Family Child Care Program

One Way is a small family child care program in a rural county in the southeast. LaKrisha Dixon is the program director. She describes how stressful it is for her to have to follow a strict schedule and to have no flexibility to be responsive to individual children's needs. Valuing fidelity to a strict schedule is not only stressful for the providers, it is also difficult for the children:

> "I am a Center Director at an infant-toddler program and I am so frustrated. I am not allowed to adjust or change the schedule and it feels like too much for a young child. Their attention span is so short, but the owner is adamant that the teachers follow the schedule exactly. The teachers are all struggling to keep the children's attention. **Help!** I tried talking to the owner but she says that we must follow the schedule if we are to work here."

Daily Schedule

7:30 Breakfast	10:15 Snack	2:15 Snack
8:00 Letter of the Week (Song)	10:30 Activity of the Week	2:45 Color of the Week
8:30 Letter of the Week (Activity)	10:45 Music Time	3:15 Clean up
8:45 Free Play	11:00 Diaper Change	3:30 Free Play
9:00 Diaper Changing	11:20 Lunch	4:00 Diaper Change
9:30 Outdoor Play	12:00 Naptime	4:30 Math Time
9:45 Gross Motor Play	2:00 Diaper Change	5:00 Storybooks
		5:00 Pickup

Reflection Questions: Stress is increased in environments when employees not only do not feel a sense of agency and control to have a voice in their daily jobs but also when they do not feel that what they are being asked to do aligns with their values and beliefs and/or if they observe that their actions are causing harm for the children and families they are serving.

- When you roll out an expectation or directive, in what ways do you first ask for input?
- How do you seek to give the employees an opportunity to share their input and to provide them with flexibility in their jobs?

Example 5: Jen Leland, Director of Partnerships, Trauma Transformed

Trauma Transformed (TT) provides training and technical assistance to programs, agencies and systems interested to become trauma-informed in their service delivery. Jen Leland, the director at TT, describes how the lack of resources and capacity in early learning programs (e.g., shortage of staff, the lack of available substitutes, and no access to time to meet with colleagues) keeps early educators in a place of daily survival with little ability to attend trainings or participate in professional learning opportunities:

> "When we are with early childhood sites, what we find is that the staff members are not able to attend trainings. And when we do show up in the classroom to coach on trauma-informed practices, we're dealing with folks in a constant and chronic state of hyper-arousal. We know that learning can't happen if you're running around making snacks, making ratios or not making ratios and begging for substitutes, looking for any warm body that comes in off the street to cover the classroom or to cover for circle time, or to put out the snacks or to serve the lunch and to change the diapers and do the instruction and create the

lesson plans for the next day, to field parent calls and to take the temperatures of sick kids...What we're seeing in early childhood programs is not only the lack of access they have to professional development, but even when we bring it to them, the lack of capacity and scaffolding needed to be part of a change process. And this lack of capacity and resources in early learning translates into directors requesting, 'Can you make this training only 15 minutes?' 'Can we send only one person to the training and have them bring it back and disseminate it across the agency?' So even if the funding stream is there to support early childhood programs to participate, there's a lack of capacity to really engage in this work and to access the resources like time and staffing needed to deeply embed this knowledge into practice. Some programs are making it work even with these conditions. For example, one group of early childhood education sites adopting our trauma-informed model is breaking up our 90-minute modules into 20-minute team coaching sessions at the end of teachers' shifts."

Reflection/Discussion Questions: When environments are consistently under-resourced and administrators and staff perceive that they are existing in a state of survival—just squeaking by or moving from one crisis to another—adults do not have the cognitive capacity to take in new ideas or to engage in the risk-taking that is necessary for learning and implementing new practices.

- ♦ How do you evaluate when embarking on a new effort or change the impact it will have on staff and if there are resources available to support them?
- ♦ How do you assess when to roll something new out and the bandwidth the staff have to fully engage in the process?
- ♦ Can you think through what it means to really fund professional development? What would an ideal budget look like? Would costs cover more than just the trainers?

Could it cover substitutes for the classrooms? Materials, supplies?
- What are some things leaders can do to reduce the stress and extend the resources for staff? What would be needed to make that happen?

Trauma-Informed Organizational Environments

Trauma-informed programs, schools and systems are environments where individuals are developing awareness and understanding of the neurobiology of stress and trauma (and their impact on children, adults and organizations) as well as building awareness about the factors that support neuroplasticity

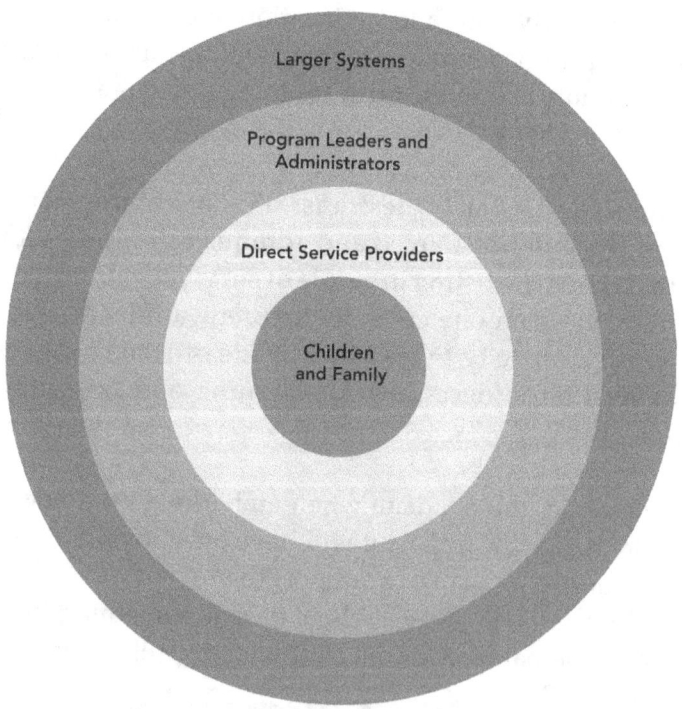

FIGURE 2.7 Trauma-Informed
Source: Hannah Shack

and strengthen resilience. Employees are being encouraged to use a common language to talk about stress, trauma and resilience. This new information is *beginning* to be used to inform policies, procedures and practices with a goal of improving the workplace culture and reducing stress for employees and the children and families they serve. These organizations have articulated mission and values statements (the "why" of their work is clear for all employees). Practical application of concrete trauma-responsive strategies is *starting to be implemented* at multiple levels of the program/school. For example, educators are learning about and deepening their listening skills and reflection skills in order to strengthen their self-awareness and to expand their understanding of a range of behaviors. Educators/staff working in trauma-informed environments may also be working on strengthening collaboration between people and teams or slowing down decision-making to be inclusive of input from a wider group of individuals—especially those who are most impacted.

Within trauma-informed environments, there is an acknowledgement of historical and cultural forms of trauma and recognition that structural and institutional forms of oppression and conscious and unconscious bias exist and result in toxic stress and trauma that impacts families, communities, organizations and systems. Trauma-informed organizations work from an understanding that addressing bias and inequity starts with increasing awareness of the way individuals and groups fit into larger structures and systems in society (e.g., the various forms of privilege and marginalization they experience based on social categories of identity). The importance of culturally responsive self-care is understood and acknowledged in these settings and is beginning to be integrated into, and supported by, the program to different degrees (this is often an area "in progress" for trauma-informed programs).

While referring to the organizational continuum and description above, read through the following examples of early childhood programs and identify elements of these environments that are trauma-informed:

Example 1. Aracely Nava, Family Engagement Coordinator for Child Development Resources

Aracely is leading a five-year project for her program to become trauma-informed. She explains how her team is starting with a small group of people and expanding each year with goals to involve people working across every aspect of the program over the course of five years. Although they are only beginning along their journey, Aracely describes how knowledge of TIP has already been instrumental in influencing how the administration at her agency responded when some destructive and fast moving wildfires tore through the community:

> "We have a five-year goal for our agency to become a trauma-informed agency. We are starting with a small cohort of staff, but the goal is to get everybody trauma-informed and trained by the end of five years. We want the line staff, the management staff, everybody, to have those skills. To sustain it, we want to be able to have the management staff and everybody go through with the training as well. We are striving to get everybody to be on the same page.
>
> First, we want to get everybody trained, to have that understanding and awareness and insight of what trauma is and what it looks like. But the second piece is the application part. So, in the second year of implementation we're proposing to have reflective groups for staff to be able to come together in small groups with our trainer to be able to talk about their work and how to apply trauma-informed knowledge with families and children and one another. The application piece is the most challenging and the part that I'm most excited about to be able to do. We are already noticing some changes. We are shifting from a deficit model to a strength-based approach. We adopted a sharing power approach, even for management and staff, we're all equal and we're here to partner with each other and support each other. So, when we work with families, we partner with you but

you are the experts in your family. You are the experts in your life, and we're here to help and support you and meet you where you're at.

Recently, our community has experienced several natural disasters that are impacting the staff and the families that we serve. We had the big Thomas fire here in California, and that really impacted our county. A lot of people had to leave their homes. For a temporary amount of time, a lot of families lost their jobs. Staff couldn't work because they had to evacuate from their homes. It really impacted all of us and our programs. Our management responded in a way that I thought was extremely trauma-informed. Their first communication was to check on everyone and to make sure that everybody was OK. They closed the centers knowing that staff were being impacted by the smoke. They checked in with all of us to see what we needed. They let us take time off as we needed to because of everything that was going on. For me, it was important that we paused, and we didn't just keep going as a program even though we have contractual requirements to meet. **We literally paused.** They made sure the staff was okay. And then after that, we came together, and we supported the families. It was a comprehensive approach. We received so many donations, diapers and water and baby things. We partnered with our mental health agency here in the county and we offered crisis intervention groups for families and staff who were impacted by the fires. We came together. Not only for the staff, but also for the children. We had ongoing groups for children to have a space and to be able to talk about their experiences in a developmentally appropriate manner with clinicians. And then the parents did the same. And the parents learned how to talk to their children about our community trauma. And so we addressed this experience with the fires from top to bottom. And for me, it was a very trauma-informed response."

Reflection/Discussion Questions: Programs, schools and systems that are trauma-informed are beginning to use knowledge of stress, trauma and resilience to influence their policies and practices. Central to the approach of any early learning program that is trauma-informed is an understanding that attuned, responsive relationships are the most powerful form of buffering stress and reducing the short and long-term consequences that result from a traumatic experience.

- Has your program had to face any difficult times together where you as a community had to build and promote coping and resilience strategies?
- How are you you currently or planning to educate staff across the system about trauma, so people are using similar language and have a shared body of knowledge?

> **"Early childhood educators are the hardest on themselves."** We did a ProQOL (Professional Quality of Life) assessment. All educator scores are high but early childhood educators have the highest scores that correlate most to burnout for sure. We did some data reflection circles with early educators and what we've heard over and over again is, "I just spend so much time worrying that I'm not doing anything right and that my mistakes are so much more crucial than the fifth grade teacher who makes a mistake in a classroom.' And we wondered, what do you think is underneath the fear of not doing anything right? What we learned is that it is the lack of training they have access to, and the lack of any time built into their schedules to connect and access coaching like K-12 educators have. And this is coupled with the complexity of the children and families that they're facing. Especially the smaller programs, they're kind of left on their own and they are so isolated. They don't have the opportunities to have partnerships or coaching and support. Some of our biggest wins have been connecting early education providers to each other and

strengthening those relationships for pure accountability and support. So that when we, as consultants leave, they still have that network.

> The other thing we spend a lot of time with is basic trauma one-on-one education, but also applying it to self-regulation and applying it to having them manage their own stress response because we've seen that their stress response is quite a bit higher based on their sense of responsibility. And frankly, the system has designed it so that they are responsible for everything, for diapers, for circle time, for instruction design, for calling parents, for snacks, for putting out the snacks for cleaning up after the snacks, to the regulation. I mean, they are running from 8:00 AM when they meet the kids out in the parking lot or out on the driveway and pull them in to taking temperatures of kids who might be presenting with a fever to being on the phone with parents in crisis to doing circle time. I compare early childhood educators to residential counselors. They're not just doing educating or counseling, **they're doing everything**. Our wins are strengthening the connections between educators so they become a network and quite frankly, encouraging early childhood care providers to organize because that is what will change the profound lack of investment that critical field, despite all the attention it's getting."
>
> —Jen Leland, Director of Partnerships, Trauma Transformed

Reflection/Discussion Questions

- What are all the avenues to provide relational connection or support inside and outside of your organization?

> - Are there any supports provided to educators so that they can manage and balance working with children/families and their other responsibilities (paperwork, tasks, outcomes and other initiatives) so they do not burnout?

Example 2. Including TIP in Early Childhood Coursework in Higher Education

Chantelle Marin, Lead teacher Omaha Educare, describes how the University of Nebraska, Omaha's early education program has begun to integrate TIP content into the required coursework for early educators:

> "Part of the reason I became a teacher is that my own childhood trauma really fueled me. I feel strongly that I need to be here for children. **I want to give them a voice.** That's why we're all in this field. We love children. We care about them. But I noticed that the University of Nebraska, Omaha (UNO) did not have any courses on trauma-informed teaching practices. None of my classes really touched on it at all. Maybe it would be like a paragraph in a book, but it really was not a focus. I started to talk about this with one of my professors. She was so gracious in allowing me to do an independent study. I read Dr. Bruce Perry's book (2017) The Boy Who Was Raised as a Dog and researched on my own. I offered to do a presentation on trauma-informed teaching practices for our department. I'm super happy to see that TIP is really starting to be brought up more. I don't know if they have course on TIP yet but it is definitely starting to be addressed by the early childhood faculty."

Chantelle's personal experience with childhood trauma and her knowledge that half of all young children in the United States experience trauma in their earliest years led her to feel passionate about the importance of including information about trauma and TIP in the early childhood coursework. She found a way to advocate for change in her department. Working to change the roots of what causes trauma in our lives and in the families and communities we serve, is a resilience-building activity. In this way, Chantelle is supporting the UNO Education Department to begin a process of becoming trauma-informed.

Reflection/Discussion Questions

- Where was your first memory of learning about trauma?
- How did you feel when you started to learn about trauma-informed practices?

Example 3. Old Elm Preschool

Andrea Estupiñan is the Site Supervisor at Old Elm Preschool. She explains how she took over her role when the center was stress and trauma-inducing and the changes that have been made over the last several years to create an environment that is now trauma-informed:

> "From the left to the right of this continuum. I am reminded of the whole process that I've had at this one center over the last five years. When I first started at this center there were a lot of the stress and trauma-inducing practices going on. There was not a mutual respect between the children and the teachers, it was very authoritarian and expectations for the children 'to just do as I say because I am the teacher and this is what you need to do, so stop doing that and follow the rules.' The impact that had was horrible for the children. A lot of them were having very challenging behaviors. They were being very aggressive with the teachers, spitting at them, pulling hair, running away and it was consistent. The first thing I did was to begin working with the teachers on how to create mutual

respect and just to have consistency with the children. We also worked with mental health consultants who helped us begin to consider where the child is coming from and really think about the child's perspective. And so that's how we started to move into trauma-informed practice. Luckily, we also had an opportunity to have training on the Teaching Pyramid (a social emotional curriculum for early childhood). Implementing a SEL curriculum and learning about TIP has helped our staff to develop a common language and understanding about children's behavior. Now we a much more positive culture in the classroom than it was five years ago. Now that teachers are building these strong relationships with the children, they have felt more confident and happier about being at work. And so that's created a more stable team. We used to experience a lot of inconsistency because of the high turnover, but we've now had a consistent team for three years. So, it goes hand in hand.

Now the teachers have more strategies for their work with the children. They also have more power because instead of me just telling them what to do, when anything comes up or any sort of change, I will always bring it to the teachers and ask them if they have an idea of what we can do, or if there's something that we need to change or to do different. I continually ask them for their input. Sometimes when there are things we have to do (for compliance), I say, 'this is what we have to do. How do you think we can make it work for you?' And everybody's on the same page instead of me just saying, 'this is what we're going to do, and we're going to do it like this because I said, so...' Well, I like to, I'd like to have our center be not just a place where you go to work, but a place where you actually enjoy your time and where you are friends with your coworkers. And we now do some team-building, we'll go out for dinner or once we took one day just for team building and we all went to the beach. Sitting in the sun, listening to the waves, looking at whales. And we played a few games out there. It was just a lot of fun and helps with our staff relationships. We also made a shift so that all the teachers share their job responsibilities and we have rotating schedule. Previously, each teacher would have one week that they were responsible for circle time and planning activities for the children in the classroom. Then the next week, they would be cleaning the classroom. But now, we have changed it up, so they have more shared responsibilities for the daily work of running their classrooms and the program.

The next change I would like to make is creating a spa type experience for teachers when they take their breaks. Painting the break room a calm blue color or having a small sofa in there too with a neck massager and/or a foot massager so they can take off their shoes and have a foot massage during their break. I want to make it feel like a place where they can just relax on their break. Another topic that has been coming up just recently is the thought of inequity and specifically, acknowledging systems of privilege and oppression and taking actions to disrupt inequity. I haven't gotten to the chance of taking any action yet, but I've been listening to a lot of the webinars that have been available lately. And there was an interesting one examining how early childhood's QRIS (Quality Rating and Improvement System) is racist. Right now I'm taking in information and listening. I have also been talking to some of my teachers to learn about their perspectives. What is clear is that women of color in our field are working long hours with young children and not getting paid very much. And expectations are going up with an increased push for early educators to get bachelor's degrees and master's degrees. And yet, they are not going to be getting paid enough even with their degrees completed to pay off those school loans. This is totally inequitable and it's important that we acknowledge this and dialogue about it."

Andrea understood that the first and most important element of a trauma-informed environment is a focus on respectful trusting relationships. This is where she put a lot of her energy as a new site supervisor—to support the teachers to build connections with one another and to communicate to them that she saw and valued them as individuals and as a team. By offering them opportunities to provide input into decision-making and dialogue about their classrooms and the program, she reinforced a strength-based approach and her value for collaboration and investing in their professional growth. Not only did this build trust between Andrea and her staff, but it reduced stress in the environment and supported job retention. She is proud of the changes they have made to become trauma-informed. Andrea is now looking forward with goals to continue on their journey and become trauma-responsive and healing centered with a commitment to support organizational care for the staff and to go beyond acknowledging inequity to taking actions to disrupt it.

Reflection/Discussion Questions

- What elements of a trauma-informed environment do you see in Andrea Estupiñan's description of Old Elm preschool?
- In what ways do you implement relational connection or team building on teams you are a part of?

The "One" is the Problem

Jen Leland, Director of Partnerships, Trauma Transformed

Jen Leland highlights a central tension that early childhood environments face in striving to become trauma-informed: children and adults heal from trauma in the context of attuned relationships yet, many early educators work in isolation or they work with others in the classroom but the teams have little to no time to meet, build relationships and plan, dialogue or reflect together on their practice. She suggests that the key to becoming trauma-informed is to "resource" the adults:

> "I would say I would love to see a team education model. I think we need circles—resilience or support—for educators. Concentric circles. Thinking about early childhood, the ratios of one to three or one to six or one to nine, **the one is the problem**. We need team teaching models, team educator models. And site supervisors also need to be coached as teams and to operate more fully as teams. We need to move from an individualism model to a collectivism model that is not only better for the kids, but also for the educators. Our ratios should be three to 12. The one should not be fixed because if you're doing team teaching, **you're going to have more relational resources to provide to children**. And we know that more relational resources means more ability for children to learn. And we know that when we're thinking about early childhood mental health or early childhood education, that happens inside of a context of an adult relationship. We say over and over again, **the most profound medicine is one caring adult**. And so we need to resource the adults and especially in early education, resourcing them so that they are team teaching. Right now we are doing a halfway approach: we'll bring in a mental health consultant for an hour a day which is not the same. For programs to become trauma-informed, we can increase the supports in the classroom, the classroom supplies and the environmental strategies but until we increase the staffing to support more teamwork and to provide mentoring, we're not going to get very far."

Trauma-Responsive Healing Centered [1] Organizational Environments

Trauma-Responsive, Resilience Building programs move past being trauma-informed to having consistent implementation and use of policies, procedures and practices at all levels that

FIGURE 2.8 Healing Engaged
Source: Hannah Shack

are informed by the science of trauma, resilience and healing. Within these environments, there is an expressed value for human connection that includes taking care of oneself, taking care of others, creating trusting relationships and building empathy. Adults are encouraged and supported to work collaboratively toward a greater good which is articulated in a program mission and a set of values or principles that guide everyone's work. There is an explicit focus on learning, growth and optimism. Joy, creativity and innovation are valued and supported. Asking for help and sharing challenges and problems of practice with the group is modeled and supported. Decision-making is inclusive of diverse perspectives, especially those who are most impacted. Staff have regular, on-going opportunities to check-in and express their needs in a supportive environment where their needs are followed up with responsive actions.

Coping, resilience and healing are strengthened in many ways. For example, trauma and its impact are acknowledged, however, children, families and communities are never defined through deficit; instead, these programs use a strength-based approach in policies, communication and practices. Staff members' strengths and assets, forms of resilience and coping, funds of knowledge and diverse types of cultural capital (see below) are acknowledged and integrated (e.g. culturally and linguistically responsive practices are integrated throughout the environment). Adults and children have opportunities for agency and control (e.g., staff are provided with opportunities to evaluate, critique and inform policies, practices and decision-making.

Trauma-responsive, resilience building programs have a culture of appreciation for people's work and their effort. These are learning organizations, where mistakes are perceived as opportunities for learning and progress/success is acknowledged and celebrated (instead of individual call-outs and competition, credit is given to all who participate). Honesty, authenticity and vulnerability are valued—people can share narratives about their lived experiences and identities and know that they will not be judged, shamed or punished. Intentional space and time is available for individuals to pause, reflect and to make meaning of, and learn from, their professional practice, especially difficult experiences. These environments emphasize not only coping and healing but also strengthen the foundations of health and well-being.

Culturally responsive self-care is intentionally integrated into policies and practices. Individuals in every role are not only encouraged to engage in ongoing self-care, the structures of the program provide supports and opportunities to make self-care accessible through organizational care routines and practices.

While referring to the organizational continuum and description above, read through the following example of an early childhood program and identify elements of this environment that is trauma-responsive and healing centered:

Little Sun People

Fela Barclift is the Executive Director and the Founder of Little Sun People, an African-centric child care program in Brooklyn, New York serving children ages two to age five. She shares the many ways her program strives to be not only trauma-responsive but also healing centered for children and adults:

> "One of the reasons why people have come to us over a number of years is that we've been a program **grounded in an African-centered perspective** that we feel connects with the student body that we serve in our neighborhood. Bedford Stuyvesant was formerly a hundred percent African heritage, African American working class, a significant number of poor people and lower working class was the largest percentage of the community here. There's been a huge disconnect with people of African heritage…it's always been a deficit lens. In contrast, what Little Sun People is bringing to the equation is no deficit, no deficiency, a very positive take on our community, on our people and the children of our community. And we felt that one of the key ways to do that—some call it culturally responsive pedagogy—but we think about it as an African centered perspective, meaning let's sort of

connect fully with who these Black skinned people are, and not only with enslavement, but with the rich and full history that goes back millennia. So that's what we do in our program in every way that we can. Even though there are two year olds, three year olds, four year olds, five year olds, they still can get a message of empowerment, of love, of belief in themselves and very high expectations.

Fortunately, now there's a wide variety of storybooks that reflect the lives and experiences of Black skin and Brown skin people in a very positive light. This wasn't always the case for the 40 years of our existence. We used to get storybooks and color the faces and hair and all that, but we don't have to do that anymore. **We find stories that center the cultures and stories of Black and Brown people.** If we're doing a math lesson, we're talking about pyramids and go straight to Egypt. When we provide children with dolls and playthings, we look for those that have Brown or Black skin. We have African dance with an African instructor who's from the Ivory Coast. He dances and drums with our children and he talks to them from his perspective as a positive and powerful Black man. We also bring African music from African Americans, the African Caribbean experience, the South American experience. Throughout their lives, our children are going to have numerous opportunities to have stories told to them where Black and Brown people are not at the center, but in the margins. The amount of white supremacy is very, very intense in our culture, in our society. It's woven through everything. So, what we try to do is just add a little balance.

We open our staff meetings by asking a few questions, "How's it going with you personally?" "How's it going with the children you're working with?" "How's it going with the parents of those children?" Even the newest youngest person on our staff will have something to say once they know that this space is for them and they're welcome in it. **We're not going to skip over you. Your voice is important to this process.** We're not expecting that a younger teacher is going to be as informed or as knowledgeable about being a teacher as the person who's been here for 15 years, but we know that everyone has something important to bring. If one of our teachers is struggling, the team here is very, very caring of each other. We will come together and surround whoever is having a hard time and do our best to make sure we provide support in whatever ways that we can. And usually there's enough intelligence, information and practice within our group of 14 people that somebody will know some way to help (e.g., "When I had that child in my group, I remember that this or that happened, you might try....)." Once everyone has spoken, then we'll start covering the business. I work very intentionally with my staff on internalized oppression and racism and internalized racism. I explain to them that it makes you impatient and not as respectful. So every two weeks at our staff meetings, **we talk about a situation, interaction or relationship where internalized racism shows up** and creates a conflict. I reinforce that we all have it. There's no way to avoid it if you're a Black or Brown person in this country. So, we have to become conscious of it and work hard to act in the opposite way.

We had a little boy join us who had previously been asked to leave three different childcare programs. Now, we didn't know this when he started with us. But we could see he was angry. We're fortunate that we have lovely people here who understand how to be with a child and to be gentle and loving and thoughtful with a child and a parent. This little one, I mean, it felt like he was resistant to kindness. He couldn't take in any of our attention. He couldn't be with the group. He would scream and kick and throw things and really try to hurt people. He was only three. We talked about it at staff meeting and of course we don't ever try to remove a child from our program. The children are not the issue. When it comes to the children, especially a little Black boy, we need to try to figure this out as a team. His teacher is very experienced with children who have massive feelings. She talks to them and she keeps helping them to figure out, "it's okay, this is a safe relationship. I'm with you. And you're with me and I love you and we're going to be okay." This wasn't working with him. So, then they brought him to me. He would come to my office and I would try to talk with him. Sometimes I would just have to just sit next to him and let him scream. I would just keep talking to him saying, "it's okay. I know that you're upset about something. Talk to me." And he would just scream and scream and scream and scream. And I would just let him do that. **He just had to get his anger out. And somebody had to listen to him.**

One day, after screaming for almost an hour, he fell asleep and when he woke up, he was ready to talk me. Afterwards I called his mom and I talked to her as well. I told her what had happened and how I thought that we had turned a corner in our relationship and that he was able to get something out that was deeply troubling him. I learned in conversation with his mom that his father was recently arrested. So, I was like, "Oh, okay, when did that happen?" I asked her, "do you think that he could be struggling with that? Was he in a relationship with his father?" She confirmed he was. "Do you think he noticed that his father's not there anymore? Even though he's in prison, he's not on the moon. Can they talk?" She said "yes, but I didn't let him talk to his father because I didn't want him to be upset. I felt like it was better to just let his father be there." So we talked about that for a long time, because I don't think people know that **children are humans. They have feelings, deep, intense feelings**. They notice everything. Even if they can't give you a full sentence, they notice what's happening. And they really notice when somebody that they love is going away.

So you have to talk with them and talk them through that and love them through that. So she helped him start talking to his father as he was allowed phone calls periodically. And I encouraged her to tell her little boy everything that's happening...when his dad is coming home, that his dad didn't leave him, that his dad still loves him. Letting them talk just really changed everything."

As Fela Barclift describes, Little Sun People is **an organization committed to a trauma-responsive and healing centered approach:** Respectful trusting relationships are at the core; children, families and the staff experience love and support and a felt sense of safety and belonging; collaboration is valued and everyone teaches and learns from one another; there is a clear program-wide mission and sense of pride rooted in history, culture and identity. There is a commitment to racial and ethnic representation among the staff, the majority whom come from the same communities as the children and families they serve; and there is an ongoing commitment to anti-racism and healing from oppression in the program.

Reflection/Discussion Questions

- What elements of a trauma-responsive healing centered environment do you see in Fela Barclift's description of Little Sun People?
- What systems do you create to help everyone feel a sense of significance, belonging? How do you hear every voice? How do you help teams manage "big emotions and stress" by having avenues to talk and share how they feel and what they experience personally and professionally?
- How do you balance getting to the "business items" on your agenda and ensure there are open-ended questions and time for staff to connect and share with one another?
- How does your program center the voices, stories, histories and perspectives of Black, Indigenous and People of Color?

What to Expect in Working for Organizational Change

Shifting a program, school or organization to become trauma-responsive requires a commitment to changing policies, practices and the culture—*how* people work together—within our diverse early learning workplaces. Making shifts from the status quo—where so many early childhood professionals experience significant stress and the toll of vicarious trauma is ever-present in their daily work–toward trauma-responsive and healing centered environments, will require a long term effort and will only be realized if staff working at all levels and roles are committed and engaged. There is no roadmap with a universal set of directions to follow. Each context will have unique conditions that will inform how decision-making, priorities and constraints inform the journey in that setting. Understanding the many roads taken, we outline a few key steps that many programs have found helpful in creating short and long-term plans for implementation and sustainability.

Key Steps in the Process of Becoming Trauma-Informed

(Adapted from Guarino, Soares, Konnath, Clervil, & Bassuk, 2009)

Set the Stage	A group of people are identified who are committed and motivated to support the process of their program/school becoming trauma-responsive (the "champions for change" or what Trauma Transformed describes as a "Reflective and Healing workgroup"). When creating this group, it is important to consider the various people/stakeholders whose support will be critical for the initiative to succeed and to have involvement from as many as possible (e.g., program administrators, district leaders, teachers' union leader, teachers/providers, parents/family members etc.). At least one of your "champions for change" should have formal authority and the ability to influence programmatic change (Dombo & Sabatino, 2019)
	Recommendations - Identify co-leaders/co-champions to facilitate the process

- Ensure that champions have dedicated time and space to dialogue and plan, discuss and reflect on the initiative over time. Without this systematic investment, the effort is unlikely to succeed.

> *"Leadership across the board I think is really key and important and having a champion for whatever it is that you want to do. To implement and sustain a new goal, we have found that leadership is key. We found that those organizations across the country who did best in implementing a new long-term strategy with positive outcomes are the ones who had strong leaders. Next, is having people at all levels of the organization weigh in and contribute to that vision. Finally, having clarity as to each person's role in executing that vision."* —Chrishana Lloyd, Senior Research Scientist, Child Trends

Note: If you are in a context where you are the only person or one of just a few (without formal authority) in your program or school interested in creating a trauma-responsive environment, consider the principle of the **"Organizing Mind"** to inspire your efforts for change. This principle is grounded in the experience of effective community organizing, "To use organizing mind means that we begin by looking around to see who is with us, who shares our desires and our vision. We then build relationships with those people. So, for example, if we find one other person to work with, then the two of us find another 2 people, then the four of us find another 4 people and so on. Organizing mind is based on the idea of 'each one reach one' in ways that build relationships, community, solidarity and movements. Using organizing mind helps us to focus on who and what is within our reach so we can build a larger group of people with whom to work and play and fight for social justice" (dRworks, 2016). Tema Okun (2020) renowned social justice leader, reminds us, "the more we can focus on the things we care about, the more our power grows. The more we focus on things outside of us, the less power we have."

Communicate a clear "what" and "why" for the initiative to support "buy in"	Begin conversations with staff across the program/agency to talk about the goal of becoming trauma-responsive. Information is shared about the science of trauma and resilience and the potential benefits of becoming a trauma-responsive workplace. This should not be a one-directional "talking at" the employees, but instead, a bi-directional conversation with teaching and learning between the staff and the leadership team. Listening and being responsive to the ideas, feedback, concerns and questions of the staff is essential not only for creating the conditions for their

engagement and "buy-in," but also for understanding how to adapt the pace and process of the change initiative to be responsive to the specific people, conditions and context of each setting.

Recommendations

- Champions communicate that the goal of the initiative is not only increasing knowledge of trauma and TRP for individual staff members but instead, to inspire changes across the organization
- Clearly communicate how each individual/group will benefit from the proposed changes (e.g., reduction in burnout/vicarious trauma; less staff turnover; improved relationships with children and families, potential access to new sources of funding etc.)
- To reduce the stress and resistance that emerges with uncertainty, it is helpful to be prepared to share a draft proposal of how the change process could begin (e.g., offering a Trauma and Resilience training to all staff) and what to expect moving forward and then to invite staff input.

> Create a brief (1–2 sentence) vision statement that provides the motivating and guiding image of what the organization will be like once it becomes Trauma-Responsive and Healing Centered. Once it's finalized, share it publicly.
> –Falvey, Epstein, & Leland (2018)

Build a shared vocabulary and knowledge-base	Building from staff discussions, it is important to provide professional learning opportunities for staff to learn about trauma (what it is and how it impacts people and organizations) and resilience and trauma-responsive policies and practices.

Research suggests that trainings alone will not lead to changed practice. Instead, trainings should be paired with opportunities for people to make-sense of the content they learn in trainings. Staff will need systematic time set aside to pause, reflect, dialogue and consider how and what it means to implement the new information into their teaching practice and/or to modify the policies and procedures within their organizations. There are many different formats where this "sense-making" can take place including

Communities of Practice, reflective book groups, individual or group coaching or staff meetings where protocols are used to support collaborative thinking and processing.

These professional learning opportunities allow staff members to build a shared vocabulary and an initial set of principles and practices that everyone in the organization can begin working toward. There are no quick fixes with TRP work. This process will be ongoing and require a sustained effort of everyone involved to continue learning and adapting.

Recommendations

It is important to create opportunities for everyone working within a program, school or system to have access to professional development opportunities (e.g., senior administrators, kitchen staff, bus drivers, administrative assistants etc.). The goal is for every adult and child who interacts with the agency to become part of creating and sustaining a supportive stress reducing environment.

> "Training coupled with ongoing support, supervision and consultation may mitigate concerns associated with training alone and facilitate lasting practice changes"
> –Melz, Morrison, Ingoldsby, Cairone, & Mackrain (2019, p. 15)

Listen carefully to concerns and try to understand what is underneath resistance

If conflicts arise and there are strong and differing opinions within the program/organization about the value or need to embark on the long and complex journey of becoming trauma-responsive, it is important to slow down and understand, acknowledge and talk about concerns early in the process to prevent the development of distrust that could undermine the entire change initiative. It is essential to create time and space to listen to the ideas, questions and concerns of staff throughout the entire process. Share power and show responsiveness to their voices and input (use their feedback and ideas to inform planning and co-construction of action steps). *Move at the speed of trust.*

Recommendations

The pace and depth of change should be aligned with the readiness factor of your staff and community. Some will be ready to dive in and make substantive changes right away. Other groups—where significant resistance or fears are present—may need to begin with small steps (e.g., implementing training to raise awareness versus discussing substantive changes to policies and practices). Plan for clear, consistent and transparent communication about the initiative: What is coming next and how staff are involved. Communication is essential to the success of all change initiatives. It is critical that employees not perceive that only a small group of people "at the top" have access to information as this will increase distrust and undermine the momentum and engagement across the program.

Conduct a Self-assessment and identify strengths and learning edges

Staff work together to reflect on their program/organization considering the new information they have gained through trainings and other professional learning opportunities. They work together to identify strengths of their program as well as their "learning edges" or areas they want to develop and/or improve. There are several methods that can be used successfully to guide and inform this process. A few include:

- Use a tool like the Early Childhood Trauma-Responsive Organizational Self-Study Tool (free to download at the Center for Equity in Early Childhood Education website: www.ceece.org)
- Design a survey to send to all engaged stakeholders to gather their input (e.g., staff, families, specialists, community partners etc.)
- Use protocols to facilitate a group through a process of dialogue and decision-making (see Chapter 7).

Reinforce that the assessments are not about individual behaviors but instead, about the daily practices and experiences within the organization.

Also, emphasize that "learning edges" are just that, opportunities for future change and growth and not judgments of people or the program.

Recommendations

Encourage staff and others providing information that it is helpful if they are honest in describing the strengths and learning edges for the program. However, they will only be honest if they feel safety in doing so. It is important to communicate how confidentiality and anonymity will be maintained in this data collection and analysis process (e.g., make sure that only aggregated data are reported and no identifying information is shared to link a person to their feedback when reporting on results)

Be responsive to what is learned from people's feedback. Be transparent in describing how the program will consider all of the information and perspectives when developing goals and action steps. This is important for building trust and for people to perceive that this is an effort worth their time and energy.

Identify short, medium and long term goals

Once strengths and learning edges have been identified, staff can be guided through a collaborative process to identify a few realistic and actionable short term, medium term and long term goals. To support the process of moving these goals from paper to changes in programs, it is helpful to:

- Outline specific action steps necessary to achieve each goal
- Identify resources and sources of support that will be necessary to achieve each goal
- Develop a realistic timeframe for making progress and/or the achievement of each goal
- Selecting the person(s) responsible for monitoring progress toward each goal

Example: Goal: "Year 1: Trauma Training"
Action steps

- All staff receive training in the neurobiology of trauma and the science of resilience and neuroplasticity
- All staff receive training in strengthening self-awareness and self-care to prevent burnout
- Education staff receive training in trauma-responsive and resilience building strategies

Resource and Supports

- Identify funds from training budget
- Interview potential training experts
- Promote the training throughout the organization
- Schedule training dates
- Ensure staff have the resources and time to attend each training

Timeframe

- Secure trainers and dates January–March
- Promote training April–June
- Execute training August to December

Person(s) Responsible for Monitoring Progress

- Administrative support personnel
- Parent representative
- School social worker/mental health consultant
- Director
- Teacher representative

Recommendations

Make sure that the goals identified are realistic given the staff, capacity and resources available within the current organization. It doesn't matter how articulate and inspiring a goal is, if the program lacks time, capacity or resources to achieve it, little if any progress will be made as people will feel deflated and immobilized in moving forward. It is much more effective to think of smaller, immediately actionable changes so everyone can see that their efforts are leading to changes right away as this builds confidence, feelings of self-efficacy and a sense of momentum that is contagious.

It is essential that the leaders/champions continue to communicate the "why" behind the changes everyone is working toward. Explicitly connect the dots for staff: "We are making changes to support the 50% of children we have identified that have experienced trauma and 67% of adults that have experienced trauma, because we believe in creating trauma-responsive and healing centered environments and equity for all" and connect the desired changes to the values and mission of the program/organization so everyone understands why and how they are working hard for outcomes that are part of something larger than their own role and contributions to the organization.

Monitor Progress toward Goals

With goals, action steps, resources and timeframes identified, it is helpful to create structures that help monitor progress in a program's continued commitment to implementing and achieving their stated goals. There are many different formats that programs might choose to support this process. A common one is to create a workgroup or committee to meet regularly, track progress and communicate what they learn to everyone in the program. This group may include but should not be limited to members of the leadership or champion's team.

Recommendations

Make sure whatever structure is set up has representation from individuals across the program or school to reinforce messages that everyone's role and participation is important and valued.

"The success rate for implementation of interventions is 80% within three years for organizations with an implementation team; in organizations without an implementation team it's 14% over 17 years" (Fixsen, Blasé, Timbers & Wolf, 2001; Balas & Boren, 2000 cited in Falvey et al., 2018)

Document Impact

It is really important that programs document progress they are making toward their goals and the *impact* these changes are having for children, families, the workforce and/or the consumers receiving the agency's services. Both intended and unintended impacts of the changes being implemented should be documented as well as the range of benefits and any challenges or concerns resulting from the initiative.

Recommendations

It is essential that the "stories" told about progress and impact are centering the voices of the individuals directly impacted by the changes. Consider methods that provide staff with "voice and agency" to participate in the documentation process (see Chapter 5).

Use various methods to communicate (e.g., staff meetings, newsletters, posters, emails, memos, inter/intranet sites and in one-on-one conversation. Using various forms of communication and multiple people to share information supports the diverse ways that people process information and increases accessibility and engagement (Falvey et al., 2018).

See Trauma Transformed (https://traumatransformed.org/) for a range of detailed guidelines and tools to support organizational healing.

Common Barriers to Implementing Trauma-Informed Approaches

- Creating buy-in
- Lack of support from administrators/leadership
- Competing teacher responsibilities
- Size of an organization (larger = more complex)
- Perception of stigma associated with trauma/mental health conditions
- Sustainability of a TRP Strategic or Action Plan
- Insufficient funding, resources and staffing
- Lack of interagency and cross-system coordination and collaboration
- Insufficient short and long-term visioning and planning, and
- *Not understanding the "why" and the benefits behind a trauma-informed approach*

(Melz et al., 2019; Thomas, Crosby, & Vanderhaar, 2019)

One of the Biggest Barriers: "They Could Never Find Substitutes"

What we find is that the early childhood staff, the workforce are often not able to attend our trainings and team coaching. It's hard to get early educators together. It's hard to get people in the same room together. So we've had to do lots of adaptations. Lots of work arounds. One district we are working in had a policy that if the early childhood staff were participating in our trauma trainings, they could have access to substitutes. We were really thrilled. This meant more resources and more practice for those teachers to learn. Unfortunately, what ended up happening is that within the substitute pool for this particular district, none of the substitutes wanted to work in the early childhood setting, so they could never find substitutes even when they had support from their leadership and funding to pay for their participation. And we're talking about half day substitutes, three hours substitutes. Even the educators know that an early childhood classroom is the hardest place to be. To be included in the substitute pools you need to have the ECE credits and most public school educators don't have ECE coursework. What I see as the biggest challenge in early childhood is the lack of resources at a systems level that significantly compromises the ability for programs and teachers to implement the TIP best practices, even if they have the funding. The severe under-resourcing of the field leaves many early childhood educators profoundly challenged in their ability to implement the changes.

–Jen Leland, Director of Partnerships, Trauma Transformed

Reflection/Discussion Questions

- ♦ Which barriers listed above do you face?
- ♦ Are there any other barriers not described above that you have experienced?

Trauma-Responsive Resilience-Building Principles for Early Childhood Programs, Schools and Systems

Guiding Principles provide a broad set of values and beliefs that guide an organization's decision-making and inform its overall culture. Establishing guiding principles can also support sustainability of an organization's vision, values and culture when there are inevitable changes in personnel, policies, initiatives and/or goals over time.

Throughout the remainder of the book we introduce readers to 13 guiding principles that we recommend individuals and groups use to guide their ongoing efforts to build more trauma-responsive, resilience building and healing centered organizations and systems serving young children and families. These principles are aligned with the most widely cited frameworks for trauma-informed systems of care for children and families and trauma-informed approaches in child serving systems including education and child welfare (e.g., Dorado, Martinez, McArthur, & Leibovitz, 2016; Sharp & Johnson, 2015 **Our principles were designed specifically with the early childhood field in mind.** We briefly list the principles below and discuss each in more depth in separate chapters:

Trauma-Responsive Resilience-Building Core Principles for Early Childhood

- Build Mutually Respectful and Trusting Relationships
- Understand Stress and Trauma
- Acknowledge Systems of Privilege and Oppression and Take Actions to Disrupt Inequity
- Create Environments that Reinforce Messages of Safety and Predictability
- Focus on Strengths and Assets
- Provide Opportunities for Agency and Control
- Intentionally Promote Coping, Resilience and Healing
- Implement Culturally, Linguistically and Contextually Responsive Practices
- Create Power-Sharing Partnerships and Community-Centered Solutions

- Use Evidence to Build Insights and Learn Collaboratively
- Work Toward Sustainability and Scale Innovation with Flexibility for Local Adaptation
- Engage People Working Within Every Part of the Program, School and/or System
- Acknowledge Today's Realities While Maintaining Hope and Imagining Justice for Tomorrow

FIGURE 2.9 Principles in Tree
Source: Hannah Shack

Top Down Pathway to Regulation

Grounding

Grounding is the process of bringing your focus to what is happening in your body internally or within your immediate surroundings in order to interrupt the body's stress response reaction and/or your worried thoughts. Grounding strategies allow you to calm your nervous system and disrupt the release of neurochemicals throughout your body. Re-focusing on your body and what you're physically feeling allows you to shift your mind away from anxious or stressful thoughts and focus on the safety and security of the current moment. Examples of grounding strategies include:

- Deep breathing
- Hold on to something and squeezing it tight or stomping your feet on the ground
- Being in nature
- Repeating a mantra (special saying or quote)
- Engaging one of the 5 senses (drinking a copy of tea, smelling an ocean breeze)

Try the following grounding activity...

When you are calm, think of a person, animal, location, object, activity, mantra or ritual that when you bring this to your mind, you associate it with such feelings as safety, belonging and calm. The moment you start to feel stress or triggered into a state of fight, flight or freeze, bring this grounder into your mind and focus on it. Focusing on this thought can be an effective top-down pathway to reducing your stress and feeling a sense of calm.

Grounders are unique for each individual. To discover your most effective grounders consider the following reflection questions:

- Can you think of one **PERSON or ANIMAL** in your life that calms you, helps you feel safe or provides grounding in times of stress? If not, can you think of a character on television, a mythical figure or a person you admire (past or present)? List the characteristics of this person and what strategies they embody to make you feel safe?
- Do you have a certain **ENVIRONMENT** or place you go that is restorative or provides a safe feeling? If not, do you have a place you can go in your imagination that you have seen in photos or that you have imagined in your mind?
- Is there an **OBJECT** you have that provides you special comfort when you see, touch, feel, taste or smell it?
- Is there a quick under 60 second OR longer **ACTIVITY** you do that provides calming when you stress systems in activated?
- Do you use a **MANTRA/SAYING/QUOTE/PRAYER/ AFFIRMATION** that you say to yourself when you feel triggered in the moment by a person, situation or event?
- Is there a particular **ROUTINE, RITUAL** or **PREDICTABLE SCHEDULE** that you repeat when you feel unsafe, worried or triggered by too much stress that helps you feel a sense of control and safety?

Note

1. We draw from Dr. Shawn Ginwright, the author of *Hope and Healing in Urban Education. How Activists are Reclaiming Matters of the Heart* and *The Future of Healing: Shifting From Trauma-Informed Care to Healing Centered Engagement.*

References

Balas, E., & Boren, S. (2000). Managing clinical knowledge for health care improvement. *Yearb Med Inform, 1*, 65–70. PMID: 27699347.

Brown, B. (2018). *Daring to lead. Brave work. Tough conversations.* Whole hearts. New York, NY: Random House.

Dombo, E., & Sabatino, C. (2019). Trauma care in schools: Creating safe environments for students with adverse childhood experiences. *American Educator, 43*(2), 18–21.

Dorado, J., Martinez, M., McArthur, L., & Leibovitz, T. (2016). Healthy environments and response to trauma in schools (HEARTS): A whole-school, multi-level, prevention and intervention program for creating trauma-informed, safe and supportive schools. *School Mental Health, 8*, 163–176. doi.org/10.1007/s12310-016-9177-0

dRworks (2016). Dismantling racism. DR workbook. Retrieved from https://resourcegeneration.org/wp-content/uploads/2018/01/2016-dRworks-workbook.pdf

Falvey, C., Epstein, K., & Leland, J. (2018). *Healing organization workgroup toolkit: Guidelines and tools to support organizational healing.* Trauma Transformed.

Fixsen, D. L., Blase, K. A., Timbers, G. D., & Wolf, M. M. (2001). In search of program implementation: 792 replications of the teaching family model. In G. A. Bernfeld, D. P. Farrington, & A. W. Leschied (Eds.), *Wiley series in forensic clinical psychology* (pp.. Offender rehabilitation in practice: Implementing and evaluating effective programs (p. 149–166). John Wiley & Sons Ltd.

Ginwright, S. (2016). *Hope and healing in urban education: How urban activists and teachers are reclaiming matters of the heart.* New York, NY: Routledge.

Ginwright, S. (2018). *The future of healing: Shifting from trauma-informed care to healing centered engagement.* Medium. Retrieved from https://medium.com/@ginwright/the-future-of-healing-shifting-from-trauma-informed-care-to-healing-centered-engagement-634f557ce69c

Guarino, K., Soares, P., Konnath, K., Clervil, R., & Bassuk, E. (2009). *Trauma-informed organizational toolkit.* Rockville, MD: Center for Mental Health Services, Substance Abuse and Mental Health Services Administration, and the Daniels Fund, the National Child Traumatic Stress Network, and the W.K. Kellogg Foundation. Available at www.homeless.samhsa.gov and www.familyhomelessness.org

Melz, H., Morrison, C., Ingoldsby, E., Cairone, K., & Mackrain, M. (2019). *Review of trauma-informed initiatives at the systems level: Trauma-informed approaches—Connecting research, policy and practice to build resilience in children and families.* U.S. Department of Health and Human Services.

Okun, T. (2020). *Unpacking Whiteness workshop* with Joe Truss. August 15, 2020. See https://culturallyresponsiveleadership.com/category/culturally-responsive-leadership/

Sharp, C., & Johnson, K. (2015). National Council for Behavioral Health's 2015 Trauma-Informed Care Learning Community. *Trauma sensitive schools.* Retrieved from https://www.thenationalcouncil.org/wp-content/uploads/2016/07/Trauma-Sensitive-Schools-webinar-10-19-15.pdf?daf=375ateTbd56

Thomas, M. S., Crosby, S., & Vanderhaar, J. (2019). Trauma-informed practices in schools across two decades: An interdisciplinary review of research. *Review of Research in Education, 43,* 422–452.

3

Core Principle—Build Mutually Respectful and Trusting Relationships

"Relationships are paramount to anything else. I don't think that anything else will happen and be effective until you have the relationship with someone."
—Krystal Lewis, Head Start Director

> When we build relationships that are attuned and compassionate, we strengthen trusting connections with others that buffer stress and support coping, resilience, healing and wellness. Young children and adults thrive in the context of consistent and nurturing relationships rooted in respect, reciprocity and responsiveness. Building trusting relationships requires skills in listening, self-awareness, self-regulation and a commitment to critical reflection, humility and continuous learning.

Consistent, Trusting Relationships that Buffer Stress and Support Coping, Resilience Building and Healing

A trauma-responsive environment is first and foremost one that values, invests in and emphasizes the importance of building consistent, trusting and attuned relationships. There is an inherent understanding that learning, development, coping, building resilience and healing is most effectively guided in the context of consistent, trusting relationships. Children and adults must have a felt sense of trust and safety in order to take the types of social, emotional, intellectual and physical risks that support the process of learning and developing. Yet, many individuals with histories of trauma develop internal working models of the world as unsafe—reinforced by bodily sensations, emotions, thoughts and perceptions/expectations—that interfere with their ability to develop trust in relationships. For this reason, **the central focus of relationship-building in trauma-responsive environments is re-building trust by creating a felt sense of safety.**

Safety is reinforced when relationships are based in respect, reciprocity and responsiveness. We draw on Barrera and Kramer's (2009) powerful work in describing the importance of respect, reciprocity and responsiveness as the base for positive and equitable relationships:

Respect: "Differences Do Not Make People Wrong"

We communicate with respect when:
"We believe that the behaviors others exhibit are the result of competent problem-solving given their knowledge and life experience within a particular situation, rather than the result of faulty or incompetent problem-solving or of not knowing what we know. Respect starts with the premise that differences do not make people wrong—they just make them different. This is not to say that we cannot or should not invite change or that all behaviors are equally life supporting and fully adaptive to a given environment. It is to say that to be respectful, we must first acknowledge the other person's resources, strengths and ability

to learn. Respect neither requires nor communicates agreement. It must simply communicate acknowledgement of the legitimacy of the ways others have crafted their lives in response to perceived and learned choices within particular circumstances. Respect acknowledges differences without being judgmental" (Barrera & Kramer, 2009, pp. 39–41)

> "I was getting escalated in a meeting with my supervisor while talking about a family I worked with. My supervisor stood up and said, 'you need to calm down' and then walked away leaving me all alone. I felt judged and abandoned in the middle of my story. Yes, maybe I was escalated but what I really needed was support, listening and an understanding and the belief from her that in that moment that I was doing the best I could."
> –Kamilla Grant, Family Engagement Specialist

> "While our program is focused on sexual abuse, respect and dignity are at the center of everything we do. In all Israeli sectors or social groups there is racism. It is important to work with early childhood educators so we can raise children who will disrupt these norms. We teach critical thinking and using their power dynamics positively to contribute to the class, to the school, to the community. We talk about how we all need to respect ourselves and to be respected."
> –Ayelet Giladi, consulting educational sociologist, Founder of Voice of the Child Association to Prevent Sexual Harassment, a program that began in Israel and is now implemented in schools around the world

Reflection/Discussion Questions

- Have you had a differing opinion with a colleague? How did you feel? How do you imagine they felt?
- Were there any ways you showed respect and acknowledged the differences without being judgmental or disrespectful?

Reciprocity: "Diversity Is Always Life Enhancing"

Reciprocity builds on respect and is based on an assumption that:
"Diversity is always life enhancing…reciprocity seeks to honor another's voice or power as a life-enhancing resource. At its core it is a recognition that the behavior of each person in an interaction is an expression of his or her competence and ability to learn rather than of an inability or refusal to learn…The essence of reciprocity is an attitude of openness to another's diverse perspective (i.e., an attitude of 'I don't have all the answers'). Such an attitude leaves room for another's voice (i.e., perspective and values) even when it disagrees with one's own. Reciprocity does not require denying that one person has more expertise or knowledge than another in particular areas or that one person has more institutionalized authority. What reciprocity does require is acknowledging and trusting that another's learning is an expression of different learning rather than deficient learning and thus, is of equal value to one's own…entering into interactions only to give—whether knowledge, support, direction or something else—with no acknowledgement of what others, [including] children, can contribute inhibits not only what we might receive, but also the full potential of what we seek to give…a lack of reciprocity erases respect" (pp. 43–44).

> "I sent my meeting agenda in advance so that staff could prepare their thoughts and ideas and opinions prior to the meeting. My email with the agenda attached suggested they come with ideas, recommendations or suggestions on how we can better promote self-care throughout our programs."
> –Adolfo Fernández, Director, County Office of Education Program

Reflection/Discussion Questions

- ◆ Imagine or remember a conversation or a formal meeting you facilitated. How much space did you allow for others voices and ideas to be shared?

- What strategies do you use to bring shared voices into a conversation? Do you ask a question? Do you use silence and a pause? Do you share an agenda in advance and request feedback? What are other ways you have cultivated this practice?

Responsiveness: "There Is Always a Third Choice"

Responsiveness begins with a value for connection. At its core it is a recognition that:

"There is always more than two choices...to be responsive is to step outside of an either-or framework...[it] acknowledges that an identified problem occurs within a particular relationship and not in isolation (e.g., Joey's behavior is not solely his problem)...to be responsive to another is to entertain the possibility of connection rather than follow the certainty of separation...to shift focus from what divides to what connects. When we see a behavior or interaction and it seems quite incompatible with what we would like to see, or when we experience things that seem contradictory to our perspectives, being responsive calls us to ask, 'where are the connections?' ...responsiveness seeks to affirm how differences are joined...by shifting perspectives from a 'you and I' perspective to a 'we' perspective. Responsiveness also entertains mystery....which requires attending to [people] with 'focused attention, patience and curiosity' in order to interact with who they truly are, not who [we] think they are. If we seek only certainty and forget mystery, [people] become frozen within our own categories and labels (e.g., the child with ADHD, the resistant mother). Practitioners are no longer in interaction with them—only with their own ideas about them" (pp. 46–47).

Reflection/Discussion Questions

- Have you ever had a difference with another adult in how you each explained or viewed a child's challenging behavior?
- Can you think of the common ground you both shared during this difference of opinion?

Trusting Attuned Relationships are more likely to Develop in Organizations that Value and Create Time and Space for:

- **Pausing.** It is important to slow down reactivity and learn to create opportunities to pause...in the action (e.g., taking a deep breath when triggered) and outside of the action (talking with a supervisor or colleague to process feelings and thoughts). This pause is essential for learning and for becoming capable of using respect, reciprocity and responsiveness in our interactions with others. Pausing creates opportunities to make new discoveries and to have new insights.
- **Collaboration.** It can feel validating when you share with others and hear their experiences. Humans thrive on connection and sharing and collaborating with others can support our coping, resilience and healing. We need individuals or teams we can go to in times of need, who make us feel less alone, who help us talk things through as we expel our intense emotion and who help us explore different solutions to our problems. As a result of this collaboration, it becomes healing for that one person and the ripple effect will likely effect so many others that day.
- **Reflection, mindfulness and inquiry:** Developing **reflective skills** allows us to explore how our thoughts, feelings, assumptions and interpersonal roots (the awareness that our past experiences may be impacting how we currently do our work) are influencing how we show up for ourselves and others in our work. With the use of reflection, adults can learn to disrupt their reactivity, assumptions, distorted thinking or premature conclusions about the motives of others' beliefs and/or behavior (Heffron & Murch, 2010). Reflective practice strengthens skills in **mindfulness** (Kabat-Zinn, 2013)—learning to notice and build awareness of one's inner world of thoughts, feelings and sensations as well as what is happening in the outer world at a specific moment in time without trying to control or judge it. Using **inquiry** involves learning to ask questions about our professional practice—especially

when we are met with confusing, frustrating or surprising interactions or situations. For example, instead of making assumptions about the behavior of a staff member or parent, using an inquiry approach, we might ask, "what do I/you think their behavior is communicating, how did I/you feel during that interaction, what do I/you see as next steps?" Reflection, inquiry and mindfulness are foundations for learning, exploring different perspectives and becoming a more intentional, equitable and healing centered early learning professional.

> "One of my Family Advocates called and texted me repeatedly that the mom she supports just told her she was experiencing domestic violence. I could tell she was worried and feeling dysregulated and needing support and guidance. I called her immediately reassuring her I am here for her and we will work on this together. When we talked it was so important that I let her unload her worries, thoughts, feelings. I could feel the steam of built-up tension slowly dissipating as we talked. As she calmed, I slowly began to ask questions such as, 'Is mom safe, does she have a plan, what community resources can we think of that might support her?' Together we came up with a comprehensive support plan to keep mom and her child safe, to connect her to community resources and to ensure she has the emotional support she needs."
> –Chelsea Paperson, Team leader modeling reflection and inquiry

> "I used to talk with parents when I was directing the center in Oakland. I used to walk down the street and have coffee with them on Thursday afternoons. That was my meeting time. And I had a little prayer that I would say to myself as I walked down to meet with them. I would say, 'Let me be completely available to this family.'"
> –Carol Barton, ECE Project Coordinator

> "I want to empower others to be trauma-informed and to build up other people's resiliency. **My flame is still going, but I'm handing a candle to them and lighting their candle.** This work is not easy, not a cakewalk. And it's definitely not a sprint. It's a marathon."
>
> –Anita Smith, Program Manager
> Mental Health Consultation

Relationship-Based Organizations are Driven by Relational Logics of Effectiveness that acknowledge:

- Staff are responsible for the whole (Each person understands and feels connected to the larger mission of the organization, not just their own roles and responsibilities)
- Competence can be recognized without a need for self-promotion
- Interdependence is a powerful and not a deficient state
- Severed relationships are an obstacle to future growth and achievement
- Outcomes are achieved most efficiently within an environment of connection and support
- Supporting the learning and growth of others requires paying attention to emotional and intellectual factors
- Authenticity (acknowledging vulnerability and need as well as strength, skill and expertise) is a necessary condition for mutual growth in connection (Fletcher, 2001)

Relational practice is motivated by strategic intention and a desire to do work more effectively. Too often organizational language excludes relational work in discussions of "outcomes" and "competence" as relational skills are mistakenly attributed to personal traits (e.g., naivete, powerlessness, weakness or someone who is caring, polite or nice...saints and angels). This devalues the power and importance of relational practice (Fletcher, 2001).

What Relational Skills are Important to Develop to Engage in Trauma-Responsive Leadership? These skills are rooted in a value for context and connection which may contrast with many work cultures that privilege individualism, independence and the hierarchical separation of roles and responsibilities:

- Building self-awareness of one's positionality (e.g., cultural perspectives, beliefs, values, intrapersonal roots, experiences of privilege and oppression)
- Learning about others' experiences and perspectives through listening, reflection and open-ended questions
- Understanding and interpreting emotional data and using it to assess situations and strategize appropriate actions or verbal responses
- Accessing and expressing one's own thoughts and feelings
- Moving easily from expert to non-expert role, with a genuine openness to being influenced by and learn from others.
- Acknowledging help and giving credit to others with no loss of self-esteem
- Admitting 'not knowing' something and seeking others' help and expertise with no loss of self-esteem
- Investing in the development of others
- Synthesizing thoughts, feelings and actions
- Engaging with and responding to others while holding on to one's own reality (thoughts, feelings, perspectives) (Fletcher, 2001; Heffron & Murch, 2010).

"Paperwork Can Wait, You Can't"

"People need to realize that it doesn't matter what position you're in within an organization. You have to see and put people first and you have to take a pause and really listen to people and what they need. And be vulnerable. It's okay. Kristina and I are like we don't know everything. Tell us, show us. I think it's the willingness to show our vulnerability. People always say, 'Oh, I know you're super busy. I don't want to bother you.' But we set the tone from the beginning that we are never busy enough that we cannot stop. Paperwork can wait, you can't. I hope that people would take this piece from your book and say, you know what, let's take a pause and really put people first."

–Kristina Adams, Program Director and Mitchell Ha, Assistant Program Director, Hayward Unified School District Early Learning Program

Reflection/Discussion Question

- ♦ What small actions do you take at work to send a message to others that you are available?
- ♦ In what ways do you show vulnerability with others to convey you are accessible, human and safe to approach?

Core Principle—Understand Stress and Trauma

"When you're in survival mode you might not have the opportunity to reflect on your actions and you might be aggressive or you might not choose kindness. When people come to me with their challenges or their stressful energy, I don't take it personally. I just try to meet them where they're at in the moment."

–Drew Giles, Director of Educare Programs with Franklin-McKinley School District at Educare California at Silicon Valley

Many children and adults experience trauma. Understanding the prevalence of trauma and adversity and their impacts on learning, development and human functioning allows educators to create more responsive and

> equitable learning environments for children and adults. Understanding how stress and trauma can affect individuals, families, communities and organizations can help to reframe otherwise confusing or frustrating behavior. When knowledge of stress and trauma informs policies, procedures, practices and intervention plans, educators are better able to provide supportive, compassionate and strength-based interactions with others. They are also less likely to re-traumatize and/or cause further harm to children and adults with histories of trauma. Educators can use their understanding of stress and trauma to provide supportive compassionate communication and environments without knowing about, or focusing on, the specific details of others' trauma histories.

Understanding the impact of stress and trauma and their impact on learning, development and human functioning is central to a trauma-responsive approach. The Substance Abuse and Mental Health Services Administration (SAMHSA) (2014) outlines four key assumptions that are acknowledged and embedded within programs, schools and systems striving to become trauma-responsive. These are described as **The Four R's: Realize. Recognize. Respond. Resist Re-traumatization.** These assumptions are a good place to start when creating the vision for a trauma-responsive early learning environment. Each program or school can determine how best to implement the Four R's in their local context:

> **Realize.** Everyone realizes the widespread impact of trauma and its impact on development, learning and functioning (for people and organizations).
>
> *Half of the world's 2 billion children have experienced one or more types of serious trauma* (Hillis, Mercy, Amobi, & Kress, 2016; Stoltenborgh, Bakermans-Kranenburg, Alink, & van IJzendoorn, 2015).

Recognize. Through training, adults learn to recognize the signs and symptoms of trauma in themselves and others (children and adults) and within the organizational culture.

"You're doing trainings with the early educators with the intention of shifting their internal dialogue and their own personal lens around the behaviors that they're witnessing. Not internalizing it, not personalizing it, realizing that really those things have nothing to do with them. But if they're being triggered in some kind of way, it's an opportunity for them to reflect and for them to heal"
–Anita Smith, Program Manager for Mental Health Consultation, YMCA

Respond. The program or school responds by creating a trauma-sensitive environment that incorporates an understanding of stress and trauma into all policies, procedures and practices.

"We've started resiliency circles at our sites with the teachers in order to create a space of transparency and of safety. We leave the management out of it. This is the first time they've been given the space to talk about the dynamics of the kids, the families and how it may connect to their own trauma."
–Anita Smith, Program Manager for Mental Health Consultation, YMCA

"Some kids test you more than others, but I keep a list of strengths of each child, things that I love about them. I think that's been helpful when I get in those moments where I get spit in the face and I just want to like pull my hair out and walk out of the building. I remember he loves to read with me. He always runs up and gives me a hug. He wants to be my helper for everything. Those are positives that help me calm myself down."
–Chantelle Marin, Lead teacher Omaha Educare

Resist re-traumatization and/or doing further harm. There is awareness that trauma may be triggered by certain language, interactions, practices and/or settings, often unintentionally and by well-meaning adults. The goal of creating a trauma-responsive program or school, is to resist re-traumatization and reduce the chances of a child's or adult's past or current experiences of trauma being triggered by something that happens in the environment (Dombo & Sabatino, 2019).

"We need to go through those trainings and see the trauma that we have"—Monique Turner, Field Services Officer, California Department of Education

> "Going through a divorce was very traumatic for me. It was hard. I'm just now truly healing from it. I went through times of hate. I went through times of crying. Times of feeling sad. And then times of numbness. And that has an effect on everything you do. My divorce brought up trauma from when I was a child because I didn't have a connection with my mother. So it brought up that trauma because it was like, 'okay, every person who was supposed to love me has treated me badly.' So even though you're an adult and you experience new trauma, it can fester and bring up things from the inside. Now I have to heal from the trauma that I had as a child but I'm going through all this while still working and trying to serve contractors and families. When we think of trauma-informed care, we often picture children and families. But before we can implement a lot of these practices with our children and families, there needs to be training for people who provide direct services. **We need to go through those trainings and see the trauma that we have** because maybe a child or a family that comes through your program or another coworker, they can trigger that trauma. We're focusing on what we should do with children and families when we really should first focus on working with the people that are working with these children and families. Just like social workers have to go through counseling before they can get their license

to counsel because they're going to deal with people that may trigger something in them. I think that's important piece for early childhood too."

Preventing Burnout and Vicarious Trauma

Burnout is common among early childhood practitioners. It can be described as mental and physical exhaustion due to work related stress (Sinclair, Raffin-Bouchal, Venturato, Mijovic-Kondejewski, & Smith-MacDonals, 2017; Vachon, Huggard, & Huggard, 2015). The World Health Organization defines burnout as "a syndrome resulting from chronic work stress that has not been successfully managed" (World Health Organization WHO, 2019). Having empathy and being responsive to the children and adults in your program is a critical component of creating a trauma-sensitive environment. However, the stressors in our own lives combined with the stresses of the job can leave us really drained causing burnout. The impact of learning about the trauma histories of others can create vicarious trauma. Both of these conditions are taxing to our physical and mental well-being. In fact, both of these conditions can lead to negativity, lack of empathy, anxiety, rigidity in thinking, detachment, low job satisfaction and other negative emotions.

There are things we can do to prevent burnout and vicarious trauma. It is really helpful to understand and maintain emotional regulation, meaning the distinction between ourselves and others, so we do not absorb others' negative emotions or experiences (Vachon, 2016). Self-care and self-compassion are two critical tools for reducing risk for burnout. Creating a self-care plan can be valuable. Select things that are soothing, inspiring or energizing depending on what you need in that moment. You may like to create lists of different self-care strategies that have worked for you so you can employ the one that will work for you when you need it whether you are in a personal or professional setting. For example, if calling your best friend and talking helps manage your stress, but you don't have time for a break, use a breathwork strategy or quick mindfulness practice instead. If being in nature helps you but you can't get outside, maybe watering your indoor plants will support you for the time being. Self-care practices are personal and can include addressing your physical needs such as eating healthier, moving more or sleeping more. Spending time alone, spending time with others, meditation, mindfulness practices, professional therapy or coaching all may be part of your self-care plan.

Compassion for others is critical in your work, but so is self-compassion. Self-compassion is treating the self with the same kindness and compassion that we would give a good friend (Neff, 2011). This requires us to be mindful of our self-talk and gently remind ourselves to speak kindly to ourselves. You may even choose to work on this with a trusted friend or coworker. Oftentimes our self-talk slips out, we my mutter to ourselves "I'm so stupid" after we've made a mistake. Having a trusted partner gently remind you to speak kindly to yourself can help you build the awareness you need to increase your self-compassion.

Creating workplace cultures and environments that encourage and support self-care practices and self-compassion are critical for supporting staff and creating a trauma-sensitive environment.

"I cried a lot over him. It's with kids like this where compassion fatigue can happen"—Chantelle Marin, Lead teacher Omaha Educare

> "We know that zero to three is so important in the development of the brain and an early trauma is the hardest to address. One three year old child in my classroom was homeless and he was placed in foster care. He had really bad food insecurities and he had a lot of very explosive behaviors. He really stood out

to me as a child who needed to be in a program using trauma-informed teaching. Once he grabbed me by the neck, scratched me and tried to choke me. A lot of times these behaviors happened right after lunch. It was a fallout about lunchtime which was a trigger because of his food insecurity. Because I understand trauma, I recognized that I needed to keep him safe. I didn't want him hurting himself or others. Instead, I wanted to help him express those emotions safely and to reassure him, 'I'm here. If you need me.' We've gone over different strategies together: If you need a hug, I'm here for a hug. If you need to just be by yourself for a little while, when you're ready, I'm here for you. The situation with this little guy just really shows that fight or flight response and how it's not intentional. Afterwards you could just see, he felt so bad. He'd come over and he would just melt into your arms. That always got me because he is hurting so bad. He can't even control his behavior. It's not something he wants to do, but that's how bad he's hurting inside. **I cried a lot over him. It's with kids like this where compassion fatigue can happen.** You really need to watch that."

"I really spend a lot of time with families thinking about their stress level because that just goes right into the child's little body"

–Jonathan Iris-Wilbanks, Certified Child Life Specialist

"If a parent or family member is showing body cues of stress like clenched hands or folded arms or they're remaining really, really close to the bed and holding onto the child's bed and their body is just saying, 'Don't take this person from me,' before I even start talking to the parent, I position my body so I'm not blocking the doorway and I'm not hovering over them. I think to myself, can I go get a chair and sit down to be at the parent's level before we even start talking? I try to neutralize the things that are stressful for the parent and send the message, 'I'm a person in this environment who's going to listen to you.' I might ask the parent, do you want to talk alone for a moment away from your kiddo? We have a private conversation where I can ask, 'How are you doing in this moment? What has been the most stressful for you? Do you feel like people are listening to you? They tell me about interactions they had in the hospital. Or sometimes, they say things like, 'I don't know where my car is parked. We came in the middle of the night to the emergency department and I just straight up don't know where my car is.' And so I ask for their consent to offer support, Can I walk with you to the parking garage to help you find your car?

I'm always trying to get a feeling for how stressed somebody is or if there are words or actions that are really stressing them out that we can address. They might not have slept. They might not have eaten. They might have their own traumas from when they were young and this is triggering all of that or a past experience in a hospital where somebody had a bad outcome or didn't live. And now all of that is flooding back in at this moment. Maybe their child only has an ingrown toenail and their stress reaction really doesn't match, but it doesn't matter. If the stress is there, it needs to be addressed. I think to myself, how is this person coping? Are they coping? What is their body telling me? Somebody who's very, very stressed needs to hear something a number of times before they understand it so I might need to repeat what I'm saying. Or I might give them the opportunity to take a break, a chance to take notes or to think of questions that they're thinking of so they don't forget them when the doctor comes around. **I really spend a lot of time with families thinking about their stress level because that just goes right into the child's little body.** So, I feel like if I can help a parent or caregiver be a little less stressed and a little more empowered in that space, the child will benefit."

How is Understanding of Stress and Trauma reflected in this vignette?

- Jonathan pays attention to the all the stress reactions by looking for clues in the parents' and family members' bodies.
- He offers them opportunities to take notes or take a break so they can continue to regulate their own body and engage their thinking brain.
- He understands the power differential of entering a place that automatically makes the parents feel powerless or out of control and this can downgrade one's brain capacity to the primitive survival brain.

Back and Knee Pain, High Noise Levels and a Lack of Adult Size Furniture

Important Yet Unspoken Factors Impacting Early Educators' Stress on the Job

"The pay gap that exists between early educators and those who work in K-12 schools is frequently blamed for high turnover in the early-childhood education field. But back and knee pain, below average cardiorespiratory health and work-related injuries might also have something to do with teachers leaving the profession. Those are among the findings of the Happy Teacher Project, a study focusing on the physical, psychological and professional wellbeing of early educators, as well as on conditions including pay, benefits and the environment in which they work. Kyong-Ah Kwon, an associate professor at the University of Oklahoma, is leading the study, which focuses on a sample of over 260 teachers working with infants and toddlers across 38 early education centers in Tulsa"

–Jacobson (2019)

Among the findings Kwon's team reports:

- The physical demands of the job, which include constant bending, kneeling, crouching and carrying as teachers pick up young children or get down to their level contribute to *musculoskeletal injuries.*
- *High noise levels* were recorded in the classrooms—at a level similar to a busy street or alarm clock—levels that likely have negative impact on stress levels.
- Teachers with more education and who were rated as better teachers were more likely to report poorer physical wellbeing and *"ergonomic pain."* They were also more likely to say they were considering leaving their jobs.

→ **80% of the teachers reported back, neck and/or knee pain**
→ **60% reported having no designated break and 33% had no place to relax**
→ **20% had no adult size furniture in their classrooms**

The authors of the study offer several recommendations for improving workplace conditions for early educators including:

- Providing teachers with space to store their belongings
- More frequent breaks from the classroom.
- Investing in adult-sized furniture in the classroom
- Offering yoga and other fitness programs
- Providing meals for teachers at their centers as many teachers struggle to their own food
- Making mental health consultants available to providers (Jacobson, 2019).

Communicate the Message that Understanding Stress and Trauma and Using a Trauma-Responsive Approach Is a Priority for Your Early Learning Organization

- Include the words, trauma, resilience, self-care and healing in your program mission statement and hand-books
- Incorporate questions about a potential employee's understanding of trauma concepts into the interview process (Guarino, Soares, Konnath, Clervil, & Bassuk, 2009)

Bottom Up Pathway to Regulation

Shaking Out Your Body

Have you ever seen mammals in the animal kingdom when they have heightened levels of stress? They shake their body during or after a stressful event. The act of a quick body shake can release built up tension and promote a greater sense of calm. It can be as simple as shaking your hands, your head (a part of your body) or your whole body. Imagine getting out of the pool or shower and you don't have a towel. Shake yourself dry.

Just Shake Your Stress Away (ACES Connection, 2018)
Simple and easy ways to shake out the stress and trauma in our bodies:

- **Ping Shuai Gong—Swing Hands Exercise:** This simple swinging-hands exercise improves *Chi* (qi) and blood circulation through the theory of "Ten fingers connecting the heart" opening all our body meridians and stimulate bone marrow, to rid toxins from the human body.
- **Kim Eng—Shaking Practice:** This simple shaking can be done anywhere, just shake out the part which feels tense. Jump, kick and throw your hand up. Surrender to the shaking. Let out any sounds that want to come out. You will feel the release of tension.
- **Crawling—The Best Mind Body-Exercise:** Just get on fours with the kids and crawl and shake away your tension.

References

ACES Connection. (2018). *Therapeutic tremoring. Shake off stress and trauma*. Retrieved from https://www.acesconnection.com/blog/therapeutic-tremoring-shake-off-stress-and-trauma

Barrera, I., & Kramer, L. (2009). *Using skilled dialogue to transform challenging interactions: Honoring identity, voice and connection* (1st Ed.). Baltimore, MD: Brookes Publishing.

Dombo, E., & Sabatino, C. (2019). Trauma care in schools: Creating safe environments for students with adverse childhood experiences. *American Educator, 43*(2), 18–21.

Fletcher, J. (2001). *Disappearing acts: Gender, power and relational practice*. Massachusetts Institute of Technology.

Guarino, K., Soares, P., Konnath, K., Clervil, R., & Bassuk, E. (2009). *Trauma-informed organizational toolkit*. Rockville, MD: Center for Mental Health Services, Substance Abuse and Mental Health Services Administration and the Daniels Fund, the National Child Traumatic Stress Network and the W.K. Kellogg Foundation. Available at www.homeless.samhsa.gov and www.familyhomelessness.org

Heffron, M. C., & Murch, T. (2010). *Reflective supervision and leadership in infant and early childhood programs*. Washington, DC: Zero to Three Press.

Hillis, S., Mercy, J., Amobi, A., & Kress, H. (2016). Global prevalence of past-year violence against children: A systematic review and minimum estimates. *Pediatrics, 137*(3), e20154079.

Jacobson, L. (2019). *Pre-to-3: Working conditions linked to high early educator turnover*. Education Dive. https://www.educationdive.com/news/pre-to-3-working-conditions-impact-early-educators-happiness/566710/

Kabat-Zinn, J. C. (2013). *Full catastrophe living: Using the wisdom of your body and mind to face stress, pain and illness*. New York, NY: Bantam Books.

Neff, K. (2011). *Self-compassion: The proven power of being kind to yourself*. New York: Harper Collins Publishers.

Sinclair, S., Raffin-Bouchal, S., Venturato, L., Mijovic-Kondejewski, J., & Smith-MacDonals, L. (2017). Compassion fatigue: A meta-narrative review of the healthcare literature. *International Journal of Nursing Studies, 69*, 9–24.

Stoltenborgh, M., Bakermans-Kranenburg, M. J., Alink, L. R., & van IJzendoorn, M. H. (2015). The prevalence of child maltreatment across the globe: Review of a series of meta-analyses. *Child Abuse Review*, *24*(1), 37–50.

Substance Abuse and Mental Health Services Administration (SAMHSA) (2014). *SAMHSA's concept of trauma and guidance for a trauma-informed approach*. Rockville, MD: Author.

Vachon, M. L. S. (2016). Attachment, empathy and compassion in the care of the bereaved. *Grief Matters: Australian Journal of Grief and Bereavement*, *19*(1), 20–25.

Vachon, M. L. S., Huggard, P. K., & Huggard, J. (2015). Reflections on occupational stress in palliative care nursing. In. Is it changing? In B. R. Ferrell, N. Coyle, & J. Paice (Eds.), *Oxford textbook of palliative nursing* (pp. 969–986). Oxford University Press.

World Health Organization [WHO]. (2019). *Burn-out as an "occupational phenomenon:" International Classification of Diseases*. Retrieved 22 June 2019. https://www.who.int/mentalhealth/evidence/burn-out/en/

4

Core Principle—Acknowledge Systems of Privilege and Oppression and Take Actions to Disrupt Inequity

"For a long time Black and Brown people have been skipped over and now that is recognized more. Our company has now released a statement. They want to create an environment where everybody is respected, because they recognize that hasn't been happening. I'm excited because they are listening, they're open, it's a conversation now and they're responsive. Just having people understand the impact that we have on others as we touch their lives, that's serious business."

–Krystal Lewis, Head Start Director

> Learning to understand and critically examine the policies, practices and decisions that create stress and trauma and reproduce cycles of oppression and then to take actions that disrupts inequity, is essential to trauma-responsive approaches that build resilience and support healing. Well-being comes from participating in transforming the underlying causes of harm within our societal institutions and structures.

> Trauma-responsive and resilience building approaches help individuals build awareness of how different forms of oppression operate in society including within our schools and early childhood programs, how privilege and oppression lead some individuals, groups, programs and communities to experience more trauma than others and the importance of understanding our individual and organizational roles within these systems (as privileged and/or disadvantaged social group members). With this knowledge, individuals and groups can articulate their values and the changes they desire, acknowledge and address biases and take actions that disrupt the policies, practices and conditions that harm children, families, educators and communities. Doing so provides people with a sense of control, agency and purpose, as individual and collective actions can strengthen resilience and support a healing process.

Trauma and resilience responsive early childhood organizations and systems acknowledge the uneven playing field for young children, families and the early childhood workforce. They strive to:

- Increase awareness of what oppression is and how it is reproduced within early childhood organizations and systems leading many children and adults to be further harmed, marginalized and negatively impacted by trauma
- Increase people's awareness of how they (personally) and the children and families they serve are positioned within systems of oppression and privilege and therefore, affected differently
- Guide people to take individual and collective actions to disrupt harm and to strengthen healing and wellness

Increase Awareness about Oppression

Building a shared vocabulary to talk about oppression and privilege is an important first step for early learning organizations committed to disrupting harm and striving to become more trauma-responsive and healing centered.

What Is Oppression?

To oppress, is to "hold down—to press—and deny a social group full access to resources in a given society" (DiAngelo, 2016, p. 61). Oppression is what happens when one group—the **dominant** (or sometimes called the "agent" group) has the power to enforce their prejudice and discrimination against another group, the **minoritized** (or the "target" group) throughout the society.

Examples of Different Forms of Oppression and Minoritized and Dominant Groups (Adapted from DiAngelo, 2016, p. 64)

Minoritized/Target Group	Form of Oppression	Dominant/Agent Group
People of Color	Racism	White (or in some cases light skinned individuals)
Poor, Working-Class	Classism	Middle-Class, Wealthy
People with Disabilities	Ableism	Able-Bodied
Elderly	Ageism	Young, Middle-aged
Women	Sexism	Men

Oppression describes a process of prejudice and discrimination that is at a societal level (DiAngelo, 2016). How is a minoritized group 'held down' by the dominant group? Through **policies, practices, traditions, norms, definitions, cultural stories and explanations** (for events and/or circumstances) **that use a deficit perspective** to represent the minoritized group and give power and benefits solely to the dominant group (DiAngelo, 2016)

$$Prejudice + Discrimination + Power = Oppression$$

Dominant group	"The group at the top of the social hierarchy. In any relationship between groups that define each other (men/women, able-bodied/person with dis/ability), the dominant group is the group that is valued more highly. Dominant groups set the norms by which the minoritized group is judged. Dominant groups have greater access to the resources in society and benefit from the existence of the inequality" (Sensoy & DiAngelo, 2017, p. 223)
Minoritized group	"A social group that is devalued in society. The devaluing encompasses how the group is represented, what degree of access to resources is granted, and how the unequal access is rationalized. The term *minoritized* (rather than minority) is used to indicate that the group's lower position is a function of active socially constructed dynamics, rather than its numbers in society" (DiAngelo, 2016, p. 61)
Prejudice	"Learned prejudgment about members of social groups to which we don't belong. Prejudice is based on limited knowledge or experience with the group. Simplistic judgments and assumptions are made and projected onto everyone from that group" (Sensoy & DiAngelo, 2017, p. 51)
Discrimination	Refers to the unjust treatment of a person or group based on biases and preconceived assumptions about that person or group. Discrimination can be person-to-person or it can be at the social and institutional level.
Racism	"A pervasive system of advantage and disadvantage based on the socially constructed category of race" (Bell, Joshi, & Valdivia, 2016, p. 134)
Privilege	Privileges are "benefits based on social group membership that are available to some people and not others, and sometimes at the expense of others. Some privileges are material (such as access to adequate health care) while others are nonmaterial (such as the ability to experience oneself as normal and central in society). The concept of *privilege* reminds us that such benefits are not earned, but rather result from social advantage relative to others' disadvantage." For example: "White men can count on being perceived as professional and their expertise as legitimate whereas women, especially working in caring professions like early childhood often have their professional skills, knowledge and expertise questioned." (Adams & Zúñiga, 2016, pp. 110–111)

Structural Racism Is a Particular Form of Oppression

Structural racism does not occur at the personal or interpersonal level (one-on-one interactions). Instead, structural racism represents the phenomenon that organizations, institutions and societal structures systematically, historically and unequivocally provide benefits to certain groups over others resulting in racial inequalities in opportunities and experiences across many systems in our society (e.g., systems of education, law/policies, finance/banking, employment/business, health care, housing, media, criminal justice and organized religion). Sometimes, structural racism might seem difficult to pinpoint, but many research studies and people's personal lived experiences demonstrate that **we do not live in a society that serves all individuals equally.** BIPOC children and adults face significant structural barriers in housing, healthcare, employment, education and within the criminal justice system that white individuals do not experience (see for instance Alexander, 2010; Bailey et al., 2017; Hanks, Solomon, & Weller, 2017).

Elements of Oppression (Bell, 2016; DiAngelo, 2016)

In order to work against oppression and to create trauma-responsive early learning programs, schools and systems, it is important to understand all of the elements of oppression and the way they weave together to maintain the inequitable systems in our society that result in systematic negative outcomes including trauma for minoritized groups.

Elements of Oppression (Adapted from Bell, 2016, P. 5)

Oppression has deep HISTORICAL roots. Oppression has deep historical roots and its effects accumulate over time. For example, the wealth gap that exists today has historical roots in slavery, the genocide of Native American peoples and the

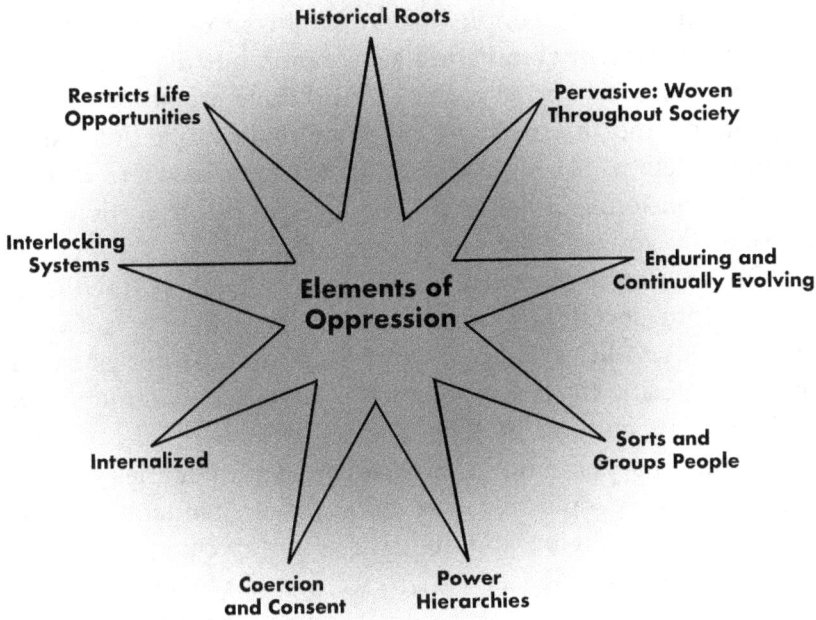

FIGURE 4.1 Elements of Oppression
Source: Alice Blecker

inequitable working conditions of many Asian and Latino workers (Bell, 2016, pp. 6–7). Because of these historical roots, dismantling oppression requires efforts from everyone—members of dominant and minoritized groups—and is ongoing multigenerational lifetime term work.

Oppression is PERVASIVE and woven throughout all of the institutions, policies and practices of our society (e.g., education, legislation, health care, justice, housing, media, law enforcement etc.). Oppression impacts the ideas we value and communicate to explain and justify the inequalities that exist in our society. These ideas are woven throughout our institutions and within our communities influencing the stories we tell, our myths, the definitions we create and the explanations we give to explain our lived experiences and our histories.

Oppression is PERSISTENT and continually EVOLVING. Oppression has been continually present in our society yet over time it changes into new forms in response to various challenges to dismantle it. For example, the civil rights movement resulted in some success in eliminating segregation but the oppression of racism evolved and in today's world there are new forms of segregation and discrimination that are more subtle but just as harmful (Bell, p. 14); e.g., as seen with the exclusionary discipline (suspension, expulsion, push outs) that disproportionately impacts our youngest boys of color in preschool.

Oppression is based in SORTING AND GROUPING people into social categories of identity. Different societies around the world sort and group people into categories based on their specific histories, geography, patterns of immigration and different cultural and political conditions. In the United States, the most common socially constructed categories used to sort and group people are based on race, class, gender, sexuality, age, language, religion and ability. The group categories upon which oppression is based—e.g., race, are not 'real'. However, our beliefs, norms and practices create perceptions that grouping people in these ways is necessary and natural. The consequences that result, treating people and distributing resources very differently based on group membership, are very 'real.'

Oppression creates and maintains POWER HIERARCHIES with dominant and minoritized groups. Social groups are sorted into hierarchies with advantaged and disadvantaged groups. The dominant group—individuals at the top of the hierarchy—are given advantages, status, resources, access and privilege that those lower on the hierarchy (minoritized groups) do not have. Those at the top of the hierarchy have the power and authority to control the institutions in society, to determine how resources are allocated, and to define what is "natural" "normal" "true" "good" and "high quality."

Oppression is maintained through COERCION AND CONSENT. Different forms of oppression in society are maintained through the dual processes of coercion (e.g., laws and policies that require compliance and benefit the dominant group) and voluntary consent from both advantaged and disadvantaged groups. Voluntary consent from individuals who are disadvantaged results from the pervasive nature of oppression that reinforces messages that the status quo is "natural and normal" and feelings of despair and hopelessness resulting from the historical and enduring nature of its impact (Bell, 2016, p. 10).

Oppression is INTERNALIZED. In systems of oppression, messages are communicated to members of the dominant group that they are superior to members of minoritized groups and more deserving of the privileges—including the access to positions and resources—they enjoy in society. This process is labeled *internalized dominance*. We see this in major companies across the United States where men hold the majority of all leadership positions reinforced with biased beliefs that they are more competent than women. In contrast, minoritized group members have to continually hear and manage messages in society that communicate to them that they are inferior to the dominant group; an experience that can result in internalized oppression. *Internalized oppression* describes the consequences of these messages as individuals begin to accept as "normal and natural" beliefs about their inferiority which influences their internal feelings (e.g., confidence, self-worth etc.) and the actions they do/don't take in the world. The internalization of oppression is often subconscious, occurring unintentionally without people's awareness (DiAngelo, 2016, p. 76). In this way, the internalized messages of subordination through which a person learns to think, behave and understand the world, become ways to maintain and perpetuate oppression. An example of internalized oppression is seen with students of color coming to believe that they are not smart as a consequence of the bias and discrimination they experience at school.

Oppression RESTRICTS LIFE OPPORTUNITIES. Members of minoritized groups have their opportunities for self-determination, personal agency and access to opportunities and resources unjustly constrained.

Oppression is held in place by CONNECTED SYSTEMS that overlap and reinforce one another. Each form of oppression (e.g., racism, classism, ageism etc.) has distinctive characteristics and specific histories that distinguish it from others forms of oppression. However, the different forms of oppression in society interact with one another as connected systems that overlap and reinforce each other. For example, although racism and ability are different systems of oppression, they also overlap and reinforce one another in ways that have impacts at structural/institutional and individual/interpersonal levels. For example, a Black male who is differently abled (deaf, in a wheelchair) would face the cumulative effects of oppression resulting from his membership in two minoritized groups based on his race and his (dis)ability.

> **"They said that they would never refer to me as doctor, and they stuck to their word"**
>
> "I'm a policy and program advisor working in a state department of education. I work very closely with our child care and early childhood programs across 200+ school districts.
>
> We all have these gremlins in our head and I think sometimes that's added stress. A voice in your head that tells you you're not good enough. You have that drum in your head and it says, 'how did I get this position? Where do you feel that those gremlins came from? Somewhere from your lived experiences. I'm sure it's some type of trauma that's happened in your life that gives you that. Like the trauma that happened when you were eight or nine and you had a teacher that said that you weren't smart. I think those gremlins come through lived experience and the trauma that you faced. Maybe you've overcome traumatic experiences, but you still have those voices in your head.
>
> I have a PhD and I've had white people tell me, 'I'll never call you doctor. Verbally they look me in my face and tell me that. Being a Black man, you're always afraid. What would be the repercussions if I asked a question, 'What would make you say that? I didn't even ask you to call me that.' For them not to even

understand how that would make me feel as a Black man... And to this day, they've never referred to me as Dr. Steele. Never, it's never come out of their mouth. I had to write a bio and send it to one of these colleagues. At the top of the bio it said Dr. Steele. and they erased the words 'Dr.' and 'PhD' and just left my name, Lionel Steele. They said that they would never refer to me as doctor and they stuck to their word. I never asked why."

–Lionel Steele, Program and Policy Analyst,
state Department of Education

Reflection/Discussion Questions

- What characteristics of oppression do you see in this story?
- What actions would you take if Dr. Steele was in your organization to interrupt the harm he was experiencing in his workplace and to create a more trauma-responsive healing centered environment?
- How could affinity groups (see below) or mentors within an organization become part of a trauma-responsive healing centered approach?

Affinity Groups: An Affinity Group is a group of people who share a common purpose, ideology, interest or social categories of identity (e.g., race, gender, sexual orientation, language, nationality, physical/mental ability, socio-economic class, family structure, religion, etc.). Affinity groups can be a place for underrepresented people in a community to come together to feel less isolated and more connected. Affinity groups are also used with people who identity as white or biracial. During affinity groups participants might share and talk about their experiences or focus on working towards a particular mission or goal.

Understanding How We Are Positioned Within Systems of Oppression and Privilege

Ibram Kendi (2019) reminds us that being anti-racist and working to create equitable institutions and systems requires self-awareness, self-examination and self-criticism that is persistent; it is a process that involves a reorientation of our mindsets and consciousness. With an emerging understanding of oppression, the next step for individuals and groups is to understand how they are positioned within the inequitable systems of society. Specifically, the various ways they experience oppression and privilege based on their social categories of identity (e.g., race, class, gender, sexuality, age, ability, nation, ethnicity and similar categories). Individuals and groups who are positioned differently within systems of power (e.g., those with privilege versus those who are held down and oppressed) will undoubtedly have different points of view about trauma, resilience and (in)equity. Most people experience both privileged and marginalized aspects of their identities (e.g., a female may experience sexism but as an able-bodied person also experiences privilege).

> ### Intercultural Storytelling Process (Tanaka, 2012)
>
> The following questions can be used with partners or small groups to raise awareness about how we are positioned within different systems of power. This intercultural storytelling process invites people to share stories of themselves, a family member or ancestor and in telling their own story and then listening to the stories of others, learn in a deeply personal way how privilege and oppression plays out in people's lives affording and constraining their access to resources, opportunities and lived experiences.
>
> - Describe how your family and/or ancestors came to the United States and moved across and within it.
> - Describe a time when you, someone in your family or your ancestors experienced privilege.

- Describe a time when you, someone in your family or your ancestors experienced oppression.
- Imagine a perfect world where the kind of oppression you just described does not exist. What does it look like?
- What's one thing you can do tomorrow to move towards that perfect world?

Oppression as Interlocking Systems

Drawing from Marilyn Frye (1983) and Robin DiAngelo (2016), we use a birdcage metaphor to describe the way that oppression is held in place by connected systems that overlap and reinforce each other.

FIGURE 4.2 Bird Cage
Source: Alice Blecker

The Birdcage Metaphor

(DiAngelo 2016, p. 71 adapted from Frye, 1983)

The metaphor of a birdcage has been used to explain the connected forces of oppression that overlap and mutually reinforce one another. The metaphor is explained in the following way:

> If you were standing close to a birdcage and pressing your face against it, you would see the bird close up but your awareness of the wires on the cage would be limited. Turning your face slightly so you could look closely at one of the wires of the cage, would take away your ability to see the other wires. If you remained looking at just that one wire, you might wonder why the bird could not escape and fly away. This would be true if you continued walking around the cage to see the bird from different positions. As long as you continued pressing your face against the cage and limited your view to this close-up perspective, you might perceive that the bird had freedom to fly away. If you take a step back so you can see the entire birdcage, you would notice the different wires and how they lock together in a pattern creating a strong barrier that holds the bird in place placing significant restrictions on its opportunities and freedom.

The birdcage metaphor can help us understand why oppression is difficult for many people to see and recognize: **We have a limited perspective and understanding of the world based on how we are positioned in society.** Just as your understanding of the bird and it's freedom (or lack thereof) would change based on where you stood in relation to the cage—and therefore, how much of the cage you could see—the same is true for the oppressive forces in society. We are socialized to focus on our own experiences, our personal intentions and individual actions when thinking about injustice (e.g., an individual from the dominant group advocating for the rights of a minoritized group). However, focusing on single events or the actions of specific people, does not allow us to acknowledge or 'see' the existence and significant impact of the broader, interlocking patterns of oppression that exist across our society.

Reflection/Discussion Questions

- ♦ Oppression can be difficult to recognize. Share with someone why you think this is the case.
- ♦ How might well-meaning adults unknowingly become part of a cycle of oppression?
- ♦ How might the birdcage metaphor help you to be more sensitive to the experiences of children, families and your colleagues daily?

> **"You can't access empathy if you are not willing to be vulnerable"**
>
> Empathy is an essential element of anti-oppression work. We have to be willing to be uncomfortable and we need to begin to listen and really hear other's experiences. It is impossible to be "armored up," closed off and guarded and be committed to this kind of work.
>
> > "We think about vulnerability as a dark emotion, as the core of fear and shame and grief and disappointment and uncertainty. Things I don't want to feel. I'm at risk, I'm exposed, I'm in grief. And so we armor up and say, 'I won't let myself slip into these dark emotions. I won't let myself be vulnerable.' Vulnerability is the center of difficult emotion but it's also the birthplace of every positive emotion that we need in our lives. Love, belonging, joy, empathy…In a culture where people are afraid to be vulnerable, you can't have empathy. Empathy is not a default response. If you share something with me that is difficult, in order for me to be truly empathic, I have to step into what you are feeling

and that is vulnerable. You can't access empathy if you are not willing to be vulnerable" (Brown, 2013).

"I've realized that within every organization, you find those people who you think that you can be honest, authentic and vulnerable with. And that is your circle that holds you. And it could be only one person, but you have to have a place where you can have a voice and to talk to someone either to get advice or just to have someone listen to you."

–Anita Smith, Program Manager,
Mental Health Consultation

Reflection/Discussion Questions
- Do you have a person in your organization where you can be honest, authentic and vulnerable? Are there groups in your program that allow you to have a voice, a place to be heard and listened to?
- In what ways do you listen authentically to others? Are you a safe space for someone else within your program?

Take Individual and Collective Actions to Disrupt Inequity and Strengthen Healing and Wellness

It is not enough to be informed. To be trauma-responsive and healing centered is to take actions to stop the harm, to disrupt inequity and to create the conditions for resilience to develop and strengthen and for healing to take place. We must have **'answerability'** or a dedicated commitment to be intentional and respond. What answerability looks like will be unique for each individual, program, school and system and highly dependent on the context. Following are a few possibilities:

Audit organizational policies and practices. Create a short and long term plan to guide learning. Scan your organization's policies and practices using the lens of trauma, resilience and anti-oppression to identify areas of strength, learning edges and short and long-term goals to set. In planning for change, talk through: What do we want to carry forward? What do we want to leave behind? (see the TR Organizational Self-Study tool at: The Center for Equity in Early Childhood Education, www.ceece.org)

Develop reflective supervision skills that support adults to pause and interrupt their reactivity, to discover their assumptions and biases and to build empathy and responsiveness in their work with others. Heffron and Murch (2010) describe several important for reflective leaders:

- **Bearing Witness:** Learning to simply listen, to be physically and emotionally present for a staff member and acknowledge the challenging situation they are experiencing without trying to fix it or offer advice and solutions. Understanding that just by sharing a concern or a problem with you, they have likely reduced their stress by feeling less alone.
- **Exploration:** Creating the ability to press the pause button and stop the cascade of reactions when faced with a challenging relational interaction. This means looping back with that person and the past interaction to understand it better. Being able to explore both one's own feelings and the feelings and perspective of others involved.
- **Reframing an Issue to Offer a Different Perspective:** Cultivating the ability to pose a hypothesis, explore assumptions, consider new information or to wonder about an alternative path of action (e.g., "I wonder if the reason she responded that way could be....," "I learned they just transitioned into a shelter, do you think that could account for what you observed?"..."What do you think this is like for the mother?")
- **Using Questions to Inspire Inquiry:** Use questions to invite reflection, information sharing, perspective taking and critical thinking.
    - What was most significant about the interaction for you?
    - What did you find yourself wondering or confused about?

- How do you imagine the child/family/person was feeling and what made them feel that way? How were you feeling? What factors or pressures were influencing your thinking or feeling?
- What ideas or information guided you? What information or skills did you need?
- Did you feel understood?
- If you could replay this scene, are there things you might do differently?
- Thinking back, are there things you understand in a different way now than when we started this conversation?

♦ **Filtering:** Listen to someone sharing a story or sharing their concerns, then focusing their attention where the greatest needs seem to be at that moment in time ("That is a lot to manage. I understand why you are feeling a bit overwhelmed. It sounds like preparing your presentation slides would be a place to start since those are due tomorrow. How can I support you?")

♦ **Containment:** Coming up with realistic and workable goals, identifying and sequencing priorities, breaking complex problems down into smaller parts so they are more manageable.

♦ **Refocusing on the Relationship:** Emphasizing that no matter what the concern, problem, dilemma, challenge that is shared, that we will get through this together. Always talking about a concern, challenge or problem to be faced with a focus on the value of the relationships of all involved.

Reflection/Discussion Questions

♦ Which of these skills are most comfortable for you? Least comfortable?
♦ Which of these skills would you like to strengthen/improve? Who could help you do this? What resources do you have available to you?

Start Meetings with a Land or Territorial Acknowledgement

"Good morning everyone. Before we begin our meeting, I want to take a moment to acknowledge that we are gathered today on the occupied and unceded territory of the Ohlone people who have stewarded this land for generations to ensure they provided for all living things. These lands were and continue to be of significance to indigenous people. Today, by giving this land recognition as we begin our meeting, we acknowledge the impact colonization had on tribal nations and recognize our responsibility to help them heal from this history and secure a sustainable future. We stand in solidarity with all Indigenous People and their right to self-determination and justice. We commit to working toward the healing of the generational trauma, theft, and dispossession native peoples' have faced and continue to face.

–Paula Garcia, Director, Little Hands Preschool, sharing a land acknowledgement at the beginning of their weekly staff meeting

What is Indigenous Land Acknowledgement? A territorial or land acknowledgement is an act of reconciliation that involves making a statement recognizing the traditional territory of the Indigenous peoples who called the land home before the arrival of settlers, and in many cases still do call it home.

What is its purpose? The purpose of a land or territorial acknowledgement is to recognize that settlers or all people who are not part of First Nations or Indigenous groups are on their land. Sharing the acknowledgement is only the first step in a learning and healing process.

The acknowledgement should lead people to **ask questions and learn more about the Tribal Nation(s) named** including how their land came to be possessed by settlers and information about the tribe(s) in contemporary times. Focusing only on historical events, keeps the discussion of oppression and colonization in the past and invisibilizes that Native Americans, First Nations and Indigenous peoples are living among us in cities and regions throughout the world today. Land acknowledgements are also intended to inspire a personal interrogation: We each need to ask ourselves, **"How am I benefitting by living on this land** that is a traditional territory of Indigenous people?"

Audrey Siegl (ancestral name sχɬemtəna:t) a First Nations activist from Musqueam cautions that land acknowledgments can be tokenism and empty words if settlers do not connect the words with the **responsibility for action**. We need to consider, as settlers, what our responsibilities are. That is, our obligations to the people who first inhabited the land we are currently on. She suggests that we ask ourselves the question, **"how I can be a good guest here?** How can we bring meaning to the fact that we are on unceded territory? Are there things that the Tribal Nation(s) whose land we are on are doing for which they are seeking public support? How can we become engaged in supporting tribal nations' local work and struggles for justice?" (Hergesheimer, 2016).

Denise Augustine, who carries English, French, Metis and Coast Salish ancestry in British Colombia on Vancouver Island, offers another extended option for a land acknowledgement:

"I want to invite you for a moment to think about and acknowledge the place that you are standing and either zooming or calling in from. I invite you to take four deep breaths and rest your eyes. And for a moment, move your attention from your mind. Let go of all that chatter about the things that need to be done today, about the challenges over the week. Just let that dissolve for a moment. You can bring it back later if you like. Bring your attention to your heart and take a deep breath there.

Now I invite you as you're moving through those breaths to bring your attention to your feet. And for a moment, imagine the building underneath you dissolving away, and your feet landing firmly on the earth below you. Imagine your feet extending deep roots into that earth that for thousands of years has birthed the animals and the plants and the people of that place where you are. I invite you as you're continuing to take those deep breaths to bring your attention to the top of your head. Imagine that expanding out to that circle of wisdom and love that surrounds this planet. That contains the histories of our ancestors and the possibilities of those yet to come. I invite you now to bring your attention to your heart and to again, contemplate the place where you are physically. Is there a connection to a river, a tree, maybe you're near the ocean. What is your connection to that physical place where you are?

Take one more breath and while holding your breath, give gratitude to the people who for thousands of years gathered around fires, raised their babies looked after the land, buried their loved ones. Those who have come before us on that land where you stand, where you work, where you live today. And when you're ready with one final breath, return to the room.

So now I want to invite you to share your name, where you're from, and to acknowledge the first nations people on this ancestral land, likely unceded land where you live and work and gather. If you don't know that, just notice it. That might be your first chance to unpack whiteness and to create some visibility for our Indigenous brothers and sisters. Also, please share a feature of the land around you that calls your heart and spirit."

Reflection/Discussion Questions

- How might you include a land or territorial acknowledgement in your convenings or meetings?

- How are you benefiting from the land your program is on? How can you be a good guest and take actions to support indigenous self-determination?

Action Steps for Equity

- If you do not know the Tribal Nation(s) whose land you are on, you can check out this Native Land resource: https://native-land.ca/ or text your town and state to 907-312-5085 and you will receive a text back.

Learn the characteristics of dominant (white supremacy) culture. When educators and race equity scholars describe the term **white supremacy**, they are not referring to extreme hate groups. White supremacy does not refer to individual white people and their individual beliefs and behavior, but to our political-economic social system that privileges, centralizes and elevates white people as a group and holds them up as the norm for humanity (DiAngelo, 2016). It is only when we learn to see how we are socialized with this message that we can begin to challenge it.

White people have may advantages in society (although they may not be aware of them as they perceive these privileges as just 'normal', 'the way things are') that are not accessible for BIPOC people to the same degree—e.g., experiences with and outcomes related to health, education, employment, housing etc. This is referred to as **white privilege** (DiAngelo, 2016, p. 108). These privileges are at structural and institutional levels, not an individual level. So, an individual person may be "against" racism but still experiencing many benefits from the systems in our society that are structured to advantage white people.

White supremacy is not about individual people. **It is the system of structural power that privileges, centralizes and elevates White people as a group.**

Kenneth Jones and Tema Okun describe several **characteristics of white supremacy culture** that show up in our organizations, including our early learning programs and systems (www.dismantlingracism.org). They explain that these characteristics are damaging for many reasons:

> These characteristics are damaging because they are used as norms and standards without being proactively named or chosen by the group. They are damaging because they promote White supremacy thinking…these characteristics show up in the attitudes and behaviors of all of us—People of Color and white people. Therefore, these attitudes and behaviors can show up in any group or organization, whether it is white-led or predominantly white or People of color-led or predominantly People of Color.

Many of these characteristics are so embedded within our programs, schools and systems that we take them for granted as 'what has to be.' And yet, we don't have to define professionalism and engage in our work in this way. In fact, many of the beliefs and values reflected in these characteristics are in conflict with the central values and ethical codes of conduct described by the National Association for the Education of Young Children (National Association for the Education of Young Children, 2005; 2011). Therefore, to allow these characteristics to shape the culture within our early learning environments undermines our mission, the collective 'why' driving the work we do. These characteristics are not associated with healing and wellness in the workplace, but instead, are more often factors that create stress and trauma-inducing environments.

Characteristics of Dominant/White Supremacy Culture and Antidotes for Creating More Trauma-Responsive Healing Centered Work Environments (Source: Jones & Okun, 2001; Okun, Nd)

Dominant Characteristic	What It Looks Like in Early Learning Environments
Perfectionism	Little appreciation expressed among people for the work that others are doing and when appreciation is expressed, it's usually directed to those who get most of the credit anyway
	It is common to point out either how a person or work is inadequate and/or to others about the inadequacies of a person or their work without ever talking directly to them
	Mistakes are seen as personal, i.e. they reflect badly on the person making them as opposed to being seen for what they are—mistakes. Making a mistake is confused with "being a mistake"
	Little time, energy or investment is put into reflection or identifying lessons learned that can improve practice, in other words little or no learning from mistakes
	Tendency to identify what's wrong with little ability to identify, name and appreciate what's right
	People learn to work with a harsh and constant inner critic
Antidotes to Disrupt Stress and Trauma Associated with "Perfectionism"	Develop a culture of appreciation, where the organization takes time to make sure that people's work and efforts are appreciated
	Develop a learning organization, where it is expected that everyone will make mistakes and those mistakes offer opportunities for learning. Separate the person from the mistake
	When offering feedback, emphasize strengths (see Chapter 7) and ask people to offer specific suggestions for how to do things differently when offering critiques
	Realize that being your own worst critic does not improve your work

A Sense of Urgency	A continuous sense of urgency that prevents people from having time to be inclusive, encourage democratic and/or thoughtful decision-making, to think long-term or to consider the consequences of their actions/decisions
	Reinforced by funding proposals and contracts that promise too much work for too little money and by funders who expect too much for too little
Antidotes to Disrupt Stress and Trauma Associated with "A Sense of Urgency"	Slow down decision-making processes to create space for individuals who are most impacted by the decisions to have opportunities to voice their thoughts and feelings. Further, realize that rushing decisions takes more time in the long run because inevitably people who didn't get a chance to voice their thoughts and feelings will at best resent and at worst undermine the decision because they were left unheard
	Discuss and plan for what it means to set goals of inclusivity and equity, particularly in terms of time. Learn from past experience how long projects, work plans and new initiatives take and set realistic time frames
	Have a process that articulates how thoughtful decisions will be made in a context with pressures and urgency
	Create realistic work plans acknowledging that things take longer than anyone expects
	"Our culture is urgent all the time. There is no time to stop, to reflect, to catch our breath. The issues are deeply urgent but we are moving at a pace that doesn't allow us to actually learn. We don't give leaders permission to take a day to regulate their bodies, to care for themselves. This is why **Rest is resistance**"
	–Tema Okun (2020)
Defensiveness	The organizational structure is set up and much energy spent trying to protect power as it exists. The defensiveness of people in power creates an oppressive culture
	Because of either/or thinking (see below), criticism of those with power is viewed as threatening and inappropriate
	People respond to new or challenging ideas with defensiveness, making it very difficult to raise these ideas

	A lot of energy in the organization is spent trying to make sure that people's feelings aren't getting hurt or working around defensive people
	White people spend energy defending against charges of racism instead of examining how racism might actually be happening
Antidotes to Disrupt Stress and Trauma Associated with "A Sense of Urgency Defensiveness"	Understand the link between defensiveness and fear (e.g., losing power, losing face, losing comfort, losing privilege)
	Engage in self-work including your own defensiveness. Acknowledge that the feeling of defensiveness or wanting to turn away is a built in protective factor that allows us (especially those with privilege) to distance ourselves from having to face, learn about and empathize with the pain that results from oppression
	Discuss when defensiveness or resistance to new ideas gets in the way of the organizational mission and values
Valuing Quantity over Quality	All resources of organization are directed toward producing measurable goals. Things that can be measured are more highly valued than things that cannot, for example, numbers of people attending a meeting, newsletter circulation, money spent are valued more than quality of relationships, democratic decision-making, and the ability to constructively manage conflict
	Little or no value attached to process; if it can't be measured, it has no value
	Discomfort with emotion and feelings
	No understanding that when there is a conflict between content (the agenda of the meeting) and process (people's need to be heard or engaged), process will prevail (for example, you may get through the agenda, but if you haven't paid attention to people's need to be heard, the decisions made at the meeting are undermined and/or disregarded)
Antidotes to Disrupt Stress and Trauma Associated with "Valuing Quantity over Quality"	Include process or quality goals in your planning; make sure your organization has a values statement which expresses the ways in which you want to do your work (how); make sure this is a living document and that people are using it in their day to day work

	Look for ways to measure process goals (for example if you have a goal of inclusivity, think about ways you can measure whether or not you have achieved that goal)
	Allow flexibility to be responsive to emergent needs and desires of the group (e.g., shifting off the agenda in order to address people's underlying concerns)
Worship of the Written Word	If it's not in a memo, it doesn't exist
	Those with strong documentation and writing skills are more highly valued, even in organizations where ability to relate to others is key to the mission. The organization does not take into account or value other ways in which information gets shared
Antidotes to Disrupt Stress and Trauma Associated with "Worship of the Written Word"	Work to recognize the contributions and skills that every person brings to the organization (for example, the ability to build relationships with those who are important to the organization's mission
	Take the time to analyze how people inside and outside the organization get and share information. Figure out which things need to be written down and come up with alternative ways to document what is happening
	Make sure anything written can be clearly understood (avoid academic language, acronyms and 'buzz' words)
Belief in Only One Right Way	The belief there is one right way to do things and once people are introduced to the right way, they will see the light and adopt it
	When they do not adapt or change, then something is wrong with them (the other, those not changing), not with us (those who 'know' the right way)
Antidotes to Disrupt Stress and Trauma Associated with "Belief in Only One Right Way"	Accept that there are many ways to get to the same goal; once the group has made a decision about which way will be taken, honor that decision and see what we (as individuals) and the organization will learn from taking that way, even and especially if it is not the way we would have chosen
	Work on developing the ability to notice when people do things differently and how those different ways might improve your approach

	Look for the tendency for a group or a person to keep pushing the same point over and over out of a belief that there is only one right way and then name it
	When working with communities from a different culture than our own or our organizations, be clear that we have some learning to do about the communities' ways of doing; never assume that we as individuals or our organization know what's best for the community in isolation from meaningful relationships with that community
Paternalism	Decision-making is clear to those with power and unclear to those without it
	Those with power think they are capable of making decisions for and in the interests of those without power. They often don't think it is important or necessary to understand the viewpoint or experience of those for whom they are making decisions
	Those without power understand they do not have it and understand who does. They often do not really know how decisions get made and who makes what decisions, and yet they are completely familiar with the impact of those decisions on them
Antidotes to Disrupt Stress and Trauma Associated with "Paternalism"	Clearly communicate and create transparency in identifying who makes what decisions and each person's level of responsibility and authority in the school/organization
	Include people who are affected by decisions in the decision-making
Either/or Thinking	No sense that things can be both/and. Things are either/or—good/bad, right/wrong, with us/against us. Results in trying to simplify complex things, for example believing that poverty is simply a result of lack of education
	Closely linked to perfectionism in making it difficult to learn from mistakes or accommodate conflict
	Creates conflict and increases sense of urgency, as people feel they have to make decisions to do either this or that, with no time or encouragement to consider alternatives, particularly those which may require more time or resources

	Often used by those with a clear agenda or goal to push those who are still thinking or reflecting to make a choice between 'a' or 'b' without acknowledging a need for time and creativity to come up with more options
Antidotes to Disrupt Stress and Trauma Associated with "Either/Or Thinking"	Notice when people use 'either/or' language and push to come up with more than two alternatives
	Notice when people are simplifying complex issues, particularly when the stakes seem high or an urgent decision needs to be made; slow it down and encourage people to do a deeper analysis. When people are faced with an urgent decision, take a break and give people some breathing room to think creatively; avoid making decisions under extreme pressure
Power Hoarding	Little, if any, value around sharing power. Power seen as limited, only so much to go around
	Those with power feel threatened when anyone suggests changes in how things should be done in the organization, feel suggestions for change are a reflection on their leadership
	Those with power don't see themselves as hoarding power or as feeling threatened. They assume they have the best interests of the organization at heart and assume those wanting change are ill-informed, emotional, inexperienced
Antidotes to Disrupt Stress and Trauma Associated with "Power Hoarding"	Include power sharing, shared responsibility and delegation in the organization's values statement. Encourage and model effective work as taking place within teams where people work together to accomplish shared goals
	Discuss what good leadership looks like and make sure people understand that a good leader develops the power and skills of others
	Plan for change as inevitable. Position challenges to current ideas as healthy and productive
	Maintain an individual and collective focus on the mission
Fear of Open Conflict	People in power are scared of expressed conflict and try to ignore it or run from it
	When someone raises an issue that causes discomfort, the response is to blame the person for raising the issue rather than to look at the issue which is actually causing the problem

	Emphasis on being polite. Equating the raising of difficult issues with being impolite, rude or out of line
Antidotes to Disrupt Stress and Trauma Associated with "Fear of Open Conflict"	Role play ways to handle conflict before conflict happens
	Distinguish between being polite and raising hard issues; don't require those who raise hard issues to raise them in "acceptable" ways, especially if you are using the ways in which issues are raised as an excuse not to address those issues
	Once a conflict is resolved, take the opportunity to revisit it and see how it might have been handled differently
Individualism	People in organization believe they are responsible for solving problems alone
	Accountability, if any, goes up and down, not sideways to peers or to those the organization is set up to serve
	Desire for individual recognition and credit. Competition more highly valued than cooperation and where cooperation is valued, little time or resources devoted to developing skills in how to cooperate
	Leads to isolation and a lack of accountability, as the organization values those who can get things done on their own without needing supervision or guidance
Antidotes to Disrupt Stress and Trauma Associated with "Individualism"	Create a culture where people bring problems to the group; use staff meetings as a place to solve problems, not just a place to report activities
	Make sure that credit is given to all those who participate in an effort, not just the leaders or most public person
	Make sure the organization is working towards shared goals and people understand how working together will improve performance
	Evaluate people's ability to work in a team as well as their ability to get the job done. Make people accountable as a group rather than as individuals
	Include teamwork as an important value in your values statement

Take Actions to Disrupt Inequity ◆ 153

Belief that I'm the Only One (who can do this right)	Connected to individualism, the belief that if something is going to get done right, 'I' have to do it
	Little or no ability to delegate work to others
Antidotes to Disrupt Stress and Trauma Associated with "Belief that I'm the Only One (who can do this right)"	Evaluate people based on their ability to delegate to others and on their ability to work as part of a team to accomplish shared goals
	"When I first came to Educare, I felt like I needed to be the expert in everything. And that was so stressful for me…So I felt a lot of pressure that I probably gave myself and no one was giving to me. When I realized that I don't need to be the expert at everything, that's why we have all of us—we have our family engagement team, we have our teachers and others—when I realized that, I was able to let go of a lot of stress and pressure." –Drew Giles, Director of Educare Programs with Franklin-McKinley School District at Educare California at Silicon Valley
Belief that Progress is Bigger and More	Observed in how we define success (success is always bigger, more)
	Progress is an organization which expands (adds staff, adds projects) or develops the ability to serve more people (regardless of how well they are serving them)
	Gives no value, not even negative value, to its cost/consequences, for example, increased accountability to funders as the budget grows, ways in which those we serve may be exploited, excluded or underserved as we focus on how many we are serving instead of quality of service or values created by the ways in which we serve
Antidotes to Disrupt Stress and Trauma Associated with "The Belief that Progress is Bigger and More"	Create Seventh Generation thinking by asking how the actions of the group now will affect people seven generations from now
	Make sure that any cost/benefit analysis includes all the costs, not just the financial ones, for example the cost in morale, the cost in credibility, the cost in the use of resources
	Create opportunities for individuals impacted to provide evaluative feedback

Belief in Objectivity	The belief that there is such a thing as being objective or 'neutral'
	The belief that emotions are inherently destructive, irrational and should not play a role in decision-making or group process. Invalidating people who show emotion
	Requiring people to think in a linear (logical) fashion and ignoring or invalidating those who think in other ways. Impatience with any thinking that does not appear 'logical'
Antidotes to Disrupt Stress and Trauma Associated with a "Belief in Objectivity"	Realize that everybody has a world view and that everybody's world view affects the way they understand things, realize this means you too. Unpack how our multiple identities (especially racial identities) influence our experiences in the workplace and our interactions with systems
	Push ourselves to sit with discomfort when people are expressing themselves in ways which are not familiar to us. Assume that everybody has a valid point and our job is to understand what that point is
Claiming a Right to Comfort	The belief that those with power have a right to emotional and psychological comfort (another aspect of valuing 'logic' over emotion)
	Scapegoating those who cause discomfort
Antidotes to Disrupt Stress and Trauma Associated with "Claiming a Right to Comfort"	Understand that discomfort is at the root of all growth and learning and welcoming it
	Deepening understanding of racism and oppression to have a stronger understanding of how your personal experience and feelings fit into a larger picture
	Not taking everything personally
	"Challenges motivate me. I embrace challenge. That's just a part of my professional fabric. In order for you to learn, you have to become uncomfortable so I continue to grow. So I look at all my challenges as an opportunity for growth." –Thomas Williams, Policy Advisor, Office of Special Education and Early Learning

Reflection/Discussion Questions

- How do any of these characteristics show up in your personal and professional life? In the culture of your program, school or agency? How are they creating barriers to racial justice and creating healing engaged environments?
- What can you do in collaboration with your colleagues to disrupt these characteristics and embrace new beliefs, behaviors and daily practices that reflect the values of anti-racism, intersectional justice and healing?

Top Down Pathway to Regulation
Internal Body Scan

This practice helps you take a moment to tune inward and notice your body. Imagine the scanners at a grocery store. It scans each product for the price. You have your own built in scanner. When we pause for a brief moment and do a mental scan from the top of our head, down to our shoulders, through the center of our body (heart, stomach) and down our hips, legs and to the tips of our toes, this mental scan helps us notice our body sensations, feelings, thoughts. All these clues can help us listen to what our body is communicating. You can ask yourself after the scan:

- Do I feel safe? Am I calm?
- Do I have small, medium or large emotions?
- Are my thoughts racing?
- Do I have a body sensation/s (pain, calm, discomfort) that may be sending me a message of how I feel and what I need?

References

Adams, M., & Zúñiga, X. (2016). Getting started: Core concepts for social justice education. In M. Adams, & L. Bell (Eds.), *Teaching for diversity and social justice* (3rd ed., pp. 95–130). New York, NY: Routledge.

Alexander, M. (2010). *The New Jim crow: Mass incarceration in the age of colorblindness*. New York, NY: The New Press.

Bailey, Z. D., Krieger, N., Agenor, M., Graves, J., Linos, N., & Basset, M. T. (2017). Structural racism and health inequities in the USA: Evidence and interventions. *Lancet, 389*, 1453–1463.

Bell, L. (2016). Theoretical foundations for social justice education. In M. Adams, & L. Bell (Eds.), *Teaching for diversity and social justice* (3rd ed., pp. 3–26). New York, NY: Routledge.

Bell, L., Joshi, K., & Valdivia, M. (2016). Racism and white privilege. In M. Adams, & L. Bell (Eds.), *Teaching for diversity and social justice* (3rd ed., pp. 133–81). New York, NY: Routledge.

Brown, B. (2013). *The power of vulnerability. Teachings on authenticity, connection and courage*. Louisville, CO: Sounds True Publisher.

DiAngelo, R. (2016). *What does it mean to be White? Developing White racial literacy* (Rev. Ed.). New York, NY: Peter Lang.

Frye, M. (1983). *The politics of reality: Essays in feminist theory*. Trumansburg, NY: The Crossing Press.

Hanks, A., Solomon, D., & Weller, C. (2017). *Systemic inequality. How America's structural racism helped create the Black-White wealth gap*. Center for American Progress. Retrieved from https://www.americanprogress.org/issues/race/reports/2018/02/21/447051/systematic-inequality/

Heffron, M. C. & Murch, T. (2010). *Reflective supervision and leadership in infant and early childhood programs*. Washington, DC: Zero to Three Press.

Hergesheimer, J. (2016). *Unceded territory*. Megaphone. Retrieved from https://www.megaphonemagazine.com/unceded_territory

Jones, K., & Okun, T. (2001). *Dismantling racism: A workbook for social change groups*. Changework. Retrieved from https://www.showingupforracialjustice.org/white-supremacy-culture-characteristics.html

Kendi, I. X. (2019). *How to be an anti-racist*. New York, NY: Random House.

National Association for the Education of Young Children (2005; 2011) Code of Ethical Conduct and Statement of Commitment (A Position statement). https://www.naeyc.org/sites/default/files/globally-shared/downloads/PDFs/resources/position-statements/Ethics%20Position%20Statement2011_09202013update.pdf

Okun, T. (2020). *Unpacking Whiteness workshop* with Joe Truss. August 15, 2020

Sensoy, O., & DiAngelo, R. (2017). *Is everyone really equal? An introduction to key concepts in social justice education* (2nd Ed.). New York, NY: Teachers College Press.

Tanaka, G. (2012). Intercultural storytelling process. Personal communication.

5

Core Principle—Create Environments that Reinforce Messages of Safety and Predictability

> Establishing perceptions of safety is central to trauma-responsive and healing centered environments. Children's and adults' stress is decreased in relationships and within environments that communicate feelings of emotional and physical safety and calm. Reducing uncertainty and increasing consistency and predictability in relationships and environments increases individuals' feelings of safety and belonging.

Creating early learning environments that reinforce messages of safety for children and adults requires attention to different dimensions of safety including:

Intellectual Safety—"I Feel Engaged"

Children and adults have intellectual safety when they have access to the full capacity of their cortex to think logically, engage in reflection, analyze and solve problems, explore new perspectives, challenge their assumptions/biases/prejudice, consider the consequences of their beliefs and behavior and be future oriented. To have intellectual safety requires one's basic needs being met because feeling hungry, thirsty, hot/cold, tired or under threat in any way, prevents full access to the cortex. It also requires that time and space and support is available for children and adults to think, reflect, dialogue, collaborate, create, innovate, solve problems, resolve conflicts and heal together.

Emotional/Psychological Safety—"I Feel Supported"

Children and adults have emotional/psychological safety in environments that recognize the signs of psychological stressors, communicate clear expectations about the importance of being a psychologically safe workplace and actively work to prevent and/or disrupt any form of psychological harm (e.g., bullying, shaming, harassment, discrimination, gaslighting). Psychological safety is created within organizations that actively promote and foster a culture based in values of anti-racism/anti-oppression, fairness, respect, kindness, belonging and support for diversity (e.g., through the development and implementation of a mission/values statement, norms, policies, practices, ethics etc.). When challenging situations and workplace conflicts/disagreements are addressed in a timely manner with an approach that emphasizes compassion, confidentiality, safety, learning, restorative processes and relational repair, psychological safety is supported. Further, people have a greater sense of safety in environments when they receive information about resources and supports that are available to enhance psychological safety at work and in the home (e.g., reflective supervision meetings, mental health consultation, peer support or mentorship, employee assistance programs, ombudsman, EAP, confidential surveys for feedback, policies for filing a grievance). It is also important for environments to have explicit policies that promote psychological safety such as encouraging staff to take time off, take their lunch breaks, consult with peers, have continued learning opportunities and so forth.

Social Safety—"I Feel Seen"

Children and adults have social safety when they experience a sense of belonging in the setting. An important foundation of social safety is feeling "seen" within the organization or setting. For a staff member this could be the safety that people recognize your strengths and contributions or that you have developed trusting relationships with one or more people in the workplace whom you can talk to. This could be creating pathways to share your ideas and feedback with leaders in the organization. It is also essential to make sure parents/families feel seen and heard. Finding ways for parents/families to connect with their child's teacher/staff in ways that work for them and make them comfortable is imperative. Some parents may like to meet face to face or one on one at a scheduled time, others may like to casually catch up at drop off or pick, some may even like to get a phone call or text message in the evening letting them know how their child is succeeding. Listening to parents/families and tuning into their needs is a way to help them feel seen and safe.

Physical Safety—"I Feel Safe"

Children and adults have physical safety in environments where they do not face risks from hazards in the workplace or any type of physical harm. Physical safety is enhanced with small but important elements (e.g., lighting in the parking lot; building security, locks on bathroom doors, locked spaces for personal belongings) and intentional plans and interventions for preventing physical threats and harm in the building/school (e.g., gunfire, threats related to domestic violence, immigration raids, emergency plans, fires, natural disasters, death). Creating learning environments that are warm and inviting may also help children and adults feel safe. You may even choose to create smaller spaces within a larger room by using low bookshelves or other furniture or boarders to help people feel secure. Recognize that many people with trauma histories need to know where the doors are within a building/room and they feel safer when they can see at all times who is coming in and out of the room.

> **Real Safety versus Felt Safety**
>
> Staff working in trauma-responsive environments understand and acknowledge the important difference between *being* safe and *feeling* safe. Think back to a time when you went through a stressful experience—e.g., a loud thunderstorm, the first day in a new job, moving into a new home or neighborhood, having a disagreement with a loved one, unexpected illness, loss, COVID-19 etc. Even though you may have known intellectually that you were safe, in that moment, you did not feel safe and this feeling was enough to activate your stress response system into a cascade of survival reactions.
>
> **Our goal in creating trauma-responsive early learning environments is to create the conditions to support children and adults to have real safety and felt safety.**
>
> We need policies, procedures and practices that establish real safety. However, children and adults also have a critical need to feel safe. Understanding the difference is essential.

How can Early Childhood Organizations Reinforce Messages of Safety and Predictability for Children, Families and Staff?

Consistency and predictability. Conditions of uncertainty and novelty can increase stress and perceptions of threat, especially for children and adults with histories of trauma. Therefore, felt safety is increased in settings that are consistent and predictable. What does this look like? There are many ways to create environments that reinforce safety through consistency and predictability. Some examples include (Guarino, Soares, Konnath, Clervil, & Bassuk, 2009, pp. 27–29):

- Keep consistent schedules and procedures. As much as possible, provide advanced notice and transparency when changes are necessary
- Have regular days of the week and times for meetings
- Keep and be on time for appointments
- Follow up on requests or concerns
- Clearly define roles and boundaries
- Provide regular and clear communication about program rules, policies and expectations
- Develop policies and procedures that outline how the organization files grievances, or complaints or a process for responding to conflicts that arise in the workplace and staff personal concerns (e.g., loss of a child's parent in a program, family member reports domestic violence, someone in the organization wants to file a grievance)
- Be balanced and empathic in the face of both successes and set-backs
- Send verbal and non-verbal messages of availability

"For families too, they also need someone to listen to them because sometimes school is that safe haven. And when they build that relationship with either their child's educator or caregiver, it really builds community. They enter a space that felt like a home space, they were able to get a little bit more comfortable. It wasn't this whole process anymore of let me just drop my kid off and pick my kid."
–Stephanie Joseph, Director, Kai Ming Head Start

Physical environment. Creating a safe physical environment is a primary component of a trauma-responsive organization. There are many factors to consider that create a climate where adults and/or children are not only literally safe but also that they experience a *felt* sense of safety. Following are several suggestions for creating a safe physical environment:

- Include welcoming language on signage throughout the building, ideally translated into the main languages spoken by your staff/community (e.g., "Please help yourself" to supplies in the art closet/kitchen area etc., "We are glad you are here. Please remember to sign in" on the sign in book or posting inspirational or encouraging quotes in the restroom).
- Keep parking lots, common areas, bathrooms, entrances and exits well lit;
- Ensure that people are not allowed to smoke, loiter or congregate outside entrances and exits
- Monitor who is coming in and out of the building. When possible, communicate in advance when staff have planned absences and/or when unfamiliar adults will arriving (for meetings, as substitutes etc.)
- Monitor noise levels and try to prevent any sudden loud noises
- Provide advance notice for scheduled safety drills (e.g., testing fire alarm)
- Use calming colors (e.g., paint on walls, artwork, Note: The most calming and stress reducing colors are usually in the blue family as well as muted shades of other colors)
- Hang photographs of nature and greenery even better, bring nature inside for decoration if possible such as potted plants, cut flowers, leaves, etc.
- Provide comfortable furniture and calming areas for adults and/or children who need time to de-escalate when stressed and ensure they know they are encouraged and supported to go there when they need a moment
- Ensure doors and exits are clearly marked (agency and control to withdraw/leave is important for many trauma survivors)
- Try to keep clutter to a minimum and the overall environment tidy and clean. Too much visual stimulation can be overwhelming and a clean environment can communicate a respect for everyone that enters into the learning space

- Create space for a break or restoration
- Promote physical safety in and around the building
- Create safety procedures for educators who are arriving and departing alone in the am and pm
- Prepare and practice for emergencies (natural disaster, restraining orders, guest or visitor entry)

Communicating Feelings of Safety from the Moment They Walk in the Building

Kristina Adams, Program Director and Mitchell Ha, Assistant Program Director, Hayward Unified School District Early Learning Program

Mitchell Ha and Kristina Adams are committed to becoming a trauma-responsive early childhood department within a large public school district. Their approach is centered on a value for building trusting relationships in the workplace. They work very intentionally to communicate their values to the families and children they serve as well as their early childhood staff. They want everyone to feel a sense of safety, welcome, belonging and respect from the moment they walk into the building. They explain how small changes they have made to the lobby in their old government building have made a significant difference in creating a positive and trauma-responsive climate for everyone who walks into their building:

Kristina: "I think it is a huge strength that we are relationship focused. To us, the most important thing is to create a really warm and comforting environment for the children and the families as they enter our building. If you walk into our main location where the majority of our preschoolers are, the entryway is decorated as if you were walking into someone's home. It's beautifully done. Most often we are playing classical music or jazz or something that's calming and uplifting when families are arriving. Usually you'll find at least one of us, if not both of us, standing in the lobby welcoming families when they come in or running out to the bus. We love to meet the kids who arrive on the bus who attend our inclusion programs or special day classes. We kind of fight over who gets to go do that…who gets to go get our babies off the bus. And **employees will walk in the door**—custodians, staff from the district office or from other schools and programs—**and just stop and say, 'wow.'** It has been Mitchell's passion to make sure that our families are welcomed and our children feel at home."

Mitchell: "I want to make sure that we **create a feeling of calm for families** when they walk through the doors. Before they arrive, they are driving on the freeway and dealing with all that traffic, but as soon as they enter the lobby it's soothing. Even though there may be chaos in our society, we try to neutralize that craziness a little. We truly practice what we preach when we say our program is family centered. When they walk in, there's a sense of family. There's a bench, there's a couch, there's wording on the wall that's encouraging and seasonal decorations that bring nature into the building. If I could control the lighting, that would be my next focus. Lighting is so important to children's feelings of safety. I always think about our children getting off the bus, coming in still half asleep and then they walk into our building with those bright fluorescent lights on their faces. I would love to dim the light in the morning and then slowly throughout the day, increase it.

One change we have made is placing **panels over the fluorescent fixtures on the ceilings.** We started this because we have children in our little family at the center who have special needs and they spend a lot of time laying on the floor or looking up in a chair facing these horrible bright lights. And just this small change has made a huge difference. So now we have done this in the hallway and in our offices too. The environment feels less sterile now. You know that awful feeling when bright light goes into your face. And if you put children in a room with horrible fluorescent lighting and no natural light, it can show in their

FIGURE 5.1 Lobby
Source: Mitchell Ha

behavior. So lighting is an important part of supporting a sense of calm for adults and children. We try to do everything intentionally to make the changes we can in this old school building.

When I first started working here seven years ago, the lobby was just the lobby. The parents would just walk straight in and walk through the classroom dropping off their kids and walk out and leave. And now I can see that parents are walking slower through the building to stop and look at the decorations and listen to the music playing. The visual and auditory changes are **helping parents to be more present with themselves and their child**, and more engaged during this important transition. The parents are also more aware of what's going on, what's on the walls, what's in the space, and we want them to be aware of what is happening in the program. They appreciate having this calming environment. They will even remind me, "it's almost winter, what are you going to do in the lobby this year?" I purposely have different decorations each year so that they have a "wow" factor but also that calming experience.

Whatever the decorations are, I tell the parents, **your child is welcome to touch anything.** Recently I put out some ceramic pumpkins in the lobby and the children are so respectful. I use those moments to point out to the parent, "It's Ok. Your child knows how to be respectful of items when they're allowed to touch whatever's out there. We're always so afraid what our child's going to do. But it's OK to trust them. That's the environment that I want them to be able to feel when they walk in. It's not like taking a child to the store and holding their hand so they don't touch anything. When you and your child enter our lobby, whatever's out there, they can touch. And if they want to change the music, they can go to the CD and change the music."

Confidentiality. Trauma-responsive environments strive to provide adults and children with as many opportunities for agency and control as possible. The way that personal information is gathered, used and stored are all important factors to consider. Although there are many situations that require adults to share sensitive information in order to access resources and services, the tone in which this is communicated is critical. Acknowledging that you understand this is personal information and offering reassurance about who will have access to the information and for what purposes can build trust and reduce feelings of vulnerability. *It can be helpful to let staff know who has access to their HR records and if and how that information will be shared. Another important example is when interpersonal conflict arises being clear about how sensitive information will be treated and how conflict will be resolved can be helpful.* Whenever possible, ask for parents' and family members' consent to talk about a sensitive topic and/or to request personal information (see Chapter 5: The Concept of the Invited Guest). Additionally, when talking about children or families, ensure the space is private and confidential.

Core Principle—Focus on Strengths and Assets

> Children and adults are complex human beings and should never be defined by the trauma they experience. Trauma-responsive and healing centered practice does not stigmatize, label or define people by their experiences of stress and trauma. Trauma and its impact are acknowledged honestly, however, it is never used to pathologize people. Deficit thinking (deficit language, stories and beliefs/assumptions about others) is disrupted and replaced with a strengths-based and asset oriented approach that emphasizes people's strengths, funds of knowledge, creative problem-solving and individual as well as collective sources of resistance, survival strategies, hope and healing. Acknowledging strengths and assets also involves recognizing and celebrating small wins, progress and accomplishments when working for change.

A strength-based approach begins with the assumption and belief that *all* **people have strengths, assets, sources of coping, resilience, creativity, brilliance and potential.** This belief leads to an intentional practice of listening, observing and learning about the children and adults in order to deepen our understanding of their beliefs, skills, knowledge, interests, relationships, cultural and linguistic practices, lived experiences and their hopes, dreams and goals. As Shawn Ginwright (2020) states, "I've been trained to see the world through problems, problem-solving and all the issues that show up in our schools. And while this may be important, we also need to pivot from problem-solving to possibility creating."

What is the #1 barrier that prevents people from acknowledging strengths and assets with the children and families they serve and/or among their staff and colleagues? *Deficit thinking.* Deficit thinking includes words/terms used, stories told and beliefs held about individuals or groups that is based on misinformation, partial information and/or misrepresentation. What are some examples of deficit thinking?

- The early childhood workforce is often described with language that represents deficit thinking (e.g., "babysitters," "they just play with kids, it's not really a profession.")
- In lower income communities families maybe described with deficit language (e.g., "they don't plan for the future," "they don't know how to care for their babies.")

One way to counter or disrupt deficit thinking, is to invite stories from people who are positioned through deficit or the families and communities who know them and love them—who can provide information, perspectives and history that is missing, invisible and/or inaccurate in the stories told and circulated about them. A good example is the Alameda County Father Corps (see http://www.first5alameda.org/alameda-county-fathers-corps), a non-profit sharing positive stories of fathers and their engagement in their children's lives.

A strength-based approach does not mean we never talk about weaknesses. It does mean that we start from strengths to address weaknesses. It means uncovering and recognizing potential resources, personal characteristics and relationships that can be mobilized to support the growth and development of a child, family or staff member. These resources are then used as the foundation from which you can work for interventions to address problems and challenges (How can this strength be used as a support or foundation?), often identified by the employee themselves. Supervisors help staff to discover their resources/strengths no matter how hard this may be to do (if situation looks despairing).

> **Deficit thinking may show up in your workplace in the following ways:**
>
> - Very little appreciation is expressed among people for the work that others are doing and/or appreciation is only directed to a small number of individuals
> - Tendency to identify what's wrong. Little ability to identify, name and appreciate what's right, what is going well.
> - Comments are made about how people or their work is inadequate and often communicated behind their backs
> - Little time, energy or money is invested in reflecting upon and learning from mistakes
>
> Research shows that in order to cultivate nurturing relationships and strong relational connections with adults, families, colleagues or children, the ratio of focusing on strengths vs. deficits should be 5:1. That is, at least **five positive interactions for every negative one** (Lisitsa, 2012).
>
> It takes effort and intentionality to disrupt deficit thinking and to focus on strengths.

Cultural capital refers to knowledge, skills, behaviors and attitudes that people acquire as they are part of their different cultural communities. Tara Yosso (2005) describes six forms of cultural capital that she describes as *community cultural wealth* that reflect some of the many talents, strengths and experiences that

People of Color bring into educational environments. Learning about different forms of cultural capital is one way to identify some of the important strengths early educators bring with them into their workplace on a daily basis:

- **ASPIRATIONAL capital** is defined as the "hopes and dreams" individuals have despite their experiences of persistent educational inequities.
- **LINGUISTIC capital** refers to the various language and communication skills (including storytelling) individuals bring with them including those who are learning to speak more than one language or more than one variety of English.
- **FAMILIAL capital** refers to the social networks individuals have within their extended families and across their communities.
- **SOCIAL capital** represents the valuable resources that are generated by the social connections and networks that individuals have access to.
- **NAVIGATIONAL capital** refers to individuals' skills and abilities to navigate "social institutions," including educational systems and their ability to cope when they experience unsupportive or hostile environments.
- **RESISTANCE capital** refers to the knowledge and skills communities of color have developed in their ongoing work to fight for equal rights and freedom seen among children, adults and within and across communities and generations.

How are early childhood staff supported to share their different forms of cultural capital in the program, school or agency?

ASPIRATIONAL capital: The "hopes and dreams" educators have. Questions to consider:

- How are staff supported to feel a sense of hope and to dream about their professional growth and future?

- What assumptions do leaders/supervisors have about their dreams and aspirations?

LINGUISTIC capital: The various language and communication skills individuals bring with them into the workplace. Questions to consider:

- How are we supporting the language and communication strengths of our staff?

FAMILIAL capital: The extended family and community social networks individuals have. Questions to consider:

- How are we recognizing and supporting our employees to draw on the wisdom, values and stories from their families and home/cultural communities?
- How are we creating environments that honor and invite families to participate and engage as partners in their children's education?

SOCIAL capital: The valued resources that are generated by the social connections and networks that individuals have access to. Questions to consider:

- How are we supporting staff to develop relationships with others (both internal and external to the program) who can provide emotional and other forms of support to ensure their professional success?
- How can we engage with individuals and community-based organizations to provide supports and resources to our staff?

NAVIGATIONAL capital: Individuals' skills and abilities to navigate "social institutions," including educational systems. Questions to consider are:

- How are we providing our employees with support and guidance to navigate this program, school and/or system?

- In what ways is this program, school or system unsupportive or hostile to employees—especially our staff of color? How are they coping despite these conditions?

RESISTANCE capital: The knowledge and skills communities of color have developed in their ongoing work to fight for equal rights and freedom. Questions to consider are:

- How are we supporting our staff to bridge the two environments between their homes/communities and the workplace?
- What opportunities are we providing staff to engage in the core processes of a democratic society (e.g., making choices, sharing their perspectives, considering different points of view etc.)?

Providing Effective Strengths-Based Feedback

We learn best by receiving feedback that highlights our effort, abilities, strengths and areas of progress. Focusing on strengths, dreams, hopes and how we might take steps to make progress in the future has been shown in research to trigger the parasympathetic nervous system. This can stimulate the growth of new neurons, a sense of well-being, better immune function and cognitive emotional and perceptual openness.

Feedback that emphasizes our weaknesses, gaps, shortcomings or mistakes often leads to the activation of our stress response system which reduces our capacity to think logically, problem-solve, expand our perspectives, take risks and engage in reflection. Triggering our stress response systems also means that we are more likely to misread verbal statements and non-verbal behavior as threatening. Essentially, our brains perceive critical feedback as a threat which then impairs our ability to hear, understand and accurately interpret what someone is communicating to us. This is why focusing feedback on concerns can shortcut people's ability to learn.

"I was new to a director position at a large organization. I was so happy to start this job and in the first 6 months I raised $20,000 and started up a few new programs by collaboration with local funders. We even coordinated a 5K walk to raise money for our program. Every step along the way, I sent an email to our Executive Directors to update them since when they hired me, they stated 'growth' of the program as a main objective. I would send daily updates to the progress. One day the Human Resources Director invited me to lunch. I told my partner that I thought they were going to ask me what I was doing to have so much progress in the first 6 months. Instead the HR Director was sent by the ED to tell me I was sending too many emails with updates and I should only send one summary per month. The entire lunch was just to give me that critical feedback. It felt like a knife was being stabbed in my heart. I could barely finish my lunch. All I wanted to do was run and never come back."
–Mayra Dorado, Executive Director, Rolling Hills Child Development Agency

In an article titled, **"How to help people excel"** Buckingham and Goodall (2019) state, "Learning happens best when we are supported to explore how we can do something better by extending or adding a nuance to what we already understand and/or do. Learning is supported by emphasizing what we are doing well, not by focusing on…someone else's opinion of what we are doing poorly" (p. 97).

Buckinham and Goodall (2019) provide several recommendations for providing effective strengths-based feedback that supports learning and growth. Their approach aligns with a trauma-responsive approach. They suggest:

- ♦ **Look for moments when an employee is successful in creating a desired skill, disposition, pedagogy or outcome** (e.g., calms down a dysregulated child; helps a parent to feel heard; supports a community member to share their story in a meeting) and bring attention to this moment. We call it a **Strength Scan**. Instead of immediately focusing on the problem, solution or moving on to the next task, pausing to comment or notice a strength, positive intention or the sharing of a new idea can go a long way in helping others feel included, seen, valued and appreciated. Doing so creates a momentary pause and helps to bring the employee's attention to something that they just said or did that was helpful or effective. This type of specific observation also reinforces to the staff member that you are invested in their success. Buckingham and Goodall (2019) explain, "When you see an employee do something that works for you, stop what you are doing and bring attention to it. Make visible to them what excellence looks like that they are already doing. Help her gain an insight into something she is already doing that is working, that she can recognize, recreate and refine. This is the heart of supporting her learning."

"People need acknowledgement. They need recognition. I know that if I give positive affirmations to somebody who's in a classroom with children, they become better at what they do. So I scan for positive attributes. This helps strengthen the wiring in their brains and their internal narratives"
    –Stephanie Joseph, Director, Kai Ming Head Start

♦ **Instead of offering evaluative feedback, share what you observed and how it makes you feel.** For example, you could respond:

"This is how that came across for me"

"This is what that made me think of…"

"Here is what I just observed …" what do you think?

Instead of "Good job" say, "When you sat at lunch with the children and were taking such an interest in what they had to say, I could see their faces light up with excitement. I can see now how much time you put in to building relationships with children and what a difference it makes."

Using positive and descriptive statements like this allows a supervisor or coach to share their honest feedback without sending a message that you are trying to "fix" someone. Instead, you are trying to "explore and understand the excellence" (Buckingham & Goodall, 2019).

- **Never lose sight of your 'highest priority interrupt'.** If an employee makes a significant mistake, you will have to interrupt him to stop something he is saying or doing that is harmful. However, your correction is likely to activate his stress responses and therefore, he is unlikely to learn from your feedback. Making corrections when someone is struggling or making a mistake, will not teach them about excellence. Comment when an employee is excelling. Stop them when they are displaying an important skill, successfully managing an interaction or communicating effectively to invite them to analyze what they are doing—"I just observed you very successfully manage to calm your colleague after that challenging interaction in the staff room. Can you rewind and walk me through how you thought that through? It was inspiring to observe your communication skills." Guiding an employee to reflect upon and break down the steps they took toward excellence will support them to feel safe in exploring and reflecting on their practice.
- **When employees come to you requesting feedback on a problem/dilemma, don't just right to providing advice. Instead:**
  - **Start with the present:** Start by asking them to share three things that are working for them right now: (maybe they are related to the situation or maybe not; they could be significant or trivial facts).
  - **Next, go to the past:** Ask, when you had a problem like this in the past, what worked for you?

- **Then, turn to the future:** What do you already know that you need to do? What do you already know works in this situation?

Reflection/Discussion Questions

- When you supervise, how do you scan for strengths of those you supervise?
- How do you communicate those strengths?
- How could these ideas inform the way you provide feedback?

Core Principle—Provide Opportunities for Agency and Control

> As traumatic experiences involve a loss of power and control resulting in feelings of helplessness, terror and often, hopelessness, trauma-responsive and resilience building practices support individuals and groups to have opportunities for personal agency, self-determination and control. This is often described as "voice and choice." These environments support children and adults to have opportunities to provide input to inform the decisions that impact them (e.g., policies, processes, procedures), to make choices and participate in creating mutually agreed upon goals and to feel a sense of control in communication, interactions and within their environments.

Before we can provide opportunities for agency and control, it is important to understand the role of power differentials and their ability to negatively impact people's feelings of safety and to trigger or activate their stress response systems. Bruce Perry (2020d) reminds us about the importance of appreciating and being aware of power differentials and how they play out in our daily interactions with supervisors, colleagues, parents/families and children. Without understanding and acknowledging these dynamics, our words, body language or actions could inadvertently communicate messages that cause others to feel unsafe or even threatened. When this happens—we may struggle to understand why our efforts to motivate change are being met with resistance, anger, frustration or behavior that is surprising and/or confusing.

Dr. Perry (2020d) describes how and why power differentials are present in our interactions with others:

> "...we have this neurobiological set of systems designed to continually monitor the social milieu to get a sense of how safe we are. Do we belong? Is this idea that I'm floating at the workplace, are people accepting it? Are they not accepting it? Do they value my opinion? Are they listening to me? Am I going to get promoted? Am I going to get fired? Who should I align with? Who's going to be competing with me? Your brain is literally nonstop doing this social monitoring to get a sense of where you fit into the group...Our stress response systems are tremendously influenced by our sense of whether or not we belong to the group or if we're getting signals that we don't belong.... Somebody who is given signals of acceptance, they feel safe. They feel like they belong...they are literally getting this bath of powerful, physiological regulation and reward and opportunities to have a fully open cortex so that they can learn things on an ongoing basis...When we are in the presence of people that we don't know, or people who are not sending us signals of inclusion and acceptance, it activates our stress response. It makes us feel threatened. And sometimes we're not even consciously aware of the threat. But it begins to influence how we are functioning cognitively, how we are functioning behaviorally, how we are feeling emotionally and how our physiology is managing our stress response...the more threatened we feel, the more the lower parts of our brains start to dominate and control our functioning."

It is essential that early educators understand that just being in a position of power (e.g., supervisor versus supervisee; teacher versus parent/family member, adult versus child) can be triggering for someone we are interacting with. The less safe or welcome they feel in our presence or in the early learning program, school or agency—and the more they perceive that they are in a sub-dominant position within the power differential (Perry, 2020d)—the more likely they are to display stress-related behaviors. And when they perceive that they are in situations where they have little power and control (a parent conference; a job evaluation etc.), the more likely you are to see dissociative or "frozen" stress behaviors like shutting down, compliance, disengagement, short comments and little responsiveness.

Just being in an educational setting or speaking to a teacher can be triggering for some adults, reminding them of their own past experiences in school or working within systems where they had traumatic experiences defined by feelings of a total loss of control, powerlessness and fear. There are many examples we could think of including a lack of safety due to racism, class discrimination, being defined through deficit, lack of cultural or linguistic alignment in the school, fear due to their undocumented status, school shooting and many others. Working with a trauma-responsive approach requires that we understand, acknowledge and work to decrease power differentials in our interactions. Similarly, if a supervisor or coach does not understand how her words or actions could lead someone to feel threatened and perceive they are at the weaker end of the power differential, you may find their response to your feedback, directions or requests for information very confusing as they behave in a state dependent manner that reflects their brain and body's attempt to survive in the midst of a perceived threat (Perry, 2020d).

> *As educators, we want to be continually aware of our positionality and considering, how can I even the playing field? How can I decrease my power and communicate messages of safety, inclusiveness and respect? We need to think about this whenever we enter a child's home, when we lead a meeting and in the many interactions we have throughout our daily work.*

What can early educators do to "even the playing field" and decrease the power differential during our interactions? Dr. Perry (2020d) offers several important suggestions:

- ♦ **Build relational regulation through repetitive contact.** The more frequently we see someone and have even brief moments of relational connection with them, the less our brains will perceive threat in their presence. Simply having repetitive contact reduces uncertainty and increases familiarity which can improve perceptions of safety.
- ♦ **Be mindful of the verbal and non-verbal signals we send in our communication.** We can build awareness of our facial expressions, tone of voice and the questions we ask and try to avoid sending any aggressive cues to others. We can also be intentional in communicating messages of reassurance and support ("You are so persistent. I know this is hard," "What can I do to support you? What do you need?").
- ♦ **Physical proximity and gaze.** Physical proximity can be an important factor in a power differential. If someone stands close to us and this is someone we don't know or do not trust, this move can be perceived as an expression of dominance and it can trigger a stress reaction, especially for someone larger than us. It is important to be mindful of your physical proximity during interactions and try to avoid making quick movements toward someone as this could decrease their sense of felt safety. Additionally, it is helpful to prevent a situation where someone has to look up to you during a conversation. Putting someone in a position where they have to use an upward gaze to communicate with you—requesting that a staff member come into your office to speak with you but having them sit on a couch that is lower than your desk—could automatically activate their brain's survival response if this signals they are in the sub-dominant position within the relationship (This is one of the many reasons early childhood providers kneel down or sit when speaking with a child).

- **Building awareness of diverse cultural beliefs and unconscious bias.** Culture has a profound influence on our perceptions of power—what we assume is natural, normal and/or desired in terms of the way power dynamics play out among individuals of different genders, races, abilities, roles, ages etc. Similarly, we all have unconscious biases that significantly impact how we perceive the world and our place within it. These biases have a profound influence on how we perceive safety, inclusion/exclusion and threat. Building awareness of cultural differences and the impact unconscious bias has in our relationships and interactions with others will help in learning how and why power differentials develop.

Building awareness of the way our beliefs and behaviors contribute to messages of dominance and sub-dominance will help early educators make thoughtful and intentional choices to decrease power differentials—a foundation for creating opportunities for people to have agency and control.

Opportunities for voice and choice. It is an unfortunate fact that 67% of adults in the United States have experienced at least one trauma before the age of 18 (Felitti et al., 1998; Koplan & Chard, 2014). Trauma impacts the majority of adults. In the past when we experienced trauma, we felt a complete loss of control. As a result, something in the present moment can trigger that trauma memory, especially when it reminds us of that "loss of control." Having no choice and no voice is the very thing that can trigger our trauma memories and send us into a fight, flight or freeze behavioral response. The antidote to this is giving voice and choice. When we can provide input, when we are asked how a new procedure may impact us, when we have choices within our daily work structure, we feel a sense of agency and control. Creating these opportunities communicates a message that employees have valued expertise and tapping into their wisdom is a worthwhile endeavor that will increase the quality of the services provided (Guarino et al., 2009). In fact, allowing for voice and choice can improve creativity, innovation and even profit as employees are more productive and more invested.

Privacy and confidentiality. It is unfortunately, quite common for adults and children with histories of trauma to have had their privacy violated and their dignity compromised—for survivors of sexual abuse, their bodies have been violated, housing insecure families may have spent nights unhoused with nowhere safe to sleep and no bathroom facilities available and children who have suffered emotional abuse may have experienced humiliation or have been publicly shamed (Guarino et al., 2009). As a result, **central to trauma-responsive practice and honoring agency and control is respecting privacy and confidentiality** for employees, families and consumers. Following are some different ways that early childhood professionals can practice respecting privacy and confidentiality (Guarino et al., 2009).

- Ask permission and outline clear boundaries before talking about sensitive topics or entering someone's home or personal space (e.g., family homes, shelters, etc.). *Note: See more on this topic in discussion of the concept of the invited guest below.*
- Provide a location where private conversations can take place free from interruption and without concern that confidentiality will be compromised.
- Ask permission before picking up, hugging, tickling or physically touching someone without their permission.
- Always be clear about what is confidential in a conversation. There are some private things you may have to share and some things that you may not think are sensitive that would make the other person uncomfortable if you shared.
- Treat people with dignity and humanity. Be calm and patient as people share with you.
- Check your biases and assumptions.

Asking for consent: The concept of being an invited guest. Bill Ketterer, author of, *Reducing anger and violence in schools* (2019), explains that an important way teachers and administrators can build trust in the early learning setting is to consider **the concept of becoming an invited guest.** The idea of the "invited guest" is based on a belief that building trust with parents and families—especially if they have histories of trauma including difficult experiences interacting with educational systems—will be enhanced when educators *ask permission to be part of the parent's/family member's life.* That is, to help the family feel as if they have choices about how things will proceed in the relationships and to allow them **the chance to withdraw emotionally** if necessary. In essence, to be an "invited guest" is to acknowledge that processing or otherwise discussing sensitive topics—e.g., feelings, behavior—requires consent and should only be done after the teacher or administrator asks permission. This small but simple act of requesting consent to open a conversation with a family about a topic that may be difficult for a parent and evoke strong emotions, provides the parent with agency by *allowing them to have a way out.* Although it may seem counter-intuitive, the invited guest concept is one of the best ways to build confidence and safety as trust is enhanced "when people have the ability to leave" (Ketterer, 2019). How does granting permission to "leave" build trust? By…

- Communicating messages to the parents and families that they have choices
- Reducing the power differential between educators and families
- Allowing opportunities for withdrawing
- Using family input to inform decisions and processes

What does "asking for consent" look like? Requesting to be an invited guest in the life of a parent/family might sound like:

- Your child said something in class today that I'd like to share with you. May I discuss this with you?
- Would you be willing to meet with us/me about your child's clothing?
- I want to share some things about your child in our classroom. Is it okay if we talk about this now?
- How much time do you have for our meeting?
- Where is best for you to meet?
- Where would you like me to sit?

Ketterer suggests that educators think of the invited guest concept like an **invitation for tea**:

"The parents may at first want a cup of tea, so to speak, but then later they decide that they don't. Of course, at a tea party, if a person doesn't like their tea, they can stop drinking it at any time. The same goes with discussions at school about behavior, emotional problems, family issues etc. *We want to be respectful of the parent and family member's right to change their mind about having that 'cup of tea.'*" (p. 87).

Communicating to parents and family members that you understand, acknowledge and will respect their voice and agency in the relationship is simply making transparent the power that families always have to disengage from educational settings and processes. Many parents find ways to withdraw emotionally and physically—and not to engage or to stop participating in an educational program in an authentic or collaborative way—when they feel inherently unsafe, unwelcome and perceive that they do not have control in determining how and when they participate.

Reflection/Discussion Questions

- ♦ What is your reaction to the idea of being an invited guest and taking a stance of "asking permission" in your work with parents and families?
- ♦ How can this concept of being an invited guest influence the way you interact with your co-teachers, colleagues or supervisees? Build trust with your colleagues?
- ♦ Thinking about a meeting with someone you supervise, how would do the following:
  - Set up the meeting
  - Welcome them to the meeting
  - Set the agenda (in advance or during)
  - Balance the discussion between your agenda items and theirs
  - Offer opportunity for input

Scaffolding Success

Creating opportunities for staff to have agency and control can mean investing in their professional learning and encouraging them to explore new roles and/or responsibilities. Doing so in a trauma-responsive manner means never using a "sink or swim" approach. Instead, supervisors carefully and intentionally plan for the resources and sources of support that will support an employee to be successful—e.g., providing relational regulation (employees do not feel isolated or alone but instead know they can count on relational support), reducing uncertainty (clear communication about expectations and roles) and striving to reduce potential triggering experiences/events. Brené Brown, author of *Daring to lead* (2018) recommends the following strategy that supervisors and team leaders can use to support the success of employees who agree to take on new responsibilities:

TASC: The Accountability and Success Checklist

T: Who owns the task?
A: Do they have the authority to be held accountable?
S: Do we agree that they are set up for success (time, resources, clarity)?
C: Do we have a checklist of what needs to happen to accomplish the task?

The leadership team is having their monthly team meeting. Over the past several months the theme of trauma-informed practices has emerged as a topic that teachers and staff want to learn more about. A decision was made to host a one day training for the organization as a great way to start to learn more about the neurobiology of trauma and trauma-informed practices in early childhood. The leadership team wanted to form a committee to take over this work moving forward. Using the TASC Checklist (Brown, 2018), the following steps were decided by the end of the meeting:

T: Melissa, Jalissa, Miguel and Anita would be on this short term Trauma-Informed Practices Committee

A: They were given the authority to research trainers, topics, experts, cost and curriculum

S: The committee agreed they could meet within 2 weeks after this meeting for 1 hour and that each member would research 1 trainer/organization and would find out what their curriculum and cost and a website link to bring back to the next leadership team meeting to present on.

C: The complete list of deliverables the committee would compile over the next two weeks: (a) name of trainer/organization, (b) website link, (c) cost, (d) time of training, (e) content or outline and description and (f) level of ECE experience and (g) amount of expertise in trauma/background, reputation, testimonials. They would then compile the data at their committee meeting in 2 weeks and prepare for a short 30 minute presentation at the next leadership team meeting in 1 month.

Following is a vignette describing how Jonathan Iris-Wilbanks, a Child Life Specialist, is working to create trauma-responsive environments in a hospital setting that provide opportunities for agency and control for the young patients and their families. As you read through the story, identify how Jonathan's beliefs and the actions reflect the essence of this principle in context:

"One Side Is Red and Says 'STOP' and the Other Side Is Green and Says 'GO'": Agency and Control for Young Children in a Hospital Setting

Jonathan Iris-Wilbanks, a Certified Child Life Specialist, who works with children who are hospitalized and their families explains how planning for young children to have agency begins by imagining the entire experience through their eyes. He explains:

> "I consider what it is like when a child walks into this setting. What is the interaction like with the check-in person? Is the child ignored and only the parent is addressed? Does the child have some say when they are told to put something on their body like a wristband? Or, are they given an option about the size, the color, the texture, the material of the gown/clothes they are asked to change into? Where they can change their clothes?" These are examples of the small touch points that we have to consider to provide agency to a child at every one of these moments.
>
> We also try to give agency and control to the parents and family members. I receive a list at the beginning of each week describing the upcoming procedures. I try to contact the families in advance and have a quick five-minute conversation about what to bring, what they might see and to reduce uncertainty for them by providing a little prep. When children have special needs, we try to make adjustments that maintain a child's sense of control. For example, some children have sensory processing challenges, and I can speak with the doctors in advance to request that they be able to wear their own pajamas during a procedure. Working with the doctors and the families, we determine whether the child's pajamas will be safe in an MRI machine (as some stretchy elastic material actually has metal in it and it could heat up and hurt the child). Just the chance to wear their own shirt, pants, pajamas, or even to wear their own socks can support a child to feel a sense of control during a very scary procedure in the hospital.
>
> In our pediatric radiology waiting room, we installed picture frames at children's heights that could be opened and closed. We have therapeutically themed art projects in the waiting room (e.g., boats on the Bay) and children

can choose to participate in the activity and then put their pictures in one of the frames on the wall. Often the children's art/drawings are a window into their thoughts and feelings. If a child draws a boat in the middle of a storm, I might look to see who is on the boat with the child in the storm, are they alone? Is their family on the boat with them? There's so much information that children can share with us if they have the chance to express it. As we walk back to their hospital room, I might ask them, do you want to tell me a little bit about your boat on the Bay? And it would tell me so much about their stress levels. It could be chaotic waves, or it could be the calmest sunny day. And we ask their permission to put their artwork on the wall. So when they walk out of the procedure, they see that they have changed the space; they've left an impact for the next kiddo. Or, they can choose to keep their artwork and take it home or they can throw it away if they want. My intention is to ask, "How can a child leave an impact on this space and actually have agency around what they do while they are here?"

I've also started to consider how a child has agency and control during our procedures. Can a child have agency to tell people to stop? We thought a lot about how to support children to have more control. One idea we have now implemented for many procedures is to provide the child with a small laminated stop sign. **One side is red and says "STOP" and the other side is green and says "GO."** We support the child to practice using the stop sign before the procedure begins. If the child holds up the red side of the stop sign, the adults stop what they are doing (if they can safely do so) and show the child their hands. If a doctor can't take their hands away, they can say, "I'm not going to move any further but I need to hold this secure so that it doesn't hurt you." Why do we hold up our hands? If a child is stressed and on the verge of losing it, they can't always tell what they're feeling and they may not know if we are/are not touching them because they might still be in pain. And so we stop and show our hands and we all take a deep breath. Then I explain to the child that it's very important for the doctors to finish and when they are ready to start again. We just need you to show us the GO sign and we'll keep going slowly. For many children just seeing the adults be responsive to the STOP sign actually helps them to say, "I'm ready," as it allows them the agency and control to cope with incredibly painful invasive procedures like tubes going in their bodies or needle pokes. For children who can't communicate by themselves (maybe they have a cognitive delay or developmental delay) agency is given to the person who knows them the best, their caregiver. So, it's really about paying respect to those little moments in our work with a child and thinking about how we can help manage stress by providing them with many small opportunities for agency and control.

Reflection/Discussion Questions

- What are some of the "small ways" you could create opportunities for agency and control in your setting?
- Can you scan your environment and look for ways to give children, families and educators input? Are their voices reflected in the environment around you?

Bottom Up Pathway to Regulation

Breathing

Biomechanics of the Breath
Breath is the remote control of regulation

Your **INBREATH** stimulates the sympathetic nervous systems which acts as the **"accelerator."** It activates the energy within your body.

Your **OUTBREATH** stimulates the parasympathetic nervous system which acts as the **"brakes."** It slows the energy responses within your body.

10 seconds of deep breathing will allow your brain to calm enough to allow you to take a more responsive, and non-reactive, approach in your interactions with other adults or children. After taking some deep breaths, early childhood providers are better equipped to ask themselves, "What is this individual communicating to me about how they feel and what they need? How can I help them feel visible, listened to, safe and cared for?"

Following are several breathing exercises you can use to immediately regulate your stress response system:

Five Finger Breathing Technique

- Hold your palm of your hand up
- Take one finger to trace from your other hand
- Start with your thumb
- Trace up–breath in 3 seconds
- Hold at the tip of the thumb—hold the breath 2–3 seconds
- Trace down the thumb—breath out 5–7 seconds
- Repeat to the next finger until you finish all 5 fingers

Tip: If the outbreath is longer than the inbreath, it will promote calm and regulation

Nose and Finger Breath

- Place the pointer finger from one hand horizontal and slightly under both nostrils
- Take one deep breath in through the nostrils
- Breath out through your nostrils and notice the breath on your finger as you breath out

Emergency Breath in a Panic—Can't catch your breath? Having a feeling of panic and your breathing becomes difficult, short or rapid? *Follow these steps to ensure quick air flow:*

- One large outbreath, as if you are blowing out a large flame (this will open up your air flow tube).
- Cup your lips as if you are sucking on a large boba straw (A **boba straw** or a **bubble** tea **straw** is used to drink milk tea with **boba** pearls. ... **Boba straws** aren't only made to sip on tapioca pearls though.)(This keeps your air tube open and sends messages to keep the air flowing in and out)
- Breathe regularly while your lips are holding on to your pretend boba straw. This allows the maximum flow of oxygen and opens up your breathing.

4-7-8 Breath (Weil, Nd)

- Exhale completely through your mouth, making a whoosh **sound.**
- Close your mouth and inhale quietly through your nose to a mental count of 4.
- Hold your breath for a count of 5–7.
- Exhale completely through your mouth, making a whoosh **sound** to a count of 6–8.

Blow Up a Pretend Balloon

- Blowing up balloons can help teach an athlete what it feels like to have a complete and full exhalation using the abdominal muscles.
- Take a deep inhale and exhale with a long, steady, forceful breath and contract the abdominal muscles to try to force the last of the air out of the lungs.
- ◆ Repeat.

References

Brown, B. (2018). *Daring to lead. Brave work. Tough conversations.* Whole hearts. New York, NY: Random House.

Buckingham, M., & Goodall, A. (2019, March–April). *The feedback fallacy.* Harvard Business Review (pp. 92–101).

Felitti, V. J., Anda, R. F., Nordenberg, D., Williamson, D. F., Spitz, A. M., Edwards, V. … Marks, J. S. (1998). The relationship of adult health status to childhood abuse and household dysfunction. *American Journal of Preventive Medicine, 14*(4), 245–258.

Ginwright, S. (2020). Healing centered. SRI Summer Virtual meeting keynote. Retrieved from https://www.youtube.com/watch?v=kPNJkr2hdQQ)

Guarino, K., Soares, P., Konnath, K., Clervil, R., & Bassuk, E. (2009). Trauma-informed organizational toolkit. Rockville, MD: Center for Mental Health Services, Substance Abuse and Mental Health Services Administration, and the Daniels Fund, the National Child Traumatic Stress Network, and the W.K. Kellogg Foundation. Available at www.homeless.samhsa.gov and www.familyhomelessness.org

Ketterer, B. (2019). *Reducing anger and violence in schools: An evidence based approach.* New York, NY: Routledge.

Koplan, C., & Chard, A. (2014). Adverse early life experiences as a social determinant of mental health. *Psychiatric Annals, 44*(1), 39–45. Doi: 10.3928/00485713-20140108-07.

Lisitsa, E. (2012). The positive perspective: Dr. Gottman's magic ratio! [Web log post]. Retrieved from http://www.gottmanblog.com/2012/12/the-positive-perspective-dr-gottmans.html

Perry, B. (2014). Rhythm regulates the brain. Retrieved from https://attachmentdisorderhealing.com/developmental-trauma-3/

Perry, B. (2020d). Understanding the power differential. *NN COVID Series 12.* Retrieved from https://youtu.be/ulwfwYDffV8

Yosso, T. J. (2005). Whose culture has capital? A critical race theory discussion of community cultural wealth. *Race, Ethnicity and Education, 8*(1), 69–91.

6

Core Principle—Intentionally Promote Coping, Resilience and Healing

"Resilience for me means that somebody has some really, really great coping skills and they're able to have an experience and put their coping skills into play and come out of it. There are times when we need assistance with our resiliency. I don't believe that anybody is an island. Building resilience is not an overnight process."

–Krystal Lewis, Head Start Director

Central to trauma-responsive practice is actively building resilience, supporting healing and creating the conditions that improve wellness. Resilience is improved when individuals and groups are supported to identify their individual and collective/community strengths, sources of relational support (family networks, generational relationships, community support systems, cultural and spiritual resources and a shared collective history and bonds that create a sense of belonging) and the coping strategies—they as individuals or their families and communities—have used to manage and survive adversity in the past. For many, an important source of healing from historical oppression and cultural

> trauma is restoration of identity through participation in cultural rooted and/or spiritual practices and rituals. An important part of building resilience for early educators is being supported to manage the multiple stressors associated with their jobs in order to prevent burnout and/or the impacts that can result from vicarious trauma.

Resilience is seen with children and adults who are succeeding, even excelling, despite incredibly difficult circumstances.

We want to create environments that are not only trauma-responsive but also intentionally plan for and build resilience and support healing for children and adults. For children, creating environments that are safe, nurturing and predictable may be one of the greatest proactive interventions we can do to build their resilience. We cannot create resilient environments without healthy adults who are self-aware and regulated. It is all interconnected and when we make one small change toward health and wellness, the ripple effect is momentous. Although there are many ways that coping and resilience can be intentionally planned for and strengthened, it is critical to name that the lack of resources in early childhood is an ever-present barrier and challenge.

What Factors Support Children and Adults to Cope, Heal and Build Resilience?

Having consistent, supportive and responsive relationships. Caring attuned responsive relationships are the most important factor to buffer stress, prevent short and long term harm resulting from trauma *and* in supporting children's and adults' healing. Perry (2017) reinforces the power of relationships to buffer stress and heal, "Just as a traumatic experience can alter a life in an instant, so too can a therapeutic encounter. The more we can provide each other these moment of simple, human connection—even a brief nod or a moment of eye contact—the more we'll be able to heal those who have suffered traumatic experience" (pp. 308–309).

Building a healthy identity and a sense of belonging. Resilience is strengthened when children and adults are supported to build healthy identities rooted in their cultural ways of knowing and being (or for those impacted by oppression and colonization, *restoration* of their authentic identities) and when they feel a sense of belonging. Participating in culturally responsive rituals, ceremonies, routines and activities builds resilience and supports healing especially for individuals impacted by trauma and oppression.

Creating resilience narratives. An important aspect of resilience is how people perceive and find meaning when making sense of, processing and metabolizing the adverse events and experiences they go through. Acknowledging what is described as *post-traumatic growth* builds resilience. Post-traumatic growth is the idea that even in very stressful and traumatic experiences, if someone can attribute at least one perceived positive change that resulted from going through and/or surviving the experience, they are more likely to cope, adjust and heal. Resilience narratives honestly acknowledge the pain, suffering and loss associated with trauma. However, they also convey the message that people and communities can and do cope, learn and grow through adversity and hardship.

We can build and strengthen resilience for ourselves and others by learning to tell stories in two parts: (a) honestly acknowledging the pain and suffering associated with a particular experience and (b) identifying at least one perceived positive change we can attribute to having gone through the experience.

Examples of Post-Traumatic Growth

Perceived positive outcomes following a traumatic experience or event can be seen at personal, family, organizational, community and societal levels.

- Improved relationships
- Healthier life-style

- Changes in the value ascribed to one's life
- Changes in spiritual faith
- Readjusting priorities
- Shift in self- image (e.g., a new sense of strength and responsibility)
- Appreciation for life
- Improved connections with children
- Creating new vision and directions in life
- Building a resilience toolbox "I lived through that so I can handle anything."
- Coming together in community

Trauma is not a life sentence! In fact, we often over focus on the trauma and the cascading effects as traumatic. But what if we looked at it also with the lens of how trauma is just one thread in the fabric of someone's life. Each one of us was born with both internal (factors within ourselves such as temperament) and external sources of resilience (factors that buffered our stress such as relationships, activities, environments, community). For this reason, focusing on trauma without resilience is incomplete and can cause more harm.

Perceiving a sense of agency and control. As perceptions of a loss of control is one of the conditions of a traumatic experience, gaining a felt sense of agency and control is essential for coping and healing. This often involves small actions people can take in their immediate sphere of influence to assert their "voice and choice" within an environment. When people advocate for policies and opportunities that address causes of trauma, such as lack of access to mental health, these activities contribute to a sense of purpose, power and control over life situations. Taking what Ginwright (2018) describes as "loving and collective actions" people not only strengthen a sense of agency and control, they are also less likely to internalize and blame themselves for the trauma they experience.

> **Examples of Loving Individual and Collective Actions that Increase Resilience**
>
> When individuals and groups take actions to change the underlying causes of the stress and trauma they experience, they have a greater sense of power and control which strengthens their ability to cope and heal. Examples of resilience-building loving actions include:
>
> - Protesting or marching to fight for racial justice
> - Testifying at a school board meeting or in front of state legislators about the need to invest in compensation for the early childhood workforce
> - Signing an advocacy letter to change policies on school discipline
> - Community coming together during a pandemic, national crisis or natural disaster
> - Donating to a cause
> - Supporting business owners who are marginalized
> - Random acts of kindness

Another aspect of how perceptions of agency and control are related to resilience concerns what Martin Seligman—a University of Pennsylvania psychologist who pioneered much of the field of positive psychology—describes as **explanatory style**, or the way they perceive and explain events to themselves and others. People can be guided to change their explanatory styles from:

- **Internal to external.** Instead of: "It's all my fault." Try: "We are struggling with enrollment at our center. This is due to many factors."
- **From global to specific.** Instead of: "I'm a total failure as a leader." Try: "It would be helpful to have some coaching/mentoring in how to provide effective feedback."

♦ **From permanent to impermanent.** Instead of: "There is no hope, year after year nothing changes." Try: "Although we want every child who qualifies to have access to early intervention services, we are making slow and steady progress. This year 200 more children received services."

Research highlights that when people explain the events and experiences in their lives—especially adversity—using an explanatory style that is external, specific and impermanent, they perceive less stress, are less likely to report feeling a sense of hopelessness (a major risk factor for depression) and have improved well-being.

Resilience and coping can change over time. The level of resilience people and groups have can change over time. Which side of the scale weighs more in your life, resilience or stressors? If stressors accumulate over time without buffers, they can easily overwhelm a person (or group's or organization's) amount of resilience—especially if there is only a focus on pain, stress and suffering and not hope and growth. However, people can also build resilience all throughout their lives, tipping the scale toward coping and healing in the face of adversity.

How Are Early Childhood Organizations Building Resilience among Staff and the Children and Families They Serve?

Early learning programs across the country are using many different approaches to reduce stress and intentionally support coping, resilience and healing with their staff and/or for the children and families they serve. One approach is scheduling **events and trainings** to increase awareness of health wellness as one Head Start program started doing with "Wellness Wednesdays."

> "We do what is called Wellness Wednesday. Every week we do different things around wellness whether it's financial, physical or mental support. I think today they did

a breast cancer workshop. We are learning and growing into this and we're getting a lot better, especially now that we are on a virtual platform."

–Krystal Lewis, Head Start Director

Some programs are creating monthly **safe spaces** (sometimes called resiliency circles) where staff can meet with one another **to share stories about their practice.** These confidential conversations are often facilitated by an administrator or a mental health professional and provide adults a chance to build trust with their colleagues and to reduce the stress of isolation as they can talk with colleagues who understand and share their context:

"The biggest form of self-care I have are my relationships. Having a safe community where I feel like I'm able to talk about difficult things and I'm not going to be judged is so helpful." I meet once a month with my co-workers to vent and work through things that you don't feel like you can always say. It's all private, nothing leaves this room kind of thing so there's that sense of like safety and security and trust which is super important. As a program to even start to address trauma, you can't do that in your classroom until you trust your coworkers. And the same goes with the teaching team, that's a really intimate relationship and one of the hardest ones to maintain, 40 hours a week in a small room and stressful situations, it can be rough. Having time once a month to get to know each other—tell me about your family, what do you like to do on your weekends, celebrating birthdays and small victories and just really encouraging each other, it helps us cope. Mental health support is something that teachers need available to them. We have very stressful, stressful jobs. With the things we are seeing, we need somewhere to vent to and someone who can offer some support and strategies.

–Chantelle Marin, Lead Teacher, Omaha Educare

Still others are creating opportunities to **engage in self-care activities at work** not only to communicate messages of care to the staff, but also to give them time and space to co-create a restorative environment at work. The essence of parallel practice: Caring for the educators in the manner we expect them to care for others.

> "I am trying to be intentional about creating spaces and opportunities for the teachers to have access to self-care. I'm mindful of what they've never experienced within this environment. After our training on self-care, I created a whole self-care bag for them. They were like, 'What is this?' They were surprised because this has never been done before. We have a training coming up **we're doing a love box** for each site. They will create a space where the teachers come together to eat, where they're creating something that reminds them about nature, about beauty and something they create and when they walk into that space and see it, will make them smile. It will make them breathe. It will give a sense of joy, creativity and innovation. Because if they don't feel that, how can we expect them to bring those things into their classrooms?"
> –Anita Smith, Program Manager, Mental Health Consultation

Reflection/Discussion Questions

- How do you think your team/staff would react to trainings or events focused on self-care or stress reduction?
- How can you build in self-care and relational connection with activities during a meeting?
- Thinking of the program you are in, what strategies are used currently that promote self-care for the adults at work? What are some ways you could include additional self or organizational care activities at work?
- How do you help staff "vent" built up emotions ("Name them to tame them" Siegel & Bryson, 2011) How do you create safety to do that?

"Giving Yourself Boundaries" as a Strategy to Reduce Stress and Promote Resilience

"In one of our resiliency circles, one of the teacher's shared, 'I'm so tired by the time I get home, I don't have any energy to give to my boys." And one of her colleagues asked her a simple question, "Why? What's happening between the time you leave work and when you arrive home?" She said she is typically talking on the phone (about work and some of the challenges of her day) on her drive home. Her colleague stated a simple fact, "maybe you need to give yourself a cutoff time. Your brain needs to breathe and think of different things. About things that make you happy, things that make you laugh, things that give you joy, things that give you peace."

Then I spoke up and said, "**What you are doing is giving yourself boundaries.**" Just the simplicity of it. It was like a light bulb went off for her, it's like a dog on your grass. You put up a fence so the dog can't get on your grass. Well, think about this like putting up a fence around your mind and your heart so that you can give (energy, love, attention etc.) to your two little boys when you arrive home.

Our resilience circles are allowing us to heal in community. We are being mirrors and reflectors—reflecting back what we hear each other say—to one another. And this community is shifting the lens. Shifting how we see the kids, the families, ourselves and our work

–Anita Smith, Program Manager,
Mental Health Consultation

> **Reflection/Discussion Questions**
>
> - How would it look to do resiliency circles in your program?
> - Have you thought about boundaries? Are you currently creating boundaries between work and home? Are there people in your life that can support you in establishing and sticking to boundaries? Are there people in your life that YOU can support in establishing and sticking to boundaries?

"Creating a Mindful Organization Is Like the Layers of an Onion"

Drew Giles is Director of Educare Programs with Franklin-McKinley School District at Educare California at Silicon Valley, a model early learning program serving low income and poor families aiming to eliminate or decrease the opportunity gaps they encounter. Drew and his staff work collaboratively to create an environment that reduces stress for children, families and staff and where relationships and regulatory strategies are learned and practiced in order to strengthen coping, resilience and healing. Drew describes what this looks like:

> "A few months ago I completed a trauma informed children's yoga teacher program. So now I have that in my toolbox and I will be able to lead a **trauma informed yoga for our children and staff.** Trauma informed yoga is being respectful and honoring of someone's lived experiences and creating a safe place for them and where they're at in the world. It's all about flexibility and choice. So if a child or staff member is interested in participating, then they are able to, but if they don't feel safe, they aren't forced to. Overall, the goal is to support their mental wellbeing and health. And I will be using a capacity-building model. I will start by teaching the kids yoga for

a six week and invite the teachers to participate so they are seeing what I'm modeling for the children so they are able to build that sustainability and capacity within their own classrooms. The idea is that I'm developing a system where in the future, the teachers will have the skills. In the past I have taught yoga after school to our staff. Traditionally, early educators have been undervalued and underpaid in our country and oftentimes can't afford a $20 yoga class. So I have been able to offer that for free to them and to our school community. This has been part of developing this mindful community and organization.

Creating a mindful organization is like the layers of an onion. At the most basic level, we have signs up around our campus that encourage mindfulness for anyone who's onsite: Signs at the doors—"**please be present for your child at drop-off**" and one crossing over a cell phone to encourage folks not to be on their phone so they're honoring where their children are at and what they're doing. So that's the approach for everyone who visits our campus, being mindful of our feelings and what we're experiencing in the moment. One of the tenets of our program is that **educators are seen as researchers.** Instead of telling someone "this is the way you should do it," we encourage them to ask questions and use inquiry. We also intentionally build peer to peer relationships and encourage staff to know that it's okay to ask for help and support. They know that they can say, '**I need to step out. Can you step in?** Because my lid is about to flip.'

In our staff and leadership meetings, **we start with connectors** so we can learn about each other. Our staff find these motivating because it allows them to slowly switch gears and mindfully transition into the meeting. We have a relatively new team because we've gone through a lot of transition. So it's a great way to build those relationships and really be present with one another. And then, at the end of our meetings we have time to do '**Ahas, appreciations and apologies**' so that staff have a safe place where they can connect, share and/or apologize to one another in our leadership group or in our teaching group. We're not just doing the celebrations—the appreciations and the Aha's, but also creating a safe place for people to feel like they can apologize because we are human and sometimes we reflect on our reactions and realize they might not have been what we wanted or intended them to be. I want them to know that they don't have to let these things steam and fizzle, we can talk about them together and then move on.

We also implemented a practice called 'community self-care,' an idea suggested by one of our staff members that is being in community and creating a culture of gratitude. In meetings, trainings and other professional learning events, we set a tone for gratitude and invite staff to call out the names of their students, families or colleagues and share an expression of gratitude. I tell my staff the wise words of William Arthur Ward, **"If you have gratitude and don't share it, it's like wrapping a present and not giving it."** I have lived my life by that. I just try to always share gratitude. If I feel it, if I think it, I need to share it. We also start meetings by **taking a breath to settle our nervous systems**. I explain that when you breathe slowly, it sends messages to your brain that you're safe. We all have the power to breathe and it is one gift that we all share together. We also want the environment to feel supportive and not intimidating. This means everything from making sure that the lights are left on and using Sunbeam circles in yoga instead of rows so nobody is behind another person and feeling self-conscious. These are a few of the ways we are actively trying to change our brain wiring to be positive and strength-based.

Gardening and food are really important to our school and community. Because we serve a community that experiences a lot of food insecurity, we know we need to meet our staff's and our family's basic needs. And one of the ways that we do that is by supporting their access to food. So we have built 24 garden boxes around our campus that our staff and our children take care of and then they can take the produce home. **So we try to incorporate the garden into our program's philosophy by making sure that the staff and families have what they need.** It's also helping with mindfulness and self-care. Whenever I have a free moment, I go out to the garden and just get some fresh air and pull some weeds and help the garden grow. And now I'm starting to see staff on their own, just taking care of the garden or watering the garden without having to be asked or anything. Children and adults are going outside to take in the beautiful smells of the fruit or the veggies or to pick the guava and taste it. We're trying to use our own context to be mindful of the importance of access to healthy food. The garden is one of our big wins right now."

Programs like Drew's that carve out time to connect, to pause, to slow down, to create mindful moments can really build in trauma-responsive strategies that support relational connection, self-awareness and self-regulation. These strategies also offer staff time to reflect on themselves, how they feel, what they need and any repairs they may need to make with others. Additionally, the rituals listed above at the beginning of a meeting reduce abrupt and rushed transitions from one activity or meeting to the next and instead, allow folks to settle slowly in mentally, physically, socially and emotionally.

Reflection/Discussion Questions

- What types of rituals do you create at the beginning or end of a meeting that allow for slow transitions? Build relational connections? Help others to feel safe? Slow things down so that everyone is regulated and can access their cortex to think, reason and problem solve?
- As you reflect, do you use any strategies in the environment that provide for these same opportunities to reflect

and slow down to regulate such as Drew's garden in the scenario above?
- ♦ What are some ways you build into your program opportunities for staff to share gratitude, strengths and/or to make repairs with one another?

Core Principle—Implement Culturally, Linguistically and Contextually Responsive Practices

> Trauma-responsive and resilience building practice acknowledges that there are many different culturally informed practices and approaches for responding to and coping with stress and trauma as well as for fostering health, healing and wellness for children and adults, groups and communities. Responses to stress, trauma and healing should be generated and/or informed by the individuals impacted by the practices. This increases alignment with the diverse values, beliefs and practices (e.g., individual, cultural, spiritual/religious, generational etc.) and primary languages that are familiar to the specific children, families and educators in the program, school and/or community. Additionally, practices need to be flexible, adaptable and adjusted to align with the different level of resources and capacities available within a specific environment or community.

Culture is a broad concept that refers to deep-rooted customs, values, beliefs, languages, social norms and practices shared among a group of people that may be transmitted across generations (Rogoff, 2003, 2011). According to the cultural psychologist Barbara Rogoff, our lives can be considered coherent constellations of cultural practices that may dynamically change over time, over social and environmental settings and across generations (Rogoff & Angelillo, 2002; Rogoff, 2003, 2011). Even without our conscious awareness, **culture plays a significant and complex role in shaping how we think, believe, behave and engage with the world including how we perceive and respond to stress and trauma as well as heal** (National Academies of Sciences, Engineering and Medicine, 2018). Guarino, Soares, Konnath, Clervil and Bassuk (2009) emphasize the connections between culture, trauma and healing:

> "Traumatic events happen to people from all racial and ethnic backgrounds, and the brain's response to trauma is consistent for all trauma survivors. However, culture plays a significant role in the types of trauma that may be experienced, the risk for continued trauma, how survivors manage and express their experiences, and which supports and interventions are most effective. Violence and trauma have different meanings across cultures, and healing takes place within one's own cultural and 'meaning-making' system" (p. 27).

How Does Culture and Language Influence People's Experiences of Stress, Trauma, Mental Health and Healing?

Culture wires our brains. Although more research is needed to examine the relationships between culture, stress and trauma, several studies have documented how different cultural beliefs and experiences influence:

- Perceptions of threat/danger
- How trauma-related memories are stored and retrieved
- Physiological arousal—the physiological processes involved in the activation of the stress response system (fight, flight, freeze)
- Recovery times after a stressful interaction or situation
- The emotional states impacted during a stressful or traumatic experience

♦ Further, research documents how individuals who are from more collectivist and interdependent versus individualist oriented cultures show differences in the way their brains are activated when they perceive others' distress (Cheon et al., 2013; Liddell & Jobson, 2016; Park & Huang, 2010).

> **A Global Perspective**
>
> **Culture shapes how people perceive and describe their lived experiences including the adversities they face.** People everywhere have traumatic experiences and find individual and collective forms of coping, resilience and healing, however, the diverse ways they make meaning of and describe these experiences are influenced by culture and language. Two of the authors recently completed a listening tour with participants from several countries who were asked: **What language/terms do you use to talk about stress/trauma and resilience in your local communities?** Below is a sample of what they learned:
>
> "We use the terms child protection and stress frequently. We also talk about trauma and marginalized communities. We do not use the word resilience. Instead, we talk about, 'looking for *solutions so we can avoid certain threats.*'" (Mauritius)
>
> "People don't talk about trauma in their lives or in their families. It happens but we don't talk about it. Sometimes the word agath kiate is used, it means being hurt or injured" (Nepal)
>
> "People are in a constant state of trauma and think of it as a normal part of life. We don't use the word trauma in Haiti. There is too much stigma around mental health issues. And we don't talk about 'family secrets.' If there was a training on 'trauma,' people would not come as they see it as very negative and not protective. Instead, we might talk about understanding the value of our emotions" (Haiti)
>
> "The word trauma is western. We use the word stress. Stress is thought to be a physical sickness. Traditional

healers and herbalists talk about how the demons have affected someone and they encourage people to come and get the demons out. The best ways to wash off stress and trauma is to get out of your ordinary circles, exercise, engage in sports activity, create social cohesion, cultivate the land together and participate in community activities like a 5k run" (Uganda)

"Trauma is not used frequently. Stress is used more frequently. Resilience is sometimes used" (Malaysia)

"Stress is the term used most often. For resilience, we talk about the ability to bounce back, help others and 'to be there.' Very few people would use the word resilience." (Pakistan)

"Trauma for young children is not something that generally is seen as an issue. We do talk about coping mechanisms. If you are speaking to people from child welfare, you will hear about psychosocial support which is what social workers say to indicate when something has gone wrong for the child" (Tanzania)

Source: Diane Whitehead, CEO, Childhood Education International (https://ceinternational1892.org/)

Reflection/Discussion Questions

- ♦ Think about the communities you work in. Do you use the words stress, trauma and resilience? Are there other words you can use? Are there other words your community uses?
- ♦ Are there stigmas around trauma in your community? How about mental health? Knowing what you just learned about culture, what are some ways you can address stigma?

There are profound **cultural differences in people's beliefs and perceptions of mental health, wellness and healing**. For example, the concept of mental health and healing for many

Indigenous Peoples is focused on restoring balance between the physical, emotional, cognitive and spiritual self through relationships with others—e.g., people (ancestors, the living and future generations), animals and the environment/land. This is quite distinct from Western perspectives where mental health and mental illness are perceived as characteristics of the mind and/or outcomes of mental activities. Linklater (2014) describes this important distinction:

> "For the most part, Indigenous trauma has been largely 'diagnosed' through non-Indigenous theories. Western frameworks of psychiatry and psychology have medicalized the experience of Indigenous peoples, applying diagnoses such as post-traumatic stress disorder, further pathologizing the trauma. Yet there are Indigenous health practitioners that utilize strategies that are rooted in Indigenous philosophies, worldviews and trauma-informed approaches; however, these practitioners are often challenged by a vocabulary that may not represent their context in an accurate way... Indigenous concepts of wellness and Western psychology greatly differ in ways of conceptualizing the person and in determining a healing process. Wellness philosophies are wholistic approaches that consider equally the spiritual, emotional, mental and physical aspects of the person, whereas Western psychology generally focuses on the mind and behavior, and Western medicine treats the mind and body as separate entities (Letendre, 2002). Furthermore, the mind-body split has influenced much psychiatric thinking...consequently, both psychology and psychiatry exclude a wholistic way of analyzing and addressing issues. Indigenous healing philosophies are based on a wellness model, while the medical model is based on illness"
>
> (pp. 20–21)

> "Trauma intersects in many different ways with culture, history, race, gender, location and language. Trauma-informed systems acknowledge the compounding impact of structural inequity and are responsive to the unique needs of diverse communities" (NCTSN, nd)
>
> **"Illness Becomes Wellness when 'I' Becomes 'We'"**
> Lea Denny, Native Hawaiian and Founder and CEO of the HIR Wellness Institute (Healing Intergenerational Roots) created a social justice-informed, culturally-rooted Intergenerational Healing Approach (IHA) in response to her research on historical trauma. She brings an Indigenous worldview to thinking about relationships and healing. Her agency motto is *"Illness becomes Wellness when I becomes We. Healing All Nations—One Tribe."*
>
> Dr. Denny coined the term, **"Persistent Toxic Systems and Environments** (PTSE):" These are everyday environmental traumatic or stressful events that negatively impact ones mental, emotional, spiritual and physical health outcomes. PTSE is repeated and regular exposure to toxic surroundings and systems that are felt, seen, heard and interpreted by the individual as inescapable barriers or hardships.
>
> Listen to Dr. Denny talk about Historical Trauma and collective forms of healing in its wake: https://vimeo.com/429647117

Adopt, Adapt, Align: The Importance of Being Contextually Responsive

Jen Leland, Director of Partnerships for Trauma Transformed, describes how they work with organizations and systems striving to become trauma-responsive using an approach they title, Adopt, Adapt and Align: **Adopt** trauma-informed principles and practices, **Adapt** the trauma-informed principles and practices to the specific organizational and community context and **Align** the organizational policies to the trauma-informed principles and practices. Using the Adapt, Adopt, Align framework is a contextually responsive approach to trauma-informed organizational and systems change. Central to this approach is listening and learning from the people working within a program, school or system to learn what language they use to talk about stress and trauma, how ready and willing they are to engage in a change process and their cultural ways of knowing, learning and making changes within their environment. She explains:

> "If someone says, 'We don't want to use the word trauma,' I welcome their comment. I say, 'Tell me more.' What happens when people talk about trauma in this setting? It's important to know, how are we defining trauma here. What is the specific language that's triggering? What is the language that feels resonant?" We are adaptive to what they say. So before we implement anything, we talk with people to understand, is it going to make sense to do this in your setting? We put people before our frameworks and models. We have tools that can get embedded in the environment. But, it's the people who make that work. It's people who are implementing these practices. So it's important to find out, how do folks in their particular program or system, how are they best able to learn and also, how can they embody and embed this in their context? "It's a dance that we're in all the time—adapting the trauma-informed principles and practices for their context while also pushing them to grow in their context."

Reflection/Discussion Questions

- If those you work with say, "we don't want to use the word trauma," how will you learn more about that so that you may adapt the trauma informed principles to the community you serve?

♦ Before you initiate or implement trauma informed and responsive work into your program, how do you talk with those who will receive these services to understand how it will make sense in their setting?

> **For an extensive discussion of Culturally Responsive Self-Care see:**
>
> Nicholson, J., Driscoll, P., Kurtz, J., Wesley, L., & Benitez, D. (2019). *Culturally Responsive Self-Care Practices for Early Childhood Educators*. New York, NY: Routledge Press.

Core Principle—Create Power-Sharing Partnerships and Community-Centered Solutions

"We have a kind of system of care. We've got lots of different entry points. If they are birth to five, we are likely going to be able to serve them on some level. Having strong community partnerships across our county and to some extent within our agency, having that relationship-based approach, that flexibility, and then that desire to work collaboratively, with others is an important part of our trauma-informed approach."

–Kathleen Kelley, Program Manager, Early Learning Institute

> Addressing trauma effectively requires creating collaborative power-sharing partnerships that lift up local/community voices and perspectives to generate community centered solutions. Collaborative power-sharing partnerships disrupt models where outside experts come in and advise communities on best practices or require programs to adhere to strict "fidelity" models that reflect a universal set of dominant beliefs and practices. Power-sharing partnerships

> balance expertise from scholars or outside experts with the place-based wisdom and lived experience of individuals within the program and/or community. Collaboration and reciprocity are emphasized—listening and learning that is bidirectional and based in respect, humility, curiosity and openness to challenge dominant "taken for granted" assumptions about universal 'best' practices and policy solutions. Value is placed on a belief that programs, schools and/or communities are best positioned to generate the approaches and solutions that are most authentic and meaningful, accessible and sustainable for them.

Power-sharing. *Def.* A policy or system in which different groups within a coalition share responsibility for making decisions and taking action.

Community-centered solutions. *Def.* A concerted, coordinated approach by local agencies to collaborate in planning and implementing solutions to the challenges faced within their communities. State institutions and federal agencies are important stakeholders but not offering prescriptive directors that constrain community voice and agency.

Why is it important for early childhood organizations—striving to become trauma-responsive and healing centered—to partner with local programs and community agencies and to participate in creating and implementing community-centered solutions? We highlight three important reasons below:

Complexity. Supporting young children, families and the early childhood workforce to thrive in contexts that are rife with stress and trauma involves meeting a range of complex human needs (emotional/psychological, physical, intellectual, spiritual etc.). It is neither realistic nor effective for program/agency leaders to presume they have all the skills, knowledge or expertise needed in the various topics and methods that support wellness and healing for the children and adults they serve, especially individuals impacted by trauma. Building partnerships allows staff to learn new information and skills and to work collaboratively to meet the complex needs that arise and require support in the wake of trauma. Drew Giles describes how his agency has developed community partnerships to help build capacity for himself and his staff to work effectively with trauma-impacted families and to provide the teachers and staff with mental health support beyond what he can offer as a supervisor:

> "Our family resource center team is working with Capacitar, a healing-based organization, to develop skills on how to talk with parents and support the families who are going through difficult situations. Right now with the pandemic, the family resource center has really shifted gears. Typically, we would have daily workshops for the community (e.g., for family child care and family/friend and neighbor providers) and for children to come in and check out books in the public library here on campus. Because of the virus, we have shifted the way that we are supporting the families. Now we are supporting resource distribution (e.g., food, formula, diapers, wipes) and holding virtual workshops. Capacitar is helping our staff to make sure that they have the skills in order to support the families right now. We also have mental health specialists who are coming to our monthly meetings, or as needed when the staff feel like they have the need for additional support, just to have someone to talk to. It's confidential and helps them with their mental wellbeing. Having these regularly scheduled monthly check-ins with mental health professionals **allows the staff to have the permission slip to reach out for help** if needed."

Reflection/Discussion Questions

- How have you connected with community-based resources to support your program in times of trauma or crisis (natural disasters, pandemics, death and loss etc.)?

♦ Thinking of Drew's comment "staff have the permission slip to reach out for help," what steps have you taken to break down the stigma of counseling, mental health and creating a culture where asking for help is encouraged?

Responsiveness. Building partnerships with local programs and inviting their voices to be included in the process of developing, implementing and sustaining trauma-responsive programs creates opportunities for the services to be responsive to local conditions and needs as well as the wishes of the specific children, families and early childhood staff being served. A major barrier to trauma-responsive approaches is prescriptive universal requirements that do not allow flexibility in order to acknowledge and be responsive to the needs of local contexts and communities. Partnering with, and genuinely including local/community stakeholders with expertise in working with trauma-impacted adults and children can support responsiveness and disrupt the inequities that arise when 'universal' best practice trainings and services that require fidelity are not aligned with the actual needs and conditions of a local community.

Do the services and resources draw upon the language/terms and stories (of trauma experiences, coping, resilience and healing) that resonate with the community and mirror their lived experiences?

Cohesiveness. Many young children and their families as well as the early childhood workforce are participating in and significantly impacted by larger service systems (e.g., housing, nutrition, health, corrections, courts, social services, child welfare, education, treatment programs etc.). Building partnerships with other service providers and agencies, creates opportunities to increase awareness and understanding of trauma-responsive approaches across the different systems that touch the lives of children and families. The more cohesion and continuity exists across systems, the less likely that any benefits children and families experience as a result of participating in trauma-responsive early learning programs will be undermined by their touchpoints with other systems. Kevin Daniel, Senior Project Manager for Urban Strategies[1] describes how as a community partner, they are actively striving to build cohesion in understanding trauma and using trauma-sensitive approaches across the various systems that touch the lives of young children and families. What he describes as a 'duty':

> "We have a duty. We're in partnership with the system: The housing authority, with the school districts, with the city and county governments. We are in partnership with the system. We cannot do our work without the system. And the system sometimes adds to the trauma of our neighborhoods, right? So one of our duties is to educate the system. It's not uncommon that the people who have the largest say in how these families live are people who have no grassroots on the ground, no interaction with these families they are serving. So it's our job in those systems, in a very respectful and kind way, to educate. It should be required for everyone to understand firsthand the trauma that their clients are going through. To understand the community needs, what the residents need, who are struggling the most. This is critical if we are ever going to get these systems right. It's our job to make sure that we continue to educate the system. It's easy for us to point our finger but it's important to remember that we really are a part of that system.
>
> So, for example, the system says we have funding to serve 500 people for housing and these are federal dollars so they are under pressure to make sure they meet their outcomes. So they cast a wide net. They need 500, so they bring 2000 people in. But when those 2000 come, the first thing the system does—because of the pressure they are under to make their outcomes happen—is try to identify the people who are most likely to be successful. So they start turning away people who really want the housing,

who really needed the housing, but the system tells them, 'I don't know if you're quite right for it.' So you just re-traumatized someone who said, 'This is the opportunity for me to change my life. I came in but you are telling me I don't meet your criteria.' And I don't think people realize how traumatizing that is for people in our communities. During COVID, the system said, 'Hey, parents we'll still give you lunches.' But what happened is when people who didn't have cars or transportation walked up they were told, 'Oh, you gotta be in a car or you can't get the food.' So that's traumatizing, right? 'Well, we are hungry. We're excited. We're going to get some food. We come out here and you said you can't serve me because I don't have a car?' So the system can traumatize or retraumatize people over and over again. They need to think, 'what are the potential consequences of the actions we are planning to take?' They need to take time to work it through and ask, 'what does it look like for a family or someone who's trying to access supports and services within our system?' And they need to include community partners like Urban Strategies, people like us, at the table when they are making these decisions. Somebody in that system was thinking, everyone has cars, everybody has a working car. Everybody has enough gas. And that's just not the case and those of us who are on the ground understand, that's not the case. In this situation and others, the system did not plan to traumatize people but it can unknowingly unwittingly retraumatize people. And so, if community partners like Urban Strategies, if we don't speak up, when we're working in a school district, we're part of the problem. If we don't speak up, when we're working with the Housing Authority, then that's a problem. We are equipped to educate the system because we know what's going on. We have the ability, the language and the data to articulate to the system. This is what's really going on with the children and families in the community."

Reflection/Discussion Questions

- In what ways do you educate the "systems of care (partners, funders, community-based organizations)" you work with about what is needed so people are not re-traumatized by the very systems that are designed to help them?
- Before launching a new initiative, what steps do you take to evaluate what you are trying to create through the lens of those who will access your services and support?

Building Power-Sharing Partnerships within an Agency

Building collaborative partnerships is not only important with external community agencies. Creating trauma-responsive approaches to serving young children and families requires making **changes within agencies to break down disciplinary silos in the delivery of support services to children and families.** Rafel Hart is the Executive Director of Educare of Omaha, Inc. with responsibility for overseeing five early learning centers. He describes how as an agency, they are striving to create more integrated and collaborative communication between their family engagement specialists, classroom teachers and the families they are serving who are impacted by trauma. Their goal is to create a more unified and comprehensive trauma-sensitive approach among all of the professionals interacting with trauma-impacted families in their centers. He is honest about the difficulties they face in achieving their goals:

> "Domestic violence is something we often work with. We may be dealing with three or four or as many as five cases in the same program. Normally what happens is the parent will speak to a family engagement specialist—who are social workers by practice and education—about challenges they're having around domestic violence at home. Often, they will not talk to the teacher about it,

however, the teachers will start observing behaviors of the child in the classroom (e.g., the child might be spanking a doll or engaging in very aggressive play with other children). When the teachers try to have conversations with the parents about their observations, it can create a friction between the teacher and the parent because the parent has not shared any information about the domestic violence with the teacher and often times hearing about their child's behavior can lead them to have a defensive or angry reaction. So, as a program, we are trying to institute an interdisciplinary approach to family engagement. And that means that without breaking confidentiality, making sure that the teacher knows what is happening with a family. We are striving to help parents understand, 'yes, my information has been shared with this teacher, but not in a gossipy way, but instead, in a collaborative way to help my child.' But this is proving challenging as sometimes the families don't want their information shared with the teachers."

Reflection/Discussion Questions

- Thinking of your program, in what ways do you break down the silos that exist and create collaborative communication and partnerships internally?
- Do you have procedures or practices that honor confidentiality but that allow information to be shared in a way that promotes the best interest of the child or family?

Bottom Up Pathway to Regulation

"Take a Breath Before We Talk"

Drew Giles, Director of Educare Programs with Franklin-McKinley School District at Educare California at Silicon Valley, supports his staff members to learn about and practice using many different regulation strategies throughout the day. He explains some of the attuned and trauma-responsive ways he responds to staff members displaying signs of activation/stress:

> "I like honoring what I'm seeing." If I see someone has big emotions and feels really passionate about something, before he begins a conversation, he will suggest a bottom up regulation strategy, taking deep belly breaths, to create a pause and opportunity to strengthen regulation. I might say, **"Let's take three deep breaths together."** He has other ways of creating a pause to support calming. "I might offer to go get them a **glass of water**. And by the time I come back with the water, the staff member had a minute by themselves which can also be calming." Drinking the water is also a calming strategy as it allows us to refocus our stress to the present moment as we engage in the small break of taking a sip of water and nourishing our bodies. Drew also uses a **calming voice to signal safety** when speaking to an adult who is stressed. He explains, "People tell me that I have a voice that is like a mindful meditation. I use a calm, soothing voice. I tend to stay pretty level. And when they hear my voice, maybe it encourages them to calm down." Drew is using his understanding of the neurobiology of stress—and specifically his awareness of the power of mirror neurons—to co-regulate and guide staff back to a place of calm and regulation.

Note

1. Urban strategies is a family-centered agency with a mission to ensure all families are thriving by focusing on case management, health education and economic mobility for people living in public housing. They are currently working in 21 cities across the United States and in two territories.

References

Cheon, B. K., Im, D. M., Harada, T., Kim, J. S., Mathur, V. A., Scimeca, J. M., & Chiao, J. Y. (2013). Cultural modulation of The neural correlates of emotional pain perception: The role of other-focusedness. *Neuropsychologia, 51*(7), 1177–1186.

Ginwright, S. (2018). *The future of healing: Shifting from trauma informed care to healing centered engagement.* Medium. Retrieved from https://medium.com/@ginwright/the-future-of-healing-shifting-from-trauma-informed-care-to-healing-centered-engagement-634f557ce69c

Guarino, K., Soares, P., Konnath, K., Clervil, R., & Bassuk, E.. (2009). Trauma-informed organizational toolkit. Rockville, MD: Center for Mental Health Services, Substance Abuse and Mental Health Services Administration, and the Daniels Fund, the National Child Traumatic Stress Network, and the W.K. Kellogg Foundation. Available at www.homeless.samhsa.gov and www.familyhomelessness.org

Letendre, A. (2002). Aboriginal traditional medicine: Where does it fit? *Crossing Boundaries: An Interdisciplinary Journal, 1*(2), 78–87.

Liddell, B. J., & Jobson, L. (2016). The impact of cultural differences in self-representation on the neural substrates of posttraumatic stress disorder. *European Journal of Psychotraumatology, 7*(1), 30464.

Linklater, R. (2014). *Decolonizing trauma work: Indigenous stories and strategies.* Black Point, Nova Scotia: Fernwood Publishing.

National Academies of Sciences, Engineering, and Medicine (2018). How people learn II: Learners, contexts, and cultures. Retrieved from https://www.nap.edu/catalog/24783/how-people-learn-ii-learners-contexts-and-cultures

National Child Traumatic Stress Network. nd. *Culture and trauma.* Retrieved from https://www.nctsn.org/trauma-informed-care/culture-and-trauma

Nicholson, J., Driscoll, P., Kurtz, J., Wesley, L., & Benitez, D. (2019). *Culturally responsive self-care practices for early childhood educators.* New York, NY: Routledge Press.

Park, D. C., & Huang, C. M. (2010). Culture wires the brain: A cognitive neuroscience perspective. *Perspectives on Psychological Science, 5*(4), 391–400.

Perry, B. (2017). *The boy who was raised as a dog and other stories from a child psychiatrist's notebook. What traumatized children can teach us about loss, love and healing.* New York, NY: Basic Books.

Rogoff, B. (2003). *The cultural nature of human development.* Oxford University Press.

Rogoff, B. (2011). *Developing destinies: A mayan midwife and town.* Oxford University Press.

Rogoff, B., & Angelillo, C. (2002). Investigating the coordinated functioning of multifaceted cultural practices in human development. *Human Development, 45*(4), 211–225.

Siegel, D., & Bryson, T. (2011). *The whole-brain child: 12 revolutionary strategies to nurture your child's developing mind.* New York, NY: Random House.

7

Core Principle—Use Evidence to Build Insights and Learn Collaboratively

Working collaboratively with programs, schools and communities to identify sources of data they believe are meaningful and relevant to evaluate their progress in working for change is a trauma-responsive approach to evaluation and continuous quality improvement. Many programs, schools and communities do not have their cultural values, beliefs and practices represented in traditional research methodologies, research/evaluation tools and literature on "best practices." As a result, trauma-responsive resilience building approaches support the expansion of sources of evidence to include both evidence-informed practices *and* evidence-based practices[1]. The process of gathering and interpreting evidence is completed in a manner that builds trust by seeking out, listening to and valuing the perspectives, skills and experiences of all those impacted by the policies, programs, services and/or practices. Analysis of evidence emphasizes a process of building insights to learn collaboratively and making adjustments in response to what is learned, not high-stakes decision-making.

Knowledge is never value neutral. Research study questions, method of data collection and interpretation of findings, descriptions of "best practices" and widely accepted screening and evaluation tools (e.g., Environmental Rating Scales, CLASS, Ages and Stages, Kindergarten Readiness Tests) in the field of early childhood are not measuring "objective" and universal truths but instead, are shaped by culturally informed ways of perceiving, understanding and documenting the world. As Jennifer Walker, Canada (2020) research chair in Indigenous Health at Laurentian University explains:

> "We tend to take data at face value. We assume that the numbers tell the story and they speak for themselves. Yet, **data are steeped in assumptions**, the way that data are collected, the assumptions that are made for the priority of data collection and the types of things that are assessed, who is in the data, who is out of the data, these things are not benign. **They establish the base for a story."**

See Dr. Amy Stuart Wells' 2019 AERA Presidential Address, *"An Inconvenient Truth About the New Jim Crow of Education."* Dr. Stuart Wells is a leading scholar of the intersection of race, schooling and inequality. She's a member of the National Academy of Education and a Professor at Teachers College in NYC. In her address Dr. Wells tells a compelling story about the mismatch between the research evidence and the policies that dominate and dictate our educational system and a racial hierarchy that removes non-European cultures, traditions and ways of knowing in our methods of education and especially, our assessment and evaluation practices. She explains how this is a problem for all students and educators because the rules of our educational system have become toxic to learning and child development and teacher professionalism. Link: https://www.youtube.com/watch?v=6kkLDhULMsI&list=PLR4xr4hFYwOm_7oECBmSUzKM_B8Ramt8G&index=2

> *The American Educational Research Association (AERA) is the largest national interdisciplinary research association devoted to the scientific study of education and learning.*

Too often, our research, evaluation and educational best practices establish the base for stories that 'Other' or marginalize our diverse children, families and individuals represented within the early childhood workforce by judging them against theories and metrics based in *Eurocentric middle class values, beliefs and norms* describing what is *typical* (e.g., how children learn and develop), *desirable* (e.g., beliefs about quality or leadership) and *measured* (e.g., kindergarten readiness, parent involvement). **There is growing awareness that traditional research, evaluation and quality improvement methods in early childhood are perpetuating racism and other forms of discrimination and oppression.** How is this done? By reproducing stories that define minoritized groups through deficit and by preventing children, families and the early childhood workforce from having more agency and authentic participation in the collection and use of data about early learning environments. When data is used to tell deficit stories (e.g., "45% of children in our city are not ready for kindergarten." "Teachers in that program have low CLASS scores." "Parents in this school are not involved in their children's education,") we not only perpetuate cycles of trauma and oppression, we take power away from children and families and the early childhood workforce serving them. As Dr. Walker (2020) describes, to prevent data from being used in a harmful manner, it's essential that the stories that are told with data are told *from the perspectives of the people represented in the data*. She provides an example specific to First Nations people:

> "If the stories of First Nations people are being told by other people (e.g., governments or well-intentioned researchers who don't understand indigenous data,

indigenous contexts and haven't spent the time understanding colonialism and the inter-generational impacts) then what happens is that the stories are shaped by assumptions and biases that continue to tell deficit-based stories. They continue to drive the narratives of disparity and difference that aren't that helpful. Especially when the scientists want to shine the light on 'problems' because they think that by shining a light on them, that something magically will happen that will change these things and help. But what actually happens, narratives about the dispossession and disparity, contribute to a narrative that, 'These First Nations people can't take care of themselves.' Or 'These people living in these remote communities have all these problems, we need to take care of them.' **So deficit-based stories take power away from communities.**"

Efforts to improve equity in the collection and use of evidence often emphasize the documentation of *counter-stories* (Solórzano & Yosso, 2002) or narratives of the lived experiences and perspectives of individuals and groups who may not historically or currently be represented in academic scholarship or "best practice" literature. Counter-stories:

- Build community among those at the margins of society by making human and familiar faces visible when considering the relevance and authenticity of educational theories and practices;
- Challenge taken-for-granted dominant beliefs, policies and practices by expanding understandings with a goal of transforming established systems
- Open new windows for marginalized individuals and groups by showing possibilities beyond the ones they live and demonstrating that they are not alone in their experiences; and
- Teach others that we can construct another world that is more equitable (Solórzano & Yosso, 2002, p. 36).

> **Methods for Documenting Counter-Stories in Research, Evaluation and Continuous Improvement**
>
> The aim of these methods is to give power back to individuals and community members who become active participants and co-researchers throughout the entire data collection process.
>
> - **Community-Based Action Research** (CBAR) (see Guillion & Tilton, 2020 to learn about CBAR)
> - **Digital Storytelling** (see Story Center for examples: https://www.storycenter.org/)
> - **Photovoice** (to learn about Photovoice, see this Blog series: https://medium.com/knowledgenudge/photovoice-blog-series-96477db68e05 and examples of using Photovoice with children and youth: https://www.childinthecity.org/2016/02/02/five-applications-of-photovoice-as-a-method-for-childrens-participation/)

Each of these methods shift the historical power dynamics in research and evaluation by demanding that **"people be seen as experts on their own experiences."** CBAR, Digital Storytelling and Photovoice "put power in the hands of individual community members" (Guillion & Tilton, 2020, p. 20) who become active participants and collaborators. Instead of being the "subjects" of research and data collection activities (traditional "power over" methods), trauma-responsive approaches position the individuals and communities being studied/evaluated/observed as **equal partners who collaborate throughout the entire process** to determine:

- Who gets to participate (Instead of just the outside researchers and evaluators, representatives from across the program/school/community can be included in the process)
- What topics/issues/problems are most important
- Which forms of evidence/data will be collected (e.g., stories, video, photographs, interviews, surveys, etc.)

and how the data collection process will proceed (e.g., methods that maintain authenticity)
- What sense to make of the data and what stories will be told to describe the insights gained and the different perspectives on what was learned
- How the data and findings will be shared with the larger community and who will have the privilege and responsibility to do the reporting
- How the data and findings will be stored longer term. That is, who will continue to have access to the data? Can they continue to tell stories using the data over time?

Disrupting "power over" models of data collection (where researchers, evaluators or the people who design assessment tools have historically held all the power) **allows different stories to be told.** Treating the individuals and communities being studied/evaluated/observed as equal partners means they **have a voice in deciding which forms of data they want to collect to examine the issues they care deeply about.** Imagine if:

- Early childhood professionals were given opportunities to determine how to define and quality in early learning settings
- Or families could explain what kindergarten readiness means to them
- Or home visitors could use their knowledge of working closely with families to weigh in on defining effective family engagement approaches
- Or coaches working with teachers in classrooms with emergent bilingual/multilingual children were asked for input in how to document teachers' professional learning

Using Data to Build Insights and Learn Collaboratively

Trauma-responsive programs, schools and systems use data to build insight and to learn collaboratively about the topics that matter to them and to make adjustments in response to what is learned. Data is not used *to judge, identify winners and losers, shame, threaten and cajole or for high-stakes decision-making* as doing inevitably induces harm. The goals of collecting and using data in trauma-responsive healing centered environments include:

- Deepening awareness of the benefits and limitations of current beliefs, policies and practices
- Creating time and space to hear different people share stories of their lived experiences and feelings related to a specific topic or issue
- Building understanding for different perspectives and ways of responding to a complex situation or challenge
- Acting upon what is learned to create more responsive early childhood programs, schools, systems and service delivery options for young children and families and healthier environments for early educators to work in

What Happens when We Collaborate with Community Members and Center Their Voices in the Collection and Use of Data/Evidence?

We learn about what is working versus shining a light on problems. Many people are very aware of the struggles and pain points in their programs, schools, communities and systems. In many cases, they are tired of outside experts coming in to shine a light on their problems without highlighting their strengths or what they are most proud of. Nobody wants to be defined by deficit. People are more interested in identifying the creative, innovative and resilient ways they are responding to the challenges they face. Instead of describing the problems year after year, trauma-responsive approaches to data collection emphasize an appreciative inquiry approach by asking, "**What's working? Where do we need to invest?**"

We learn about the types of support people really want and need versus what others *think* they want and need. As Guillon and Tilton (2020) caution, "Researchers often have good intentions...but when we claim to want to make positive social change, we need to ask ourselves, change for whom? When we say, we want social justice, we need to interrogate the question, social justice for whom? My notion of a just society could look different from yours. It is important that we are in dialog with the people we research with, that we have agreed upon goals and hope for outcomes. **We need to conduct research with people.**" (p. 13). We could revise the final line in this quote to say "We need to conduct quality ratings 'with people.' We need to conduct evaluations 'with people.' We need to identify funding priorities 'with people.' Otherwise, research, evaluations, ratings and/or funding decisions will be used in a manner that takes power away from people and in doing so, creates additional work, emotional labor and in some cases, toxic stress and trauma as they try to manage the gap between what they actually want and need and the priorities determined by outsiders and imposed upon them.

Krystal Lewis, Head Start Director in a large urban center explained how part of her role is pushing back on the resources that are given to them that are not helpful and to ask that funders and decision-makers truly listen to the needs of the staff and families in her program. In one example, she explained that at one point, the greatest need in her program was to have help paying for funerals as so many families were suffering losses in the face of community violence. She explains:

> "We were revising our family strengths assessment so we gathered focus groups of families from the community and asked them about their needs. What are your biggest challenges? What kinds of support do you need? When you think about planning for your future, what do you most need? The program staff assumed that support with educational and economic attainment would be on the top of the list for families. But overwhelmingly, families asked for support with funeral planning. There were so many violent crimes and drug related deaths in the community that many families knew that at some point they would need to have money available to pay for a funeral. This changed the strength assessment. Now as part of our enrollment process, we ask families directly if they need support saving for or planning for a funeral."

Through this experience and others, Krystal realized that an important part of her role is pushing back on the demands and expectations that funders and decision makers have for the families and staff in her program. She asks that instead, they need to really listen to what families and staff are saying about their life experiences. Only through listening, Krystal states, will we learn how to be truly responsive to others' needs.

Core Principle—Work toward Sustainability and Scale Innovation with Flexibility for Local Adaptation

> As programs, schools and systems plan for change, it is important to make decisions that build local capacity and work toward sustainability. When moving toward scaling innovations and learnings, flexibility and adaptation are supported while requiring some adherence to key principles. A trauma-responsive resilience building approach to scaling prioritizes local and community resources, accessibility and the importance of local capacity building. Emphasis is placed on creating innovative approaches and solutions that are practical/doable and accessible, i.e., not overly complex or complicated but instead, easily shareable practices. Programs, schools and systems are always allowed to make adaptations to practices scaled from other contexts in response to their local and community needs. This flexibility and allowance for local modifications—while maintaining an adherence to some agreed upon core principles of Trauma-Responsive Practice—acknowledge that individuals within a specific environment are best suited to learn and determine what 'works' for their community and context.

"We have an adopt, adapt and align framework… a model for both embodying trauma-informed practices and embedding those into your organizational structures and systems."
    —Jen Leland, Director of Partnerships,
                        Trauma Transformed

Paquin, Coburn, Catterson and Higgs (2019) describe four approaches to scaling (program, initiatives, innovations etc.), three have been widely used in educational research and in practice—adoption, replication, adaptation—the fourth, reinvention, is an emerging strategy:

- **Adoption.** The goal of scaling as adoption is the widespread use of a new practice or innovation. However, the focus is only on whether individuals and groups choose to use the innovation, not on *how* they use/implement it.
- **Replication.** The goal of scaling as replication is when a new practice or innovation is widespread, implemented with fidelity, and produces expected outcomes.
- **Adaptation.** Scaling with adaptation is the widespread use of an innovation that is adapted or modified according to the needs of specific users and local contexts. Typically, modifications are supported as long as the innovation or practices adhere to a set of pre-defined "core principles." In order to allow for local adaptations, this approach does not require strict fidelity to a universal set of best practices or methods. Continuous improvement is aligned with an adaptation approach to scale where iterative cycles of design, testing, reflection and modifications—based on local needs and conditions (Morel, Coburn, Catterson & Higgs, 2019)—lead to innovations that are shared and expanded within a local context. Because the adaptation approach to scale is so highly contextualized, only the core principles are expected to generalize to multiple settings.
- **Reinvention.** Reinvention is when innovations serve as a catalyst for further innovation. Instead of reproducing or adapting an innovation, people "remix" the innovation to create something new, including "radical transformations" from the original innovation. That is, "what the innovation looks like, what it means, how it is used, what problems it solves and what outcomes it produces all depend on the creative appropriation by local actors… scale as reinvention involves intentional and systematic experimentation with an innovation" (pp. 370–372).

Prioritizing local and community resources, building capacity within programs and/or communities (versus relying upon outside experts), providing people with the trust and power to adapt an innovation based on their knowledge of what 'works' for their community and local context—e.g., adaptation and reinvention approaches to scaling—is best aligned with the principles of trauma-responsive and healing centered practice. In contrast, strict fidelity models (replication) can be stress and trauma-inducing if the adherence to the 'right methods' of using an innovation limit and/or prevent people from engaging in relationship-based practice and having a felt sense of safety, flexibility, voice and choice and alignment with their cultural and linguistic ways of knowing and being.

Core Principle—Engage People Working Within Every Part of the Program, School and/or System

> "Our intention is to make a shift. Not only the teachers, but every staff member in our program including the person who's at the front desk and the people working in facilities. We are aiming to shift the lens, to have a different sensitivity toward families and kids. And we are involving everyone who's in this building."
> –Anita Smith, Program Manager,
> Mental Health Consultation

Trauma-responsive and resilience building programs, schools and systems create opportunities for people working at every level to have authentic and sustained engagement, especially during change initiatives. Involvement from individuals working across every part of the organization, school or system is essential for building trust (and preventing distrust) and for creating, implementing and sustaining a learning environment embracing growth and change.

> Distrust arises when a subset of individuals "at the top" make decisions for others in less powerful positions within a program, school or system preventing their participation and ability to inform decision-making and policy changes. When only some people are allowed to make decisions *for* rather than *with* others in the group/community², their decisions are less likely to be responsive to the actual needs, demands and/or desires of their program/community; thus, sowing the seeds of distrust, preventing critical buy-in and inspiring individual and group resistance to change.

For a program or school to become trauma-responsive, it is critical that there are opportunities for people working at every level to have authentic and sustained engagement in the initiative for change. Meg Walkley, who co-coordinates the 0 to 8 Mental Health Collaborative, a multi-disciplinary group of early childhood practitioners in northern California, has worked for many years in collaboration with others to create a trauma-responsive early childhood system in her county. She emphasizes that involving people in all roles within a program or school not only builds a common language among staff, shared knowledge also allows for trauma-sensitive communication to be woven into the culture of an early learning environment. She explains, "Training everyone—administrators, direct care staff, case managers, support staff etc.—about trauma and trauma-related topics ensures that all staff members are working from the same level of understanding and are capable of providing the same types of trauma-sensitive responses."

As services for young children often involve professionals collaborating across sectors and disciplines, coordination and alignment of services and care is improved when multi-disciplinary team members have access to training and professional learning opportunities with systems change initiatives. Information on trauma and trauma-responsive practices is valuable for a wide range of diverse professionals who collaborate in the delivery of services for young children and their families including social workers, foster or resource parents, public health, child welfare, mental health providers, counselors, after school program coordinators, early interventionists, infant mental health specialists, home visitors, and child life specialists among others.

Reflection/Discussion Questions

- ♦ What specific ways do you include input and the voices of those at all levels of the organization?
- ♦ In what ways do you include voices of stakeholders outside the four walls of your systems of care?

Core Principle—Acknowledge Today's Realities While Maintaining Hope and Imagining Justice for Tomorrow

> "Being hopeful ties into resiliency and positivity. That's difficult for a lot of people, especially when they've had any kind of adverse experiences. For me, hope is a coping skill. Some people never develop coping skills. We try to provide our staff and our families with hope, I think that's our role."
>
> –Krystal Lewis, Head Start Director

Working with an honest acknowledgement of today's realities while also maintaining hope that inequitable conditions can and *will* be improved over time, is essential for a trauma-responsive and resilience building approach. This involves dreaming and imagining that the future holds potential for positive change, new growth and innovative possibilities where children and adults, families and communities are healthy and thriving. Maintaining a sense of hope improves our ability as individuals and groups to cope, to strengthen our resilience and to heal as imagining a better future provides individuals with feelings of agency and control and motivation to take courageous actions to create a more just, loving and equitable world.

To bring about change, early educators must perceive a sense of hope for the future of our children, our families, our communities and our field. The enormity of the task involved in shifting mindsets and the stress and trauma-inducing policies and practices that are woven into the fabric of the institutions and structures of our child-serving systems in the US., could easily lead to a sense of despair that could make even the most passionate advocate wonder if their efforts are destined to fail. Working for justice is a journey with no beginning, no end, no roadmap to follow and no guarantees that what is desired will be realized. Creating trauma-responsive healing centered early childhood environments is emotionally and physically draining and extraordinarily complex work. And yet, as Freire (Horton et al., 1990) reminds us, **our road forward to justice can only be made 'by walking.'** Despite the lack of certainties, we face in our route or destination, we have a moral obligation and responsibility to the children and families we serve to maintain a sense of hope and to take loving actions to work for change within our sphere of influence.

Hope is an important form of political resistance (Ginwright, 2016) in responding to harm and oppression. Hopefulness is strengthened when people believe that they have agency and opportunities to work for the changes that matter to them. To build a sense of hope against a backdrop of a seemingly impossibly complex task, it is critical to shift attention to the small steps individuals and groups can take—the tasks they do have some level of control over—that move them closer to their dreams and aspirations versus focusing on what is not yet accomplished. As Glass (2008) states, "Should I despair over what remains unachieved? No. I only hope to fight another day. If each of us were dedicated daily to the tasks immediately within our reach, the wheel of history would turn more quickly; the dream of justice would be pursued...despite the obstacles to its realization" (pp. 339–340).

Describing the road to healing and justice, Ginwright (2016) recommends that we **shift from thinking about hope as individual beliefs and actions toward a collective or group orientation.** When people in community have a sense of collective hope, they are more likely to work for change despite the barriers they face. What is collective hope? Collective hope is a "shared vision of what could be with a shared commitment and determination to make it a reality. Collective hope can be likened to the soul of the community...collective hope focuses on those aspects of community life that provide meaning, purpose, happiness and joy...it is the fuel that drives community efforts toward the struggle for a higher quality of life" (p. 21) Ginwright describes three essential activities groups and communities can engage in in order to build and strengthen a sense of collective hope:

- **Storytelling: Creating time and space to talk about shared experiences.** Creating opportunities for people to share stories of their lived experiences, to discover what is shared in the conditions and experiences of their daily lives provides a foundation for envisioning changes they seek for their group/community.
- **Resistant or radical imagination.** Inviting people to dream together about how things should be in a more just, equitable and caring world allows them to have freedom in moving beyond the overwhelming conditions of the status quo, to imagine resistantly (Medina, 2013) how things *should* be
- **Loving and critical actions.** Once a group has imagined their version of a better tomorrow (their "Northstar"), they can begin thinking about small actions they can take—changes in mindsets, policies and practices within their reach—that foster feelings of movement, engagement and a sense of control over their future. Strengthening a group's sense of future orientation is critical for the development of hope.

"To me, there is a connection between faith, hope and love. Hope is when you write out something you want to happen. Faith is work. That means I can write down the change I want to see but if I do nothing to work toward that change, it's just going to sit there as hope. And having love for yourself and for others is the driving factor that helps you to take those steps to bring to fruition what it is that you've written down, what you want to see happen in your life."

–Anita Smith, Program Manager,
Mental Health Consultation

Relational Pathway to Regulation

Attunement and Deep Listening

Attunement involves what Bronwyn Davies (2014) calls emergent listening. In most of the conversations throughout our day, we "listen in order to fit what we hear into what we already know" (p. 21). We do not expect, and therefore, often we do not allow, our underlying worldviews and central beliefs about "the way things are" to be shattered and rearranged in our day-to-day interactions. Davies calls this *"listening as usual."* In contrast, emergent listening, involves, "opening up the ongoing possibility of coming to see life, and one's relation to it, in new and surprising ways" (p. 21). **Emergent listening is about "being open to being affected" by what one hears, rather than simply responding.** It requires the listener to be open to being changed by what they hear or experience, possibly in a fundamental way that challenges their convictions and worldview. This is a deep form of listening that creates opportunities for transformative learning to occur. When we remain open to changing our minds after tuning in to truly listen to someone else, and open to whatever we learn as a result, we communicate a powerful message to children and adults that they are seen, heard, respected, validated and safe.

   To engage in emergent listening requires effort and commitment. It demands that we are open to moving beyond our initial assumptions, biases and judgments in order to take a risk to imagine the world through another's perspective, to expand our awareness, to let go of the status quo in the service of increasing empathy and understanding for others. Emergent listening is an aspirational skill—we never master this practice, but instead, we are always emerging and striving to strengthen our capacity to engage in it.

Using Protocols in Meetings and Professional Learning Can Support the Development of Deep Listening Skills

Protocols provide simple structures that allow adults to know what is expected of them in discussions or professional learning experiences. They create systematic openings to support equity of voice—allowing everyone to participate at equally meaningful levels and in the ways that are most authentic for them—and to prevent inequitable patterns of participation (e.g., disrupts patterns of one or a few people dominating and centering their voices, stories and perspectives). Protocols create the conditions to support adults to listen to one another and/or to analyze a topic/interaction/data set/dilemma or text from multiple perspectives. How? By creating a systematic process that invites each person to share their perspectives or experiences without evaluation, judgment or debate from others. Why? Because too often our learning is prevented when people's words/ideas are questioned, critiqued, doubted or compared to someone else's. As protocols structure turn-taking, they provide opportunities for adults to practice pausing, interrupting their reactivity and to strengthen their reflection skills. Protocols also help groups to use their time efficiently and to avoid analysis-paralysis as they can be used effectively to guide people to collaboratively move through complex data analysis and/or decision-making.

TRY the Constructivist Listening Protocol

Purpose: To create a safe space to become better at listening and talking in depth. Constructivist Listening supports adults to work through feelings, thoughts and beliefs that sometimes produce anger or passivity, undermine confidence or cause interference in relationships with others.

Listeners do not interpret, paraphrase, analyze, give advice or break in with a personal story while someone is talking/sharing. Instead, the commitment listeners make when using the constructivist protocol is....."*I agree to listen to and think about you for a fixed period of time in exchange for you doing the same for me. I keep in my mind that my listening is for your benefit so I do not ask questions for my information.*" By agreeing to listen and not try to 'solve' someone's problem, you send them the message that people can often solve their own problems. This protocol acknowledges that many times what people find most helpful is to have a space to be with trusting others who can listen in an attuned manner and bear witness to their stories, emotions and sharing without moving into 'fix' it or offer advice as often there are no easy solutions for the challenging and complex situations we face.

Confidentiality is maintained to reinforce messages of safety. Participants using the Constructivist protocol agree that they will not share anything they hear outside of the protocol conversation. This is critical as people need to know they can be completely authentic.

Access to the Constructivist Listening Protocol and other free downloadable protocols can be found here:

- National School Reform Faculty (NSRF): https://nsrfharmony.org/protocols/
- School Reform Initiative (SRI): https://www.schoolreforminitiative.org/protocols/

> **Intentional Disconnection Pathway to Regulation**
>
> *Guided Imagery*
>
> Let's go on a journey together in thinking about our dream early learning program that is adequately funded and resourced:
>
> Imagine you are employed at Sunshine and Stars child care program. Staff in this center are attuned to the needs of children, families and their fellow educators. The philosophy and core values places the collective community at the heart of program outcomes and the environment is healing centered. All classrooms are able to freely select from the top notch state of the art vendors when enriching the indoor/outdoor environment whose play materials are both trauma sensitive and culturally responsive to the children served in the program. The program has its own internal substitute pool so educators are able to easily schedule vacations and medical appointments knowing classroom coverage is not a concern. Continuous program quality improvement focuses on educator voice in all decision-making. Educators and families serve on the Senior Leadership Team to inform programmatic goals, fiscal stewardship, organizational operations, as well as family and community supports.
>
> What thoughts come to mind imagining working in this environment? What feelings?

Notes

1. *Evidence-informed* = Approaches and techniques supported by research findings *or* informed by the lived experiences and perspectives of individuals and groups that may not be represented in academic scholarship or "best practice" literature. *Evidence-based* = Approaches and techniques supported by research findings, typically quantitative studies.

2. Schultz, K. (2019). *Distrust and educational change.* Teachers College Press.

References

Davies, B. (2014). *Listening to children: Being and becoming.* New York: Routledge.

Ginwright, S. (2016). *Hope and healing in urban schools.* New York, NY: Routledge.

Glass, R. (2008). Staying hopeful. In M Pollack (Ed.). *Everyday anti-racism: Getting real about race in school* (pp. 337–340). New York, NY: The New Press.

Guillon, J., & Tilton, A. (2020). *Researching with: A decolonizing approach to community-based action research.* Boston, MA: Brill Sense.

Horton, M., Freire, P., Bell, B., Gaventa, J., & Peters, J. (Eds.). (1990). *We make the road by walking: Conversations on education and social change.* Temple University Press.

Medina, J. (2013). *The epistemology of resistance: Gender and racial oppression, epistemic injustice and resistant imaginations.* New York, NY: Oxford University Press.

Morel, R. P., & Coburn, C., Catterson, A. K., & Higgs, J. (2019). The multiple meanings of scale: Implications for Researchers and practitioners. *Educational Researcher, 48*(6), pp. 369–377.

Paquin, R., Coburn, C., Catterson, A., & Higgs, J. (2019). The multiple meanings of scale: Implications for researchers and practitioners. *Educational Researcher, 48*(6), 369–377. Doi: 10.3102/0013189X19860531.

Solórzano, D., & Yosso, T. (2002). Critical race methodology: Counter-storytelling as an analytical framework for education research. *Qualitative Inquiry, 8*(23), 23–44.

Walker, J. (2020). Talkin' tech, dabblin' in data. Media Indigena (Episode #221). Canada. Retrieved from https://mediaindigena.libsyn.com/talkin-tech-dabblin-in-data-ep-221-0s

8

Case Study: "Do You Mind if I Bring Plants into the Center?" The Power of Grounders for Regulating Stress

Kristina Adams, Program Director and Mitchell Ha, Assistant Program Director, Hayward Unified School District Early Learning Program, describe how they support one of their staff members, Emilia, to use a grounder while at work to help reduce the increased stress she is experiencing as the caregiver for her ailing mother. Bringing plants from her mother's garden to the child development center helps Emilia feel safe and calm so she can focus on her work caring for young children. Mitchell explains:

> One of my staff, Emilia, has been taking care of her elderly mom the past few years. She is someone I would describe as having an extremely high stress level. She shared with me how stressful it is for her to manage work and running home to take care of her mom. We have an hour in between our morning and afternoon sessions. She has to run home, make sure her mom's eating, and make sure her mom is taking her medication. And so Emilia is

always running. I could tell she's running herself in to the ground. She asked me, "do you mind if I bring plants into the center?" Emilia's mom loves plants and she grows huge orchids in her home garden. Emilia often brings orchids into the center from her mom's yard. I spread the orchids throughout the center so that she can feel her mom's presence while she is at work as that helps her to calm herself, the orchids help her to self-regulate. So when she asked if she could bring her mom's plants into the center, I told her, "oh yes, please do." And like before, I placed them down a hallway she uses so she could see a piece of her mom's garden while she was at work. She would say to me, "Mitchell, you know what? As much as I worry about my mom, I look forward to coming here. This is a calm place for me."

Kristina continues:

When Emilia's mom passed away, I think we were able to really help her through that transition as well. I lost my mom right around the same time as Emilia's mom passed. And so we have a connection although her mom had been ill for a long time and my mom's death was unexpected. Sometimes Emilia comes into my office or calls me to say, "This is hard." Other times she says, "I'm supposed to calm down and breathe right?" And I will respond, "yes" and reassure her. These kinds of things wouldn't happen if we didn't have a strong relationship. I try to figure out unique connection points with staff. This is one of the ways I try to help our teachers deal with stress. I try to meet them where they are.

Mitchell and Kristina describe how Emilia would have never felt safe if they had not built a relationship with her. They figure out unique connection points with staff throughout the day to build relationships. These small connections promote relational safety which is a trauma-responsive and healing strategy.

During hard and stressful times, Emilia felt safe to go to Mitchell and/or Kristina for grounding and support. Sometimes it is the simplest gestures that can make someone feel safe and cared for. In this example, all it took was the flexibility and responsiveness of a director to ensure that their staff member was able to manage her stress. It is easy to get stuck in the way things are "usually done" or have been done in the past. But, in this case, knowing about Emilia's stressors and being creative and responsive allowed a staff member to feel safe and comforted while at work.

Reflection/Discussion Questions

- In what ways to you find simple, small or unique "connection points" with children throughout the day? With colleagues? With families?

Case Study: "What's the Context of the Child?" Creating a Trauma-Responsive PreK

Caroline Jones, Early Learning Principal, for a state subsidized preschool in Oakland Unified School District, has been working with her staff for several years to create a trauma-responsive early learning program. Caroline enthusiastically participates in trainings along with her staff so she can learn the content and strategies alongside her teachers. Caroline describes that one of the most important changes she has observed in her program to date is the shift away from a deficit perspective of young children toward a more inquiry-based reflective approach. Now, she explains, teachers seek to understand the meaning of a child's behavior and to learn more about a child. They no longer ask "what's wrong with this kid?." instead, as a staff they ask, "what's the context of this child?" She explains, *"We're not stigmatizing children. We are taking time during our staff meetings to talk about kids."* "Why is she biting on her shirt, biting her hand, biting her friends? What's going on there?" "It's not, what's wrong with that kid, but what's happening with the child? Is it developmental? Is there something else going on? And we bring the instructional assistants into these conversations too." Caroline also coordinates time for her teachers to have access to a mental health consultant and she participates in these meetings with her staff.

Caroline regularly communicates to her staff that she values their safety, wants them to feel a sense of belonging at school, and that at least while they are at work, she will ensure that their basic needs will be met. Understanding that some of her staff are food insecure, Caroline regularly provides *healthy nutritious snacks in the staff lounge*. She added *lavender hand soap* to the bathroom knowing that aroma therapy can be calming and hung *aspirational quotes* on the walls in the staff lounge and in the staff bathroom ("I deserve to be healthy and feel good" "I am worthy of my dreams."). The teachers also bring in their own items to support self-care for one another (e.g., hand painted rocks with inspirational messages, healthy snacks). The lounge is space dedicated to teachers and their self-care. The room includes a *comfy chair and a massage pad, healthy snacks, fun lotions* and a library with books about trauma for teachers who want to read and expand their knowledge about TIP content and strategies.

Twice a year, Caroline holds an offsite *staff retreat focused on healing and restoration* which she plans with help from their mental health consultant. They close the preschool site for the morning and drive to a nearby beach. The teachers are provided with a healthy box lunch from a local restaurant. This past year, after eating they formed a circle in the sand and took turns answering a prompt, *"what did you appreciate about the year?"* Each teacher received a candle with a card attached. They passed the candles around the circle and wrote an appreciation about each of their colleagues on the various cards. When the activity ended, everyone on the staff had a candle and a card filled with positive messages from their colleagues about their strengths and the various ways they were appreciated for their work and contributions at the center. The circle and candle exercise reinforced the value of relationships and collaboration and a strength-based view of staff. The retreat also reinforced to the teachers that their supervisor truly valued their self-care.

Caroline and her teachers serve many children impacted by trauma. They ensure that the children have access to big body play, play with loose parts, outdoor play and play that provides proprioceptive and vestibular input throughout the day; all forms of play that research documents are most effective for the development of coping skills, resilience and healing. They arrange the environment to support children to feel welcome and safe and to offer opportunities for them to release the extra energy in their bodies resulting from toxic stress and trauma. They also encourage children to develop body awareness and notice when they need to go outside and/or engage in specific types of play to release energy; steps they are taking to support the trauma-impacted children in their care to develop self-regulation. Caroline explains: *"We're working on creating a sensory playground. We have chunks of redwood and the kids roll them. So instead of punching each other, we have log rolling contests across the lawn. And then I put up a hammock outside because we needed a place for some vestibular play. We also have a small trampoline outside. Children have agency to tell us when they want/need to go outside and we always try to respect their requests."*

Caroline is now focusing her attention on trauma-sensitive family engagement: *"This year my focus has been really with the families. I know all the parents' names. I know the kids. I know who's in their homes and the teachers know this information too. We're really trying to build more meaningful relationships with the families."* Similar to the space she created for teachers to engage in self-care, there is now has a space in the school just for families. Caroline shares why this is important, *"I think having a safe space for families is really important because some of my families don't have a safe place to go. And when it's in between classroom sessions, they know that they can just go to the family room as long as the school is open that they're welcome here."*

Becoming a trauma-responsive school requires that staff engage in continual reflection and dialogue. Caroline understands that learning to reflect is an important skill for teachers to develop and that her staff has different levels of experience with reflection. As a result, she accepts that part of her responsibility is using staff meetings as time where she can support her staff to strengthen their reflection skills, *"Some of the staff are already expert reflectors. And for some of them, this is something brand new. You can see it's kind of like flexing new muscles and having some soreness, but we're working together and I'm beginning to see it happen."*

Reflection Questions

- ♦ What opportunities do you have in the workplace where you are able to "pause" and reflect on dilemmas, challenges or small wins (a shout out for something that went well)?
- ♦ If you find this time for reflection has not been a regular part of your practice, can you think of one small way that you could start to build it in each week for yourself and/or others?
- ♦ If you supervise, what opportunities do you create in the workplace that offer your staff access to self-care? How do you build in organizational care routines and communicate that you care about their health and well-being?

Case Study: "I Would Go Home and Remind Myself that My Job Was Not to Judge"

London Hess, a preschool teacher, describes what it was like during her first year of teaching.

> In my first year of teaching, I had a rocky start developing a positive relationship with Sheila, the mother of a four year old girl, Henrietta, in my class. I was hired over the holiday break so the families arrived and there I was, a new

teacher that appeared in the new year. On my first day of work, Sheila grilled me at the end of the day, "What have you noticed about my child? Why did you do set up the classroom like this today? What church do you go to?" She shot questions at me one after the other and made it known she was very unhappy with my presence. I was really taken back.

Sheila and I struggled for several months. It was very difficult but every night I would go home and remind myself that my job was not to judge, assume or meet her anger with beliefs and actions that would make things worse. I learned to do a lot of deep breathing, to talk with my supervisor about how hard the situation was for me and to remind myself why I was doing this work, my "why," what I cared about most which was being a responsive and attuned teacher for young children and their families. Not some families. Not only the "easy" families. But all families. And what I have found over the years, is that the families that have the most trauma in their backgrounds and challenge me the most to align my teaching practice with my professed values, are always the families I become the closest with. I think this happens because I have to work hardest on these relationships.

Eventually, I learned from Sheila that her daughter had experienced some domestic abuse. I came to understand that Sheila's initial questioning of me was coming from her desire to ensure that she was not putting Henrietta in harm's way. One day Sheila shared with me that Henrietta was scared of doors being shut because she would go into her room and shut the door when she would hear the sounds of abuse at home. So doors being shut were a big trigger for this little girl. Sheila asked me, **"Hey, with the door situation, can you just not shut the door when Henrietta goes to the bathroom?"** I reassured Sheila and thanked her for sharing this sensitive information with me. We spoke together and problem-solved a few options. As one of our bathroom stalls has a door that is cut in half horizontally, we decided to encourage Henrietta to use that toilet and to keep the top half of the door open so she would have some privacy but also feel safer when using the bathroom.

A lot of times we won't know the details of a child's trauma history, but that's why it's so important to look at patterns. **I don't necessarily need to know the reason to observe that it's a trigger.** When I observe the pattern, what can I do to change the environment to support the child to feel safe and to prevent them from experiencing a trigger that could be re-traumatizing? Without understanding how trauma impacts young children's behavior, if/when Henrietta triggered in the classroom, I would have been like "girlfriend, why are you freaking out?"

Oftentimes families will display their frustration, greatest concerns and fears for children in a range of big emotions that can be displayed through adversarial daily communication that arises from a previous lived experience. Providers and the systems that touch them are not always given those immediate insightful clues and patterns about children's and families' needs. In the midst of building any new relationship, including ones that are not yet centered on trust, we are called to listen, show compassion and remain open to learning about how to be responsive in our work with a child, parent or family member or colleague.

Reflection/Discussion Questions

- What is one specific strategy you use to build relational connections and safety with a child you work with when faced with a dysregulated behavior? A family you work with? A colleague you supervise or work with? With yourself?

Case Study: Trauma-Responsive Environments Everywhere (TREE Project, Humboldt County)

> **TREE Core Concepts "Creating Safety, Reducing Triggers and Supporting Regulation"**
> - Relationship based
> - Family-strengthening
> - Reflective practice
> - Developmentally responsive
> - Neuro-developmentally informed
> - Trigger and temperament responsive (safe spaces)
> - Self-regulation & resiliency promoting

Meg Walkley is a credentialed school social worker, endorsed infant-family and early childhood mental health specialist and co-coordinator of a multi-disciplinary group of practitioners, the 0 to 8 Mental Health Collaborative, in Humboldt County, a rural area in Northern California. She explains that **the decision to put the words "mental health" in the title of their collaborative was strategic with intention to normalize mental health supports and reduce stigmatization.**

Working collaboratively with her colleagues, Meg wrote and received a small grant to fund the **Trauma-Responsive Environments Everywhere** or TREE project. The goal of the TREE project was to create neurodevelopmental and trauma-responsive environments and to create consistency of practice for young children and families impacted by trauma across their county. The initial outreach was to the people and organizations that they already had connections with and/or those who showed an interest and a spark to become more trauma-responsive. The participants included early childhood professionals working in settings serving children birth to 8 years—e.g., public school Kindergarten—2nd grade classrooms, a public special day class, a developmental playgroup, a counseling clinic serving families of young children and a preschool site.

Participants in the TREE project participated in a **professional learning community** once a month where different topics were discussed (e.g., early brain development, sensory processing strategies, social and emotional development, intro to reflective practice, risk and resiliency, providing family-sensitive services, how to create trauma-responsive environments and factors impacting relational health). The topics were partially determined by surveying the participants to learn about their interests and knowledge of trauma). These monthly meetings allowed participants to learn about the topics and to network with one another. Additionally, the **participants had coaches** assigned to their site who could provide them with support ("how can we make changes to make this room for sensory responsive to children?") The TREE project grant funding also provided pilot sites with **tangible materials** including foldable, camping, rocking chairs and mini-trampolines. Although they initially only planned for the trampolines to be for the children, after observing how they were also valuable for parents' regulation, they decided to make them available to the parents and family members as well. Meg describes the materials they purchased and the rationale behind their selections:

> So we purchased folding rocking chairs for teachers who didn't think they had space for rocking chairs in their classrooms. And we had mini trampolines. At one of the playgroups, one of the dads really wanted to jump too. And so we were able to buy an additional trampoline that went up to 350 pounds so parents could jump right alongside their children. He was a stay at home dad and he came into playgroup and he just marched right up to the trampoline, spent about five minutes jumping up and down, got off and said, "Oh, I feel so much better." We used the trampolines as a strategy for parents to regulate themselves and then to model that for their children. We were also able to purchase sensory tables, riding toys, dolls, expanding/contracting balls, physio balls, toy horses with manes and tails and other "hairy" animals to brush and brushing tools, drums and

other percussion items, soft mats suitable for infants to be placed upon for play or massage, match games and other games that build executive functioning and self-regulation skills. Staff were also provided with the book "Doodles, Dances and Ditties" which includes neurodevelopmental and trauma-responsive activities. Of course, we also provided training to teachers on how to utilize the new materials and the "why" behind these choices. They learned that these materials were selected based on what research demonstrates is helpful with the really ancient parts of our brain that are connected to our regulatory system.

Meg and her team discovered that it was really important and helpful to initially **pilot the TREE project** with a small group of programs. They shared what they learned from these pilot sites to create buy in with a larger group of organizational leaders across the county. With the Superintendent's help, they began shining a light on how the TREE project was having a positive impact with young children and families. It did not take long before there were requests to expand and replicate the TREE program across the county.

Despite the success of the TREE project, Meg and her colleagues faced a significant barrier: **The lack of sustainable funding for critical infrastructure**—funds to pay for Project Coordinator and Training Coordinator positions. Meg explains, "we can get grants to bring in trainings and we can get grants to do some piloting of programs but it's hard to get funding for the leadership positions that are essential to creating and sustaining a project like TREE." Another challenge that is particularly acute in their rural county is the lack of a robust early childhood service delivery system. Children and families may qualify for trauma-related services, however, too often there are **no clinicians to refer them to**. Meg shares, "We have such a lack of mental health clinicians in our county that they can choose which population they want to serve. And unfortunately, many clinicians do not choose to serve children zero to five and their families."

Reflection/Discussion Question

- Reflecting on your environment, do you have sensory materials for children, families or staff that help regulate as Meg mentions, "the ancient parts of our brain that are connected to our regulatory system?"
- How will you fund the infrastructure and materials needed to support and sustain your efforts to become trauma-responsive?
- How can you plan to pilot your new project with a few select programs and then learn from successes and struggles?

Tree Project Materials Master List

Note: Not all programs chose or were budgeted for all materials. Each program prioritized their expenditures

- Cozy cubes or materials to make cozy spaces
- Bouncing Horses
- Adult folding Rocking Chair
- Child-sized folding rocking chairs
- Mini trampolines with bars that hold up to 350 lbs. (to encourage use by both adults and children)
- Large "Pillow Pets"
- Washable cover bean bag chairs
- "Pea pod" chair
- Sensory tables
- Sensory bins
- Sand and other sensory materials
- Children's books about feelings/yoga/mindfulness
- Double sided book display with wheels
- Various Fidget/Busy Toys
- Teeter Totter- 3 person
- CD players and CD's
- Musical instruments
- Cooperative games (Hoot Owl Hoot, Snug, Bug, Rug, etc.)
- Foldable ball pit and balls
- Sensory/textured balls
- Toddler safe doll house with diverse array of dolls
- Exercise balls (12", 18" and 24")
- Interlocking floor mats to create soft flooring in sensory room space
- Small rug(s), in different soft textures.
- "Sensory Sox" body sock
- Oversized soft stacking blocks
- Buddha/Zen Board, for fun calming activity time.
- Large parachute
- Playdough
- Spot IT game
- Art box
- Blocks
- Dolls and stuffed animals with "hair" that can be brushed and combed
- Resource Books. Hiebert, Platt, Schpok, & Whitesell (2013) *Doodles, Dances and Ditties: A trauma-informed somatosensory handbook.*
- Mind Body Skills: Activities for Emotional Regulation
- In Sync Activity Cards

Case Study: "I Think We can Make This a Better Experience for Children."

Jonathan Iris-Wilbanks is a Certified Child Life Specialist and a child and family therapist. He describes how an essential part of his work in the hospital is building collaborative relationships with the doctors and nurses, physical therapists, social workers, spiritual care providers and all the different people in the space that interact with families. It is the strength of these relationships that allows Jonathan and his colleagues to work collaboratively to create a more trauma-responsive environment for young children and families in the hospital. He describes what this looks like:

> Consider the doctors and technicians who operate the MRIs, CT scans, ultrasounds, x-rays, imaging and nuclear medicine. There so many different spaces where children have procedures. Hospitalized children interact with many different professionals and types of equipment every single day. And because of the relationships I have with the doctors and the technologists, I am invited to observe and share my recommendations for each of the environments children are in for procedures. I am able to pause and reflect on the experiences of children I have worked with and offer ideas to improve the environment to make it more responsive to children's needs. As I observe, I tried to put myself in children's shoes as much as I can. Where are the moments where children are experiencing pain? Where are the moments where the child has choice and agency? **What part of a child's experiences might be more or less stressful?** I share my observations through a discussion with the team. I learned early on that the best way to share my knowledge as a Child Life Specialist is to empathize—not to say, "this is happening and it's wrong, you need to stop what you're doing"—instead, I say, "It must be so hard to continue to do this procedure in this way and to see children in pain. My goal is to communicate empathy and then to give the message," **"I think we**

can make this a better experience for children." I respect their training and expertise in operating the machine and doing the procedures, but they are not trained in child development. That is my contribution to the team. So I tell them, "We can make it so your work is not only easier, but it won't be as upsetting to children. It must've been so difficult to do this work for so long in this way and to see children in discomfort, fear and pain in the process. Let's collaborate together and make it easier for everyone."

As one person, I can only reach so many people so what I try to do is to take my knowledge and skills and build capacity among the hospital staff. I am always looking at the environment and thinking, **"How can Child Life be here when the Child Life Specialist cannot?"** A good example was with hospital badges. We developed small laminated cards that hospital staff could tuck behind their badge that had pictures of cartoon characters or objects that children would be familiar with (e.g., Paw Patrol, Bob the Builder or Dora the Explorer). I provided a very brief training so staff could learn how to use the cards to create a distraction during an uncomfortable procedure or stressful situation. The idea is to give the child the little card and while the doctors are doing the procedure, they would distract the child with questions, "who's your favorite character?" "who do you think runs the fastest?" "Oh, Donald Duck is faster than Lightning McQueen? Well, who do you think throws the best birthday party?" So now **the child's talking, they're looking at this little card and the procedure is happening all at the same time.** And so this little piece of laminated paper became a Child Life intervention that every single person in the department could carry in their badge. To support change, I've also printed stickers for staff members to wear who attended one of my Child Life trainings that said things like, "Ask me about comfort positions" (ways to hold a child that increases their comfort) or "Ask me how to use the cards for distraction." So we created little community incentives that would essentially communicate, "I can make needle pokes less painful."

There's always people within a system that are going to have resistance. They don't want to change something. They feel like they're doing it well enough. I decided at some point I wasn't going to spend too much energy on them. **I was going to look for the people in that system who were really wanting change**, because I knew that if I taught them to use Child Life techniques, they'll tell their colleague and then their colleague will tell another colleague. And then eventually the one person who's really resistant will be the only one who is not offering comfort positioning or using distraction to reduce pain or any other tool in my Child Life basket. So I look for the people in the system who are more inclined to be collaborative and I spend more time with them. I take my time with a more resistant person and build a relationship with them in a different way.

Jonathan's Approach as a Child Life Specialist Reflects Several of Our Trauma-Responsive Principles

Provide Opportunities for Agency and Control. Jonathan gives children a voice in a situation where they might not otherwise have one. He scanned the environment for moments the child may be more vulnerable to an emotional trigger or feel pain the most. He used that information to inform his recommendations. Then he made his recommendations not in a directive and corrective way but in a trauma-responsive way.

- When working with children, can you scan your environment noting times children may have been triggered by something they perceived such as a loss of control (i.e. drop off and pick up, transitions, a stranger enters the room, subs, unexpected changes, loud noises)?

- Can you think of one small change you can make in the environment to <u>prevent</u> children from being triggered or to <u>support them to feel safe</u> in vulnerable moments?
- When working with adults, can you scan the environment for situations that might trigger a loss of control or vulnerability (i.e. being called on in a meeting, transitions, not receiving an agenda before a meeting, rolling out new policies without advance notice, being told they are not performing, visiting with no notice, not providing opportunity for input to a change etc.)?
- Alternatively, do you recall a time an employee was triggered emotionally? Can you think of one small change that could have been made to <u>prevent</u> them from being triggered or to <u>support them to feel safe</u> in this vulnerable moment?

Jonathan could have taken his information back and told the medical professionals what is wrong and how to do it right (correction or direction). Instead, he approached it with a trauma-informed and responsive lens.

- Can you think of 1–2 strategies Jonathan used that were trauma-responsive?
- How did he help the medical professionals see how it would help them? Help the child?
- Do you have an example when you moved from a correction/direction to an approach that was trauma-responsive?

Understand Stress and Trauma. Jonathan understood that during certain procedures children may feel more vulnerable or triggered into their fear responsive and reactive brain (fight, flight or freeze) in attempt to protect themselves from a real or perceived danger.

- Thinking of your organization or scope of work, can you think of a time when you created a sense of safety (e.g., when rolling out a new expectation or policy, making

new changes within an organization, sharing difficult information)?
- Does your program have policies, procedures or protocols that help make expectations clear and promote a sense of safety for others (ex. emergency preparedness, responding to a crisis, handling of a complaint, employee performance, a child with persistent challenges)?

Work toward Sustainability and Scale Innovation with Flexibility for Local Adaptation. Sometimes organization roll out new initiatives (e.g., social-emotional, trauma-informed, etc.) and they focus on an implementation plan that starts with the programs that need it the most. Jonathan on the other hand, focused on early and eager adopters. Those who were most willing to engage and participate. He helped create momentum and through small steps he achieved success with the early adopters implementing these trauma-responsive strategies that promoted safety and relational connections. He recognized the concept of "mirror neurons." A positive buzz of changes and attitudes was contagious. This positive new initiative was working, and others wanted to be a part of the new strategies being implemented.

- Can you think of a time when you had to implement something new and longer term for your program? What steps did you take to get input from others across all levels of the organization?
- How did you consider the capacity for staff to take on a new task without being overwhelmed?
- How did you break down the implementation plan into small and measurable steps so as to not overwhelm everyone at once?
- What creative ways can you use to create a "buzz" or energy around your project to help others see the benefits and successes?

Bottom UP Pathway to Regulation
30–60 second Rhythmic Somatosensory Activities that Regulate an Activated Stress Response System

*"The only way to move from these super-high anxiety states, to calmer more cognitive states, is **rhythm**…we need patterned, repetitive, rhythmic somatosensory activity literally, bodily sensing exercises"* (Perry, 2014)

- Swaying forward and back or side to side
- Chewing on food or gum
- Snapping fingers
- Squeezing and then relaxing fists
- Engaging the 5 senses (sight, sound, touch, taste)
- Tapping on knees (left to right; 9–12 times) while thinking of a positive image in your mind

- Humming a song
- Swinging
- Laughing
- Blowing bubbles
- Pushing hands against the wall with all your strength
- Stomping a few times as hard as you can on the ground
- Finger and toe wiggles

(Perry, 2014)

References

Hiebert, M., Platt, J., Schpok, K., & Whitesell, J. (2013). *Doodles, Dances and Ditties: A trauma-informed somatosensory handbook.* Denver, CO: Mount Saint Vincent Home.

Perry, B. (2014). Rhythm regulates the brain. Retrieved from https://attachmentdisorderhealing.com/developmental-trauma-3/

Conclusion

Uncover your mirrors and windows (Bishop, 1990). You probably picked up this book for a reason. Perhaps you stumbled across **"mirrors"** and felt excited to uncover what you were already doing that was trauma-informed. Maybe you unveiled the **"windows"** and envisioned new opportunities to become a program, school, center or organization that is trauma-responsive and healing engaged. As you read this book and found your strengths and learning edges, you may wonder where to go next on your journey. In working for change…

Keep the focus on your individual and collective "Why." As you work with your program, school, agency or system to become trauma-responsive, resilience-building and healing engaged, it is critical that you remain connected to your vision, goals and mission statement. Take time to return to a few critical questions: Why is it important we embark on this journey? How will doing this work help our children, families, staff, program, community and/or the greater society? Susan Raffo (2017) has wise words to consider, "Healing is about taking the time to notice what gets in the way of feeling connected to your life, your community and your sense of possibility. Healing, at its core, is about slowing down so that we can better listen, to ourselves and each other." (p. 199).

Focus on your sphere of influence (where you *can* make changes) and realistic action steps you can take right away. We all need a GPS and a road map to our final destination. Creating a vision and a longer-term plan to guide us with an overarching north star gives us a sense of hope and something to work toward that will make a difference for so many. Then, we have to work backward and map out a plan of action to get there. It is important to create the larger vision, but real change happens with those first small steps. Momentum builds for change when many people take relatively simple actions within their sphere of influence. Many small actions can combine and be a powerful force that leads to large-scale change. As Mary Pipher (2005) reminds us, "Social change is a million individual acts of kindness. Cultural change is a million subversive acts of resistance." So ask yourself, what change can I influence? What are some small steps I can take individually or with others right and be successful at implementing right away?

It takes more than an island: Include the voices and input of others. Don't' do this alone! Engage staff internally (children, families, staff) and external stakeholders (community partners, resource and referral agencies, funders) and seek their input and contributions. The leadership/champion team needs the support and involvement of the individuals who are employed and interact with the organization to execute this approach successfully. Ask your team, who do we need to engage internally and externally as we seek input in our journey of becoming a trauma-responsive, resilience building and a healing engaged program? Where are our learning edges and what do we need to do to support our learning and skill development so we can do this work better?

Remember to give yourself and others grace. At least 67% of the adult population in the United States have experienced at least one trauma before the age 18 (Felitti et al. 1998; Koplan & Chard, 2014). The long-term adverse impacts of trauma—socially, emotionally, mentally, physically and spiritually—for individuals, families, communities, organizations and systems makes trauma an urgent public health crisis for our nation. Despite being the most important process an early learning program can embark upon, creating trauma-responsive healing centered early childhood environments is complex and long term work. Huge amounts of grace are required to sustain this journey! Kristina Adams, Program Director from Hayward Unified School District describes this beautifully *"My mantra has been about grace...In all of our staff meetings I say, "This is hard work. Give yourself some grace. And go find somebody else you can give some grace to."* We hope you start with grace. We thank you from the bottom of our hearts for being a courageous advocate in working to create environments that support children, families and the early childhood workforce to feel safe, respected, welcomed and visible so they can learn, heal and thrive in the presence of consistent and responsive relationships.

References

Bishop, R. S. (1990) Mirrors, windows, and sliding glass doors. Originally published in *Perspectives*, 1(3), ix–xi. Accessed on January 22, 2019 at https://scenicregional. org/wp-content/uploads/2017/08/Mirrors-Windows-and-Sliding-Glass-Doors.pdf

Felitti, V. J., Anda, R. F., Nordenberg, D., Williamson, D. F., Spitz, A. M., Edwards, V., Koss, M.P., & Marks, J. S. (1998). The relationship of adult health status to childhood abuse and household dysfunction. *American Journal of Preventive Medicine, 14*(4), 245–258.

Koplan, C. & Chard, A. (2014). Adverse early life experiences as a social determinant of mental health. *Psychiatric Annals, 44*(1), 39–45. doi: 10.3928/00485713-20140108-07

Pipher, M. (2005). *Reviving Ophelia: Saving the selves of adolescent girls.* New York, NY: Berkley Publishing Group.

Raffo, S. (2017). In Menakem, R. *My grandmother's hands: Racialized trauma and the pathway to mending our hearts and bodies.* (p. 199). Las Vegas, NV: Central Recovery Press.

Resources

APPS for Mindfulness and Self-Regulation

- **Calm** They are rated the #1 app for sleep and meditation using various sources of support like music, visuals, videos and lessons to support you on your journey.
- **Headspace** Learn the life-changing skills to bring calm to any situation with sessions as short as one minute.
- **Stop, Breathe & Think** Recommends activities that are right for you whether you are anxious, sleepless, hopeful, angry or anything in between.
- **UCLA Mindfulness** With guidance from the UCLA Mindful Awareness Research Center, they use scientific research to help you manage stress-related physical conditions, reduce anxiety and depression, cultivate positive emotions and help improve overall physical health and well-being.

Other APPs

- **Help Kids Cope** Helps to assist parents and adults in talking to their kids about different disasters they may or have already experienced. It does cover early childhood through adolescents.
- **Provider Resilience** Gives users an overall resilience rating generated through user self-assessments—and a countdown clock showing how long until the user's next restorative activity. Provider Resilience also features stress-busting and compassion satisfaction-building tools.

Websites

- **Center for Equity in Early Childhood Education** (www.ceece.org). CEECE aims to create early learning environments and systems that end the intersectional racialized predictability of outcomes for young children.
- **Center for Optimal Brain Integration** (www.optimalbrainintegration.com). At the Center for Optimal Brain Integration, we provide training and a range of services to support individuals, programs and communities to become trauma-responsive and build capacity for coping, resilience and healing.
- **The National Child Traumatic Stress Network** (www.nctsn.org). NCTSN.org is a resource for the public, professionals and others who care about children and are concerned about child traumatic stress.
- **Trauma Transformed** (https://traumatransformed.org). Infusing healing into the DNA of our human serving systems, including both public and community-based organizations, so that the people who make up the systems can bring their whole, human selves to the important work they do to care for others.
- **Zero to Three Toolkit** (www.zerotothree.org/resources/2896-getting-started-with-mindfulness-a-toolkit-for-early-childhood-organizations). In this toolkit, learn more about the case for implementing mindfulness techniques into your daily work and organizational culture, try hands-on strategies for doing so, and learn more from organizations that have begun this journey.

For Product Safety Concerns and Information please contact our EU representative GPSR@taylorandfrancis.com
Taylor & Francis Verlag GmbH, Kaufingerstraße 24, 80331 München, Germany

www.ingramcontent.com/pod-product-compliance
Lightning Source LLC
Chambersburg PA
CBHW052219300426
44115CB00011B/1748